NoFear

No Fear

A POLICE OFFICER'S PERSPECTIVE

Robert R. Surgenor

PROVIDENCE HOUSE PUBLISHERS
Franklin, Tennessee

Printed in the United States of America

03   02   01   00   2   3   4   5

Library of Congress Catalog Card Number: 99–67602

ISBN: 1–57736–159–8

Cover design by Gary Bozeman

The author's sons posed for the cover—Robert is a police officer, Matthew is a freshman in high school.

PROVIDENCE HOUSE PUBLISHERS
238 Seaboard Lane • Franklin, Tennessee 37067
800-321-5692
www.providencehouse.com

To
My Parents

Two God-fearing people who used common sense instead of theory to raise my brother and me, and who prayed for us every day of our lives.

To Dad—Who demanded, and got, respect for his authority.

To Mom—Who was so quick to forgive our immature mistakes.

To Dad—Who set limitations on my behavior and insisted on discipline when the rules were broken.

To Mom—Who worked together with my dad to create an atmosphere of cooperation and unity.

To Dad—Who made me feel safe and secure by establishing those well-defined boundaries.

To Mom—Who never had any trouble making me understand that her love for me was immeasurable.

To Dad—Whose efforts to teach me honesty were reinforced by the example that he lived.

To Mom—Who domesticated me at a young age. Today, I'm the best dishwasher in the household.

To
Mom and Dad
Who trusted the wisdom of Solomon and spanked me
when I deserved it.

Thanks Mom and Dad!

Contents

Foreword

I never expected this book to be published. The information contained in this book was originally intended for the large number of parents with whom I deal with on a daily basis. These parents, like millions of other parents in this country, are confused about why their child is out of control. Sitting in my office, some wringing their hands, some crying, these parents pour out their souls to me. Why doesn't my son listen to me? Why did my daughter get mixed up with that bum? Why did my child burglarize that house? Why is my child so violent?

I felt a great deal of compassion for those mothers and fathers who loved their children, but had failed them miserably in the areas of structure and discipline. I got used to hearing the parents say "I was told that I couldn't discipline my kid in that manner," or "I didn't want to go to jail for correcting my child!" I became aware that the modern philosophical ideas introduced into child rearing were taking their toll.

I began compiling laws, statistics, and personal information on my trusty computer. I began giving parents copies of the information I had so diligently gathered. Suddenly, everything began coming together into a well-organized document, loaded with the type of specifics that parents were thirsting for. The single page of state laws and crime statistics that I passed out to parents of out-of-control children turned into a complete book, including suggestions on how to control your child, and the child abuse laws from all fifty states.

My intent in publishing this book is the same as it was when I was distributing those single pages to those parents sitting in my office. I believe we need to educate parents as to their authority, responsibility, and liability. We need more advocates of parents' rights. We need parents to understand that when they are right, law enforcement and the courts are always on their side. I hope this book empowers those parents who are just simply afraid to control their children.

Preface and Acknowledgments

I will be forever grateful to the many people who helped me in writing this book. To my father, whose insight into the true meaning of scripture was an invaluable resource. To my mother, whose proofreading skills uncovered a plethora of my mistakes. To my three biological children, Rob, Dawn, and Bryan, and my two adopted children, Mike and Matt, whose present day status exemplifies my message of the rod and reproof. To the officers on my department whose support and friendship over the years inspired much of my writing. To those who planted ideas in my head that eventually turned into the words in this book, Mark Inman, Don Andrukat, Jon Matej, Mark Schultz, Bob Reitman, Bob Bushok, Dan Barth, John and Patti Kuczkowski, and Joe and Jennifer Hudock and Terry Nall.

To the officers who helped me put together the photographs for the book, Joe Grecol, Tim Milter, Chris Holmes, Rob Surgenor, Matt Vanyo, Mark Adam, and the K-9 unit, Odin.

But there is a special thanks to my wife, Nancy, whose support while this book was being written was exemplary. Putting up with a husband who is pounding away on the computer keys is not easy when the chores aren't done. Thanks redhead!

Introduction

It took the help of five other police officers to assist me in getting the handcuffs on the fifteen-year-old boy who had just broken his mother's nose, knocked his father to the floor, and thrown a table through the front window. As I compiled the information for the report, the mother indicated that they had lost control of the boy at an early age. Time-outs and groundings just never worked. When I asked the mother if they had ever tried spanking the boy when he defied their authority, she replied angrily "We don't believe in spanking. Violence begets violence!" I wondered if she realized how foolish she sounded.

I, for one, am fed up! During the years that I have served my community as a police officer, I have come to the realization that law enforcement and the courts bear the brunt of social experimentation. In an era of theory, yesterday's youth are becoming tomorrow's criminals. Since 1982 when I joined the police department, and especially since 1995, when I was placed in charge of the detective bureau's juvenile crime unit, I have observed the rapid deterioration of attitude in today's teenager and adolescent. There are times when I feel as though all of my efforts are futile. It's like I'm rearranging the chairs on the Titanic. Although I try to educate parents about structure, discipline, and the law, it seems as though my advice falls on deaf ears. In many of today's young people, there is no fear. No fear of consequences. No fear of their parents. No fear of their teachers. No fear of the cops or the judge. No fear of God.

A friend of mine in the field of psychology once told me something very disturbing. He stated that although he believed in spanking as a form of discipline, he would never dare say it aloud in his line of work. If he did, he would be blackballed by the profession. It's sad when a person who has convictions about an issue like corporal punishment can't say how he/she feels. It's sad that a few psychologists with a few "theories" have turned the world of parenting upside down. As a Christian, I also realize that man's "wisdom" is not wisdom at all. First Corinthians 3:19 states, "For the wisdom of this world is foolishness with God." The secular world, and in numerous cases, the Christian community, has fallen for the rhetoric of a few ungodly men whose agenda is not easily recognized. When Sigmund Freud, an atheist and the father of psychoanalysis, introduced his theory that man is motivated by pleasure, he began laying the groundwork for our modern-day permissive society. Following Freud's lead, most present-day psychologists have brainwashed parents into believing that corporal punishment is counterproductive and harmful to children. Parents are being taught that children should not fear their parents. The resulting defiance by our youth has turned family life into an agonizing experience that is a nightmare for parent and child alike.

The city I work for is located in Cuyahoga County, Ohio, which includes metropolitan Cleveland and surrounding suburbs. It has the highest crime rate in the state. Its juvenile court is understaffed and overburdened with juvenile crime. More than once, while attending criminal trials, I have heard judges, magistrates, prosecutors, and probation officers say, "These kids have no fear." The "in your face" attitude amongst those juveniles being charged with crimes is becoming more and more prevalent.

In March of 1998, I attended a meeting of local police officers, juvenile detectives, juvenile court personnel, and judges to discuss a new "get tough" procedure being instituted by the Cuyahoga County Juvenile Detention facility. The reason for the new policy was to instill some "fear" of consequences into the local youth. The discussion turned to the subject of disciplining children, as it usually does when a group of juvenile officers get together. The consensus amongst all present was that although there are many factors involved, the major factor in the rising defiance and lack of fear of consequences in today's youth is the absence of corporal punishment in the home. A lieutenant from one of the suburbs got a chuckle from everyone when he said, "When I was a kid, what really got me to move, was when I heard the leather coming out of my father's belt loops." It was the fear of pain that made us obey the rules and treat others with respect.

I'm not suggesting that we abuse our children. I don't believe spanking is abusive. I'm also not suggesting that parents never use any other form of discipline. If grounding the child or making them sit in the corner helps change their negative behavior, then that form of discipline should be used if the infraction was something other than an illegal act or one of defiance. When I look back on my childhood, I can only recall three spankings that I received from my parents. I also remember being grounded and certain privileges being taken away for certain violations of the rules. I recall vividly the penalty for defying my parents' authority. I learned at a very early age that I was never to say "no" to an order from my mom or dad. By the time I reached the age of responsibility, I knew better than to refuse to do what I was told. The consequences were stinging.

Unfortunately, by the time children reach their early teenage years and begin to flagrantly defy their parents' authority, it may be too late to implement corporal punishment into the discipline plan. Some children are easy going and need very little correction, whereas others are extremely strong willed. A parent may feel that they can control a four year old's defiance by making him spend a "time-out." A parent may feel that it is not necessary to spank the small child who talks back. Other forms of discipline may work with a toddler, but by the time that child reaches puberty he/she has already formed the ideas of authority and the fear factor that goes along with it. When children reach the early teenage years, they are stronger, smarter, and can easily dial the telephone. If not conditioned to fear the consequences of violating the rules, the older child may be unable to be controlled by the parent. I believe that a child should be spanked for obvious defiance of the parent's authority or for illegal acts such as stealing. Those parents who fall for the nonsensical nit-wittery of the antispanking "experts" end up in my office, unable to control their children.

At the present time, our society is being bombarded by suggestions from professionals that we seek alternative forms of discipline, rather than spanking our children. Studies conducted by "experts" indicate that we are causing irreparable damage to our children by spanking them for any reason. It's strange that as we spank our children less, we are experiencing more defiance from our youth than ever before. In this book, you will notice that I refer many times to the wisdom of King Solomon, who wrote in Proverbs 29:15, "The rod and reproof give wisdom: but a child left to himself bringeth his mother to shame." I find it very difficult to argue with the wisdom of Solomon. Although there are many other factors that parents must consider when rearing their children, such as creating a supportive, loving relationship with their children, and using positive reinforcement for good behavior, to fall for the claim that spanking as a form of discipline will harm children can result in disaster.

We, as parents, have been inundated by numerous sources that have made us believe that we are powerless to control our children. When I first started this book, I had planned for the cover to say, "How modern-day psychology has produced a generation of out-of-control children." As I researched studies conducted by psychologists, I was surprised to find a large number of those in the field who endorse structure and discipline in the upbringing of our youth, including corporal punishment. There are psychologists like Dr. James Dobson of Focus on the Family, and others, who realize that a permissive approach to child rearing results in disaster. But it appears that the professionals who advocate spanking are becoming outnumbered.

At first, I felt that the movement against corporal punishment was born of concern for the children. I assumed that the professionals and "experts" who were telling us that spanking is counterproductive and harmful to our kids were concerned about the welfare of the children in our society. As time went on and I studied the nonspanking philosophy, I began to better understand what this group stands for. I now believe that the agenda of the antispanking bunch is much more ominous than many of us suspect. The nonspanking crowd is a close-knit group who have developed "peer-reviewed published research" they claim proves that corporal punishment is harmful to children. Their attitude is one of arrogance. Their movement is humanistic. Their religion is atheistic.

These nonspanking advocates are like those mentioned in Romans 1:22, "Professing themselves to be wise, they became fools." Modern-day "experts" have inundated our culture with "foolish wisdom" that is not wisdom at all. In direct conflict with God's way, these "fools" have brainwashed a large portion of our society into believing their ideas—ideas that have not yet withstood the test of time. In truth, these ideas are "theories." Webster's Thesaurus lists the term "theory" as synonymous with "a doctrine, guess, presupposition, assumption, or speculation."[1] Many of these experts proclaim their theory as fact, when in fact it is a "guess," an "assumption," or pure "speculation." I might add that the concept that spanking harms a child has become, in effect, a doctrine. Because God's word clearly advocates corporal punishment in child rearing, the nonspanking advocate attempts to discredit the Bible as a source of knowledge. They attempt to show that the Bible is contradictory and unreliable. They attempt to discredit God.

Ephesians 4:14 tells us "That we henceforth be no more children, tossed to and fro, and carried about with every wind of doctrine, by the sleight of men, and cunning craftiness, whereby they lie in wait to deceive." We can trust God's word to keep us from being "carried about with every wind of doctrine." The doctrine of the nonspanking movement is dangerous. We cannot allow ourselves to be deceived by its rhetoric.

One of the sergeants from our department once told us a story about his six-year-old son, who discovered an unguarded twenty dollar bill on the kitchen counter as he walked out the door one morning on his way to school. Mom discovered after he had left that the money was missing. Mom later received a call from the school lunch monitor, reporting that the son was buying everyone "extras" in the cafeteria with a twenty dollar bill. We all chuckled as he conveyed the scene when his son arrived home that afternoon. The son received a spanking and was grounded for several days. The small son humbly apologized for his dishonest action and was soon engulfed in his father's loving arms.

I seized the opportunity to convey my thoughts about the incident to the rest of the detective bureau. "You know," I trumpeted, "the only difference between sarge's son and Bill Jacob's son," (one of the local youngsters who has been labeled the community's juvenile public enemy number one) "is the consequence he receives from his parents when he violates the rules." I went on to make my point that every child will violate the rules and commit dishonest acts. It's how the parent handles the infraction that decides how that child will act further on in life. The parent is the deciding factor in how a child turns out. The problem is, there are a very large number of parents who would like to take control of their children, they just don't know how.

It's time someone stood up and proclaimed very loudly "Parents, take control of your children." The law demands that parents be responsible for their children's actions. Responsibility without authority is futility! Because parents are liable for everything their child does, the same law gives that parent a great deal of latitude in dealing with the juvenile, including the use of force. This book deals with that issue—parents and their out-of-control children. My laboratory is an entire city consisting of rich and poor, black and white, young and old. All of the data that I collect is unsolicited. I don't have to look for it; it's dumped right in my lap. I believe my findings are more accurate than any psychologist's theory that is untested by time and unproven by statistics. Psychologists, the department of children's services, and public school counselors are telling us that we can't touch our kids. The resulting confusion has produced children with "no fear" of consequences and parents feeling helpless and alone.

Parents need to be educated about the law regarding parental liability and responsibility. I have seen parents lose everything they have worked for because their child drained them financially. I have talked to parents who have had to reach deep into their bank accounts to pay for damages incurred by their child. I have encountered parents who have spent thousands of dollars retrieving their runaway offspring many times over from areas far from home. I have worked with parents in court who have gone into debt to pay for the legal costs of their child being prosecuted for crimes committed. I have counseled parents whose child has reached that last stage of defiance and has just quit obeying. These are parents who love their children and would give anything to have their child follow the rules and stay out of trouble. These parents have fallen for the lie of a few so-called experts, "Don't touch your kids." And it doesn't work. God's word states that corporal punishment is a necessary part of child rearing. It's time for someone to say, "Enough is enough."

We will examine corporal punishment from three aspects. First, we will examine what God says about spanking and cite examples from God's word to substantiate the claim that corporal punishment is not only helpful, but necessary, in rearing a child. Second, we will examine the law. Does the state in which you reside allow you to spank your children? Third, we will look at the argument of the nonspanking expert from a "common sense" viewpoint. Does what the antispanking crowd say make sense?

This book is designed to educate parents as to their liability, responsibility, and authority. A parent must know the *limit* of his or her power to avoid exceeding it, and the *extent* of the power to exercise it fully. Once parents know to what extent they can go to control their child, they can move forward without fear of arrest or interference from the authorities. And once the child realizes that the parent is in total control, the will is broken and compliance results. I hope this book will help those of you who are desperately making an attempt to change your child's behavior. Your child's future depends on it.

1

SPANKING

Like every rookie just out of the police academy, I wanted to hit the road in a police car and catch bad guys. But like every other rookie before me, I was assigned the parking ticket detail in the central area of the city. The afternoon was just lovely as I walked the beat in the downtown area looking for the everdangerous parking violator. With ticket book in one hand and pen in the other, I carefully scrutinized the "no parking" areas for any flagrant fool daring enough to chance my presence. Since every rookie got this job on nice days, I figured that I may as well make the best of it. I smiled and waved at an elderly lady, glaring at me as she ripped a citation from her windshield.

Suddenly, the air was shattered by a bloodcurdling scream. "No, no, no" the young voice bellowed. It seemed to be a small child in distress, the sound coming from municipal lot number one. I raced toward the commotion as fast as I could as the child's voice screamed "No, stop." As I rounded the corner of the building, I heard an older female voice state gruffly "Get in, now!" Wow, I thought. I've stumbled upon a kidnapping! This is going to make me famous. From rookie to hero in a matter of months. I thought of drawing my firearm as I rounded the corner, prepared for the worse scenario imaginable.

What I observed in the parking lot didn't exactly settle my mind. A well-dressed woman was struggling to wedge a child of about three years of age into the front seat of a car. She was having a difficult time accomplishing her objective due to the thrashing legs and arms of the child. Every time the adult would gain the upper hand, the child would manage to land a pretty good shot with a fist or foot. Whammo, and the woman would back off for a second. Placing as much authority in my voice as possible, I yelled in the direction of the struggle, "Hold it a minute here."

The woman spun around, her flushed face an indication of how high her blood pressure was reaching. She squinted in the sunlight as she strained to see who was speaking to her in such authoritative tones. "Oh officer," she exclaimed, "thank God you're here!" Since your average kidnapper seldom enjoys seeing a policeman arrive on the scene of the kidnapping, it was fairly safe to assume that this woman was not a criminal. Perhaps she was the child's mother, or at the very least, her nanny. I took it upon myself to investigate further to establish whether this adult had the right to be woman-handling this child.

Several photographs later it was apparent that this child belonged to this lady. The woman sorted through ten or fifteen pictures from her purse, each one of her darling daughter, each one with the little angel's tongue stuck out at the camera. Aside from the tongue, I realized that the little girl even resembled the woman, enough evidence for me to prove a genetic connection. At that point I was pretty well satisfied that a kidnapping was not in progress.

"Officer," the woman said, "would you please make my daughter get in her car seat?" So that's what this is all about, I thought. It's just a poor mother trying to get her child to comply with her wishes. Having three of my own children, I realized that this was an opportunity for me to impress this woman with the wisdom of today's policeman. Here's a chance for me to really use all of that authority that the city gave me. I bent down and leaned into the front seat of the car. I immediately recognized the tongue I had just seen in all those pictures. Just a slight obstacle to overcome, I thought. Nothing to get too concerned about.

"Sweetheart," I began. "You know that your mother loves you very much." I paused to observe any reaction that I might get. Nothing. The child just stared at me without expression. I continued. "You know that mommy doesn't want you to get hurt now, don't you?"

"Shut up!" was the reply. My recoil caused the back of my head to crack on the inside of the roof of the car. The child stuck her tongue back out and blew saliva all over my face. This was a little tougher than I had expected. I knew how to handle my kids when they talked back, but this was a different experience. I figured I would have to try the tough approach. "Young lady," I stated, "I think you had better do what your mommy says and sit in this car seat!" The little girl scrunched up her face, crossed her arms, and hollered, "No!" It was evident that this kid wanted to play tough. My next move was to explain the blow by blow description of a high speed crash. When I got to the part about how her pretty face would slam into the dashboard and knock her pretty teeth down her pretty throat, she responded by giving me the raspberries again.

I quickly exited the car to avoid the saliva spray coming my way. The mother, standing nearby, leaned down and yelled "If you don't get in that seat, I am going to have this policeman take you to jail!" That threat didn't even phase the little demonette as she continued to shout "no" and "shut up." The mother stood up, wringing her hands. "I have no idea what to do with her," she moaned. "I've tried everything, and she just won't do what I say." What I said next couldn't have had more of a negative effect if I had slapped the mother in the face. "Why don't you try spanking her," I suggested.

There was a long pause as the woman's eyes narrowed to slits. She took a deep breath and clenched her teeth. "That's all you guys with guns think about," she growled, "is violence." The astonished look on my face probably tipped off my thought at the moment as the woman continued to struggle with the uncooperative child. I was wondering how much more violent this little urchin could get. Long past the point when my young ones would have gotten an emphatic little slap on the bucket, this woman was trying to work some kind of deal with the mini-terrorist. "Look honey," she said, "if you get into the car seat, I'll give you a nice treat when you get home." This attempt also failed, as the youngster stuck out her tongue and shouted, "No!" The mother tossed the child's seat into the rear of the vehicle and slammed the door. "Excuse me, ma'am," I said softly. "You are aware that it is against the law to allow your child to ride in your car in that manner?" The mother crossed her arms (much like the little demonette had) and sighed. "Well," she said, "you'll just have to give me a ticket then, won't you!"

I didn't give the woman a ticket. I ended up shaking my head as the car drove away, the woman screaming at the child to let go of the steering wheel as they pulled out of the lot. I actually felt sorry for her. The mother had been defeated by a creature one tenth her age, one fifth her weight, and only a fraction of her intelligence. She was actually going to allow this small child to have her own way, totally unaware of how dangerous it could be standing on the front seat of a moving car. I was imagining the problems that this mother was bound to encounter when her daughter reaches the age of thirteen. At the age of three, the daughter was already dictating policy and procedures, even though those decisions endangered her very life. The mother was absolutely powerless over her daughter with the use of threats and promises.

The first thirteen years of my career I spent as a patrol officer on the road. Since then I have been assigned to the detective bureau, in charge of the juvenile crime unit. I have observed firsthand what happens when a child is allowed to do whatever he/she pleases, with little or no restrictions set by the parents. I am constantly amazed at the attitude of parents who have allowed their offspring to rule the roost. I have responded to many domestic violence calls that involved the abuse of a parent by a child. The common denominator amongst these cases is the lack of parental discipline as the child was growing up. I have asked parents the same set of questions in every case. When did you start having trouble with your child? Why do you think he is acting like this? How do you discipline your child when he gets out of line? The answers are always the same. What astounds me is the feeling by these parents that spanking small children makes them violent when they get older. There is only one thing wrong. Almost every one of the domestic violence incidents that I have responded to involving abused parents reveals a child who was never spanked. So how do you explain this?

As I mentioned in the introduction, I once responded to a call of a fifteen-year-old kid who just busted a ceramic lamp over his mother's head, hit his father with a fire poker, threw a coffee table through the front picture window, and wrestled with five policeman before he was finally subdued in handcuffs. Being the junior man on the call, I was required to compile the information for the police report. As I talked with the mother, she explained to me how they had always experienced problems with their son obeying them. I asked her at what age she had noticed this defiance in her son, to which she replied, "Oh, about two or three years old." I pursued the subject and asked her what type of consequences they had imposed when their son defied their authority. She explained that they had tried "time-outs," but they had never been very successful. They had attempted to make him sit in a chair, but he would just get up and walk away. I decided to ask her if she had ever spanked her son as a small child when he misbehaved. She became very angry as she replied, "We don't believe in spanking. Violence begets violence!" I wondered if the woman realized how utterly ridiculous she sounded. Why in the world was her kid so violent? Because he was spanked as a small child? No. This kid had never been spanked. And he was one of the most violent children I had ever encountered.

Although there is a growing concern in this country about the problem of child abuse, there is also a movement to convince the population that all parents are overreactive and dangerous to the well-being of their children. There is nothing that could be further from the truth. I believe that if an accurate survey could be conducted that would indicate the percentage of loving, caring parents who incorporate corporal punishment into the training and rearing of their offspring, the numbers would be higher than realized. The reason is that most of the older parents today were reared with the same philosophy. Unfortunately, many are being deceived by the liberal permissive attitude becoming more and more prevalent in our culture. For centuries, parents have used spanking as a form of loving discipline. Now, with the parents reading Dr. Spock while they allow their children "freedom of expression," the problem of children's behavior has worsened instead of improved. The "permissive" parenting concept has bred a generation of uncontrolled self-centered spoiled children who have no idea how important it is to comply with the wishes or demands of their teachers, bosses, police officers, and judges. The temper-tantrum-throwing five year old has grown into the temper-tantrum-throwing twenty-five year old, who has few friends, has been in trouble with the law, cannot hold a job, and cannot control his temper. In most cases, the parents were truly concerned about the future well-being of their child; they simply were deceived into believing the lie of modern-day psychology.

While visiting a group of friends one evening, the subject turned to child discipline. One of the couples in the group had differing views on discipline. The husband had no problem swatting the bottom of the two year old when he defied their authority. Mom had a slightly different view and expressed "difficulty" spanking her two young children. As we discussed juvenile crime and the direction our culture seemed to be headed, the mother stated that she had "the feeling" that by using physical discipline on her sons, they would grow up to be violent. She felt that if her son was spanked as a child, he would grow up to be aggressive and would get in trouble "hitting" other people. She felt that she would be teaching her son to be aggressive if she were aggressive in her discipline.

I pursued the subject with her and asked her if she had ever been spanked by her parents when she was a child. "Oh yes," she answered. "If I got out of line, I got whacked a good one." I advised her that I had also been spanked by my parents when I was a child. I then asked her "How many times have you been arrested as an adult for walking up to someone and slugging them a good one?" She looked confused. "I take it you're an aggressive person who can't control your urge to hit people?" She frowned slightly and then smiled. "No," she replied, "I'm not aggressive at all." When I suggested to the mom that she "think about it," she admitted that her theory was not one that was born of experience. It was something that she had heard from someone else. A "theory" that has never been proven.

There was a man who lived long ago named King Solomon; he was divinely inspired by God to write the Book of Proverbs. Considered one of the wisest men who ever lived, he wrote in chapter 29 and verse 15, "The rod and reproof give wisdom: but a child left to himself bringeth his mother to shame." This verse is what I would consider child rearing in a nutshell. Much like John 3:16 is to the gospel, Proverbs 29:15 is to rearing children. It covers the elements needed to rear a child, the elements necessary to destroy a child, and the end result of the action or lack of action taken. The ability to intentionally change the meaning of this verse is nonexistent. The original Hebrew text makes it very clear that a combination of physical discipline (the rod) and nurturing and advice (reproof) results in a child with the culpable mental state to make conscious decisions as to what is right and wrong (wisdom). Parents who eliminate either of these elements from their discipline plan will foster a child who is submissive but unemotional (all rod and no reproof) or defiant of authority (all reproof and no rod).

King Solomon also wrote in Proverbs 13:24, "He that spareth his rod hateth his son: but he that loveth him chasteneth him betimes." In this verse, God is instructing parents not to search for alternative forms of discipline when the circumstances warrant a spanking. The parents' instincts tell them that a five-year-old child should be spanked when he/she says "no" to a direct order from the parent, yet many parents attempt to change this negative behavior by sentencing the child to a "time-out." Proverbs 13:24 tells us that a parent who fails to use corporal punishment in this situation shows a lack of love for the child.

The rod and reproof give wisdom.

As a police officer in charge of our city's juvenile bureau, I have observed firsthand the results of the recent "philosophical doctrine" on our culture. In fact, law enforcement often bears the result of social experimentation. According to F.B.I. statistics, during a recent ten-year period, murders committed by juveniles increased by 150 percent. Is this because more parents are spanking their children than in the past? I think not. The F.B.I.'s Uniform Crime Reports indicates that during that same period, there was a 97 percent increase in felony assaults committed by juveniles. Is this due to a larger percentage of parents incorporating corporal punishment into their disciplinary measures? Not on your life!

During the past ten years in my city alone, we have experienced a 700 percent increase in children committing domestic violence offenses against their parents. A statistic that alarms me more is that of those children charged with physically assaulting their mothers and fathers, only 1.9 percent were ever spanked by their parents. This is more glaring evidence that the lack of corporal punishment is contributing to the increase in juvenile delinquency. Years ago, when more parents used spanking as a loving form of discipline, a child would never dream of swearing at or hitting his mother or father. Now I see it on a regular basis due to the lack of fear the child has of the parents' authority. King Solomon's words, "He that spareth his rod hateth his son" is proving to be accurate. Parents who don't incorporate corporal punishment into their discipline plan all too often end up with angry, frustrated teenagers who are looking desperately for control in their lives.

Many pediatricians endorse spanking, including Dr. Den Trumbull of Montgomery, Alabama, who states that sophisticated studies have consistently shown that corporal punishment is effective and not harmful to long-term development of the child.[1] Parents have spanked their children for thousands of years. It is a time-tested form of discipline and has been effective in instilling responsibility into millions of children. For those "experts" who contend that spanking harms a child, Proverbs 23:13 addresses that very issue. The verse reads "Withhold not correction from the child: for if thou beatest him with the rod, he shall not die." How many times have we instructed our children to do something that was not very popular, but necessary, then added "It's not going to kill you!" Remember the cut on the elbow that needed the antiseptic, and you knew it was going to sting the youngster when you sprayed it on. You knew the pain was part of the cure, and all you could say was "Settle down, you're not going to die!" God is telling us in Proverbs 23:13 that although the rod of correction causes pain, it causes no other negative side effects. That pain instills one thing in the mind and heart of that child—a fear and respect for authority.

In the majority of kids that I see in my office and in court standing in front of the judge, there is one common similarity. Those kids have no fear. There is no fear of punishment for wrongdoing, no fear of consequences for negative behavior, and no fear of authority. Why does a thirteen-year-old boy sneer in his father's face and spew obscenities? Why does a fourteen-year-old girl call her mother filthy names and defy her authority? Why does a fifteen-year-old child punch a parent with a closed fist? It's because there is no fear of consequences. Many of these kids come from homes where the parents attempted to place restrictions on the child's behavior. Some of these out-of-control kids were grounded when they misbehaved. Some of them had privileges (like the television, telephone, and freedom on the weekends) taken away when they disobeyed. Yet they still developed an in-your-face attitude toward their parents. Why?

In almost every case I have worked with that involves a child or teenager who has completely defied the authority of his or her parents, the child did not experience any type of corporal punishment growing up. Time and time again, when questioning parents about the type of upbringing the child had, I find that the kids with the worst attitudes are the ones who were never spanked.

Think about it. When you were growing up, what did you fear most as punishment from your parents when you got caught doing something wrong? Were you really afraid of being grounded or losing privileges? Although it was boring for a few days, those penalties did not instill fear into your soul. It was the dreaded spanking that we were afraid of. It was the fear of being sent to your room, with the information that dad would be there shortly to deal out a spanking as punishment for your wrongdoing. It was the fear when you heard the leather snapping out of dad's belt loops. There was nothing that made you move faster or made your heart beat harder. You were *afraid* of the consequence. You feared your parents' authority. It acted as a deterrent to negative behavior.

Another trait that I have recognized in kids who have never been spanked is an uncontrollable anger and a hatred toward the parent who has reared them in such a manner. This correlation became very obvious to me very early in my career. Today's researchers are attempting to convince us that a spanked child is an angry child. My findings are the *complete opposite*!

One of the children that I dealt with over the years began her final stage of defiance at the age of thirteen. For the purposes of identification, we'll call her Barbara. She was the offspring of a marriage that didn't work out and ended in divorce when the girl was two. The mother remarried a year later to a soft-spoken man who attempted to introduce some structure and discipline into Barbara's life. The mother, who did not feel that spanking was an option, prevented her husband from using that form of discipline. The couple had another child, a son, when Barbara was five years old. Dad soon found out that he was not allowed to use corporal punishment on his biological offspring either. When Barbara began reaching the young teenage years, her parents began to notice that final stage of defiance. The husband attempted to take control of the daughter by dishing out discipline when there were obvious acts of defiance. It soon became apparent that the mother would not tolerate her husband even touching the children. On three occasions, the mother reported the father to our department for child abuse. Further investigation by our department and the department of social services determined that what the father was attempting to do was within the guidelines of the law. The father reported that the children were refusing to follow any of the rules and were swearing at him and the mother, yet the mother was trying to protect them from any kind of physical discipline. The father stated that the mother would attempt to ground the children or take privileges away, but her efforts seemed ineffective.

The relationship ended in divorce. Like most domestic relations cases, custody of the two children was granted to the mother. Although efforts were made by the father to gain custody of his biological son, he was denied the request by the court. The father then began calling our department with horror stories about the mother and son being abused by the teenage daughter. When our officers questioned the mother about the allegations, she denied them. We advised the father that we needed proof that Barbara was committing acts of domestic violence against her mother and brother. I decided to meet with Barbara and her mother, and set up an appointment for them to come into my office.

It was obvious from the get-go that Barbara had a chip on her shoulder. She sat defiantly in her chair with her arms crossed and a sneer on her face. Mom fidgeted in her chair while I talked, apparently afraid that something was going to go wrong. Mom's new boyfriend sat next to mom. He had already indicated to me that he felt Barbara was out of control. My intent was to explain to Barbara mom's liability and the daughter's responsibility. I was only into the spiel about five minutes when mom meekly attempted to point out one of Barbara's recent violations of the rules. Barbara at that point flew into a rage. She began spewing obscenities at her mother and came up out of her chair in an aggressive manner.

There is one thing I make very clear to those families who meet in my office. While you are there, you follow my rules. Everyone will treat everyone else with respect. There will be no yelling, no swearing, and no getting up and leaving. Barbara was already aware that I did not tolerate the behavior she was now exhibiting.

Barbara soon found out that I wasn't kidding around. I leaped out of my chair and grabbed her by the neck, lifting her up and into the wall behind her. Nothing that I was doing was hurting her, but you should have seen the look of surprise in her eyes. With the scariest "mean cop" look I could muster, I gritted my teeth and made it clear that one more outburst like that and I was going to place her under arrest for fourth degree disorderly conduct and we would be hauling her in handcuffs downtown to the detention center. I then slowly lowered Barbara into the chair by her lapels.

Barbara burst into tears. She sobbed uncontrollably for several minutes while mom's boyfriend restrained the mother from comforting her. I had reached this point numerous times with little tough guys. I was silent for several minutes until the sobbing quieted. I then asked softly, "Barbara, what makes you act the way you do?" Barbara looked down at the floor and answered, "Because my mom isn't tough enough on me." Mom looked at me with amazement. I thought for sure that I had made my point. After our meeting with Barbara was over, mom talked with me privately. I told her that what her daughter had admitted was profound, and it would be wise to take her daughter's indictment seriously.

About one month later, our officers responded to an anonymous call that an altercation was taking place in front of a convenience store in the middle of town. Our officers arrived to observe Barbara, duking it out with mom and the boyfriend. The officers had to use quite a bit of physical force to place the girl under arrest and place her in the police car. Mom explained that she had asked the girl to return home, and Barbara had refused. When they attempted to force her into the car, the fight ensued. Because Ohio has a preferred arrest policy for domestic violence offenses, mom's objections to her daughter being taken to the detention home were ignored, and Barbara was whisked away to kiddie jail. It was not until I received the case dispositions from juvenile court that I discovered that mom later refused to testify against her daughter, and the case was dismissed.

Our department kept receiving reports from the ex-husband that his son was in danger. Because mom covered up any wrongdoing by her daughter, it was difficult to compile any type of case, by either the police department or the department of children's services. Then one day to my surprise, mom called me in my office. She had reached the point where fear for her life was pushing her into taking action against Barbara. She explained to me that she had installed a dead-bolt on her bedroom door to protect herself against her daughter at night. She had recently installed a telephone tap on her line to record conversations her daughter was having with her friends. Much to her surprise, she recorded her daughter making arrangements with a friend to hire a hit man to kill her. During the same week, the younger boy had been beat up by his older sister because he told his mother

The juvenile court is understaffed and overburdened with juvenile crime.

about something his sister did. Barbara was now involved in the ritual of smoking marijuana in pages torn out of the Holy Bible. I'm sure in her eyes, this was the ultimate defiance of authority. In a very short amount of time, our officers were placing Barbara under arrest, charged with conspiracy to commit murder and domestic violence. Barbara is another subject in my study that is proving more and more that spanking a child doesn't make them angry and aggressive. Not spanking them does.

There's a tendency to use the term "spanking" when referring to any type of corporal punishment, when we should be more specific in our terms. A spanking to me when I was growing up was a swat on the buttocks or the back of the legs. My parents used something besides their hand to make contact with my derriere, usually a belt or wooden spoon. I remember my dad once saying, "This is meant to hurt you, not me!"

Dr. James Dobson, in his book *The Strong-Willed Child* states, "When spankings occur, they should be administered with a neutral object; that is with a small switch or belt, but rarely with the hand."[2] Dr. Dobson goes on to say that he has always felt that the hand should be seen by the child as an object of affection rather than an instrument of punishment. (There are exceptions to this rule, such as when a child's hands are slapped or thumped for reaching for a stove or other dangerous object.)

I was never slapped in the face as a child, although I remember being slapped on the back of the head. Although some advocates of corporal punishment do not condone face slapping (and at least one state prohibits the practice, considering it child abuse), I know numerous parents who have given the open palm to the cheek of a sassy offspring with no noticeable adverse effects. Some of you might recall the recent domestic assault case in Michigan, where a mother slapped her adult daughter for swearing at her. Although the parental discipline law no longer protected the mother because the daughter was past the age of emancipation, a jury found the mother not guilty of domestic assault, even though the criteria was filled to satisfy a violation under the law. When the jurors were interviewed by Court TV after the case, they basically stated that no daughter should talk to her mother as she had and that she "deserved what she got." Here was a case that involved an actual violation of the law, but because of the public sentiment about parents being treated with respect by their children, the jury returned a verdict of not guilty.

Dr. Dobson also refers to what I call "pain compliance." In law enforcement, pain compliance comes in handy when you encounter a person you plan to arrest who plans not to be arrested. Once you announce to the suspect that they are under arrest, you had better plan on taking them into custody, even if they don't intend on going along. It would be embarrassing after the suspect told you that he was not going to jail, to have to say, "Oh, I'm sorry to have bothered you, you are now unarrested. Have a nice day." Police officers use whatever tools are available to them, nightsticks, flashlights, and handcuffs, to place pressure on certain parts of the body to cause pain. Pressure on the wrist, fingers, forearm, or other sensitive parts of the body will cause your prisoner to wail, "Alright, alright, I'll go, just let up a little." Dr. Dobson states,

> Minor pain can provide excellent motivation for the child, when appropriate. You see, the parent should have some means of making the child want to cooperate, other than simply obeying because he was told to do so. For those who can think of no such device, I will suggest one: there is a muscle, lying snugly against the base of the neck. Anatomy books list it as the trapezius muscle, and when firmly squeezed, it sends little messengers to the brain saying, "This hurts; avoid recurrence at all costs." The pain is only temporary; it can cause no damage. When the youngster ignores being told to do something by his parent, he should know that mom has a practical recourse.[3]

For thousands of years, parents have used pain as a motivator for positive behavior in their children. For thousands of years, parents have utilized switches from trees, belts, razor straps, and wooden spoons. For thousands of years parents have squeezed that trapezius muscle and boxed those ears. For thousands of years kids have gotten cracked a good one when they talked back. For thousands of years kids have gotten spanked with the belt when they got caught shoplifting. And do you know what? They turned out alright. In fact, they turned out normal. Remember the kid at the family reunion who had never been spanked? While he screamed and had temper tantrums, his mother smiled at everyone and proclaimed that he was a "spirited child." Everyone else was hoping they could get just two minutes alone with this brat without anyone else seeing them. Maybe they could teach him the lesson his mother wasn't teaching him.

With the advent of the digital age, most of us have learned how to use a computer, either at work or on our own personal machines. We have all encountered the dreaded lockup, when the computer, seeming to have a mind of its own, refuses to comply with our commands. When nothing else works, we hit the reset button. Kids also have a reset button. It's located on the rear side of the body directly below the waist and above the thighs. A good whack on the "control-alt-delete" bucket restructures their thinking and restores the program to its original direction and order.

Look around, folks. What do you see? Are children better behaved now than when we were young? Do children treat their parents with more respect now than thirty years ago? The implementation of the liberal philosophical and psychological "theories" has resulted in a society that is more violent and less respectful of authority and the rights of others. I believe it's time to trust the wisdom of Solomon rather that the theories of modern psychology.

2

TRAINING

"Train up a child in the way he should go, and when he is old, he will not depart from it" (Proverbs 22:6).

Officer James Mayer was found lying on the ground next to his police cruiser in the parking lot beside the bank. He had been shot three times in the upper torso, one of the bullets severing the carotid artery in his neck. Death had occurred within seconds after he was hit with a hail of bullets from the bank robber's gun. Little did Officer Mayer know, as he responded to the bank alarm, that his life would end within minutes.

Investigators cordoned off the area as they tried to determine how Officer Mayer died. Detectives who responded to the scene went to the body, lifted the sheet, and peered down at the lifeless form that had been a few hours earlier a partner in the war against crime. How in the world did he allow himself to be placed in such a compromising position? How did he allow the bank robber to get so close as to get three well-placed shots into a vital area? In his right hand was his service revolver, a .357 magnum with the cylinder open and no rounds in the gun. Investigators then noticed that his left hand was in his left pants pocket.

As investigators pulled Officer Mayer's left hand from his pocket, six shiny .357 caliber brass shells fell out onto the pavement. They were empty rounds, the brass remains of bullets that had been fired. Each piece of brass was worth about one cent. This was the brass that was usually recycled and reloaded with new powder and new lead in order to save money. Reloads, they were called. Most departments saved their brass when they trained on the firing range in order to save on the

Officer Mayer lost his life reacting to a shootout exactly as he had been trained on the firing range.

budget when ordering new ammunition. So while training on the firing line, officers were instructed to open the cylinder of their revolver, empty the brass into their left hand, place it in their pocket, and then reload with new ammunition. At the end of the range detail, the officer then dug all of that brass out of his left pocket and placed it in the brass bucket. It was something all officers did every time they qualified with their weapon. It became part of the training procedure.

Considering the fact that every police officer knows that an empty brass round is worth about one cent, you would assume that under life threatening conditions during a gun battle, an officer would disregard the part of his training that conditioned him to place his empty brass in his pocket. You would think that a police officer would place his life first before worrying about saving six cents worth of brass. You would think a police officer would empty the brass from his gun onto the ground quickly without looking down and placing himself at risk during a gun battle. You would think that a police officer would be intelligent enough to figure out the difference between training and reality.

King Solomon wrote in Proverbs 22:6, "Train up a child in the way he should go, and when he is old, he will not depart from it." Notice that the verse doesn't say, "when he is old, he *might not* depart from it," or "when he is old there is a good chance he will not depart from it." The verse reads "when he is old, he *will not* depart from it." This isn't a simple suggestion. This is a promise. I once challenged my father on this verse, advising him that I had observed teenagers whose parents were very diligent in their structure and discipline and had been disappointed with the actions of their eighteen year old who moved out and seemed to abandon the values that the parents had tried to instill in him. My father was quick to point out that the promise does not say, "when he is going through puberty, he will not depart from it," or "when he is a teenager, he will not depart from it." The verse promises that "when he is old, he will not depart from it." Case after case proves that even though that child tears himself away during that last stage of defiance and independence, when he finally matures, he will revert back to the instruction and teaching of his parents.

Like the police officer who lost his life trying to save six cents worth of brass, we become conditioned as we are growing up to react certain ways to certain types of stimuli. When police departments began realizing that their officers respond under fire exactly as they were trained on the firing range, training officers began to modify their training scenarios. Officers were no longer required to save their

Officers are now trained on the firing range under conditions that are as close as possible to conditions encountered on the street.

brass when reloading their guns. They were trained to dump the empty shells out onto the ground without taking their eyes off the enemy and reload with new ammunition as quickly as possible. As a parent, if we see that the method of training we are using on our children is failing, it is our responsibility to modify that training until a more effective method is discovered.

A person who "trains" other people always knows more about the subject that they are demonstrating than the person who is being trained. It would be foolish for a rookie police officer just out of the academy to attempt to train the veteran shift sergeant how to handle domestic violence calls. It happens the other way around. The person with the experience and knowledge is the one who teaches or trains the one with no experience and no knowledge. Parents always know more than their child. I have only been involved in one case where the child was smarter than the parents. It involved a fourteen-year-old boy who had a mentally handicapped mother and father, each with the mentality of nine or ten year olds. But even in that case, the life experiences that both parents had lived through gave them the instincts to know when their child was in trouble and headed in the wrong direction. That mentally handicapped mother, sensing something was wrong with her boy, searched his room one day and found a bag of marijuana in his dresser drawer. Within minutes she was calling me on the telephone, "Detective Surgenor, I need your help!"

Parents instinctively know what is best for their children. Children, even in their late teenage years, don't know what is best for themselves. And even if they do know what is in their best interest, they will usually make a decision to do the opposite. And I can prove it.

Every time I have a kid in my office along with the parents, I try to get the brain cells working and everyone thinking. My intent is to prove to the kid that his parents are smarter than he is. If I can prove that to him, I'll have a better chance of convincing him that his parents should be the people in charge. I say to the child, "Let's imagine that tomorrow, the principal of your school makes an announcement that Friday is an optional day to attend school. Friday is not a mandatory attendance day. The teachers will be here, the classrooms will be open, but no one will get in trouble if they stay home on that one day." The kid usually looks at me as though I should know the answer to my next question before I ask it. "How many students," I ask, "do you think would be in school on Friday?" The answer is always "Not many!"

My next question drives the point home. "Now, Johnny, be very honest with me. Is it in your best interest to go to school, or is it in your best interest to stay home?" I have not had one child argue the fact that going to school is very definitely in their best interest. The point is not hard to make. There are times when even though children know that a certain type of action is in their best interest, they will elect to take the irresponsible action. Children are fortunate that there are parents who can control their behavior. From my observations, I have found that unless the parent "trains" their children to make responsible decisions, children will grow into adulthood continuing in an irresponsible manner, unable to make decisions that are in their own best interest.

As previously mentioned, one of the most evident differences in many of today's children, as compared to those of thirty or forty years ago, is the lack of fear of consequences. These children have not been trained through the use of discipline that they are afraid of. Many of today's "child experts" have made us believe that a parent should never be "feared" by their children. What we are now experiencing is the result of the "no fear" attitude. It's something that has even taken hold in the marketing world. We see it on baseball caps and on the rear windows of cars being driven by teenagers. No fear. Parents are experiencing the defiance of the "no fear" attitude, along with school teachers, employers, police officers and judges. We have a generation of "no fear" kids who have never been trained to fear the consequences of defying authority.

I have talked to hundreds of other police officers, many of them working juvenile units, who agree that the one missing component in delinquent youth is the fear of consequences. If children are afraid enough of the penalty for their wrongdoing, they won't commit the offense. If they don't have any fear of what will happen to them, the offense is easier to commit.

When I was a patrol officer on the road, I soon got to know many of the local teenagers who drove their cars recklessly. Many of them came from wealthy families, with parents who were quick to bail them out of trouble. One kid in particular received, on three separate occasions, three traffic citations from myself. Other officers on the department also kept an eye out for the youngster who had a heavy foot and flagrant disregard for others on the highway.

Then one day, while patrolling in a semi-marked police car (one that was very difficult to identify as a police car), I spotted the young man operating his souped-up vehicle down the main street of the city.

I pulled in behind him, confident he hadn't recognized my car as a police cruiser. It was soon evident that Sam Speedy was obeying every traffic law on the books. He was using his blinker to change lanes. He was stopping completely for every stop sign. He was obeying the speed limit. I was flabbergasted that the young man was behaving so.

I then thought of a possible reason as to why Donnie Dragster was trying so hard to comply with the law. I picked up the radio microphone and asked dispatch to run the young man's name through for a traffic record check. It only took seconds for dispatch to confirm my suspicion. Our carefree driver wasn't so carefree anymore. He had ten points on his driver's license. In Ohio, you lose your driving privileges when you collect twelve points on your driving record. Since most moving violations, such as speeding or running a stop sign, are two points, one more violation would push him over the top. The state of Ohio would suspend his driving privileges, and mommy and daddy couldn't do a thing to prevent it. The parents had been quick to pay their son's fines and court costs, but they had no control over the state. And junior knew it. He was afraid of the consequences of violating one more traffic law. And to confirm my "theory," as soon as some of those points started to drop off his driving record, he started operating his car like a maniac again. The real fear of a consequence controlled the young man's behavior.

A police lieutenant once made a comment to myself and a group of officers about the missing fear factor. "When I was a kid," he said, "when my parents would ground me, it was a real inconvenience. When they took my television privileges away, it was real boring. But what really got me to move, was when I heard the leather coming out of my father's belt loops. That's what made me respect my father." Another officer piped up, "For me, it was the wooden spoon out of the kitchen drawer."

That lieutenant is one hundred and ten percent correct. If you think back to your school days, and you consider all the teachers that you had as you went through school, the teacher that was the toughest was the one who gained your respect. I remember teachers who were constantly bullied by the students—teachers who were back-talked and did nothing; teachers who were made fun of to their face and turned away. I did not have much respect for those teachers. But those strict disciplinarians, who didn't take any guff and put the disrupters in their place, gained the respect of all of the other students. In fact, they gained the respect of the clowns who didn't behave in any other class.

And their class was always orderly and comfortable to learn in. These students had been trained to act properly. There was a fear of consequences for violating the rules. And everyone felt good about it.

A friend of mine, Bob Reitman, who counsels families who are referred to him by our police department, has a great analogy to demonstrate the importance of consistency when it comes to training or conditioning children. I first heard this analogy during a seminar the two of us held titled "How to Change Your Child's Behavior."[1]

"Why do people play slot machines" Reitman asked the audience. "What would happen if every time you put a quarter in a slot machine, you lost?" The audience, already conditioned to hear information on rearing children, began to get the picture. "If every time that you put a quarter in a slot machine, you lost the quarter," Bob said, "you would eventually quit playing the slot machine and walk away. What keeps you putting those quarters in that machine and losing quarter after quarter, is the one time you win the jackpot. Win one time, and you will start pumping more quarters in that machine, hoping that you will win again."

Reitman went on to make his analogy. "Consistency is most important when it comes to discipline," he said. "Every time your kid violates a rule, he's pulling that handle. And every time you let him get away with it, he wins. But if every time he loses, eventually he will give up and walk away. If he can't win, he'll eventually quit trying."

Bob Reitman is absolutely correct. This is what is referred to as "intermittent reinforcement." If children can avoid the consequences for negative behavior just once in a while, they will take the chance to win again. If a parent enforces a rule and imposes consequences with consistency, a child becomes conditioned to associate the consequence with the negative behavior. That child will eventually "give up," and that particular negative behavior will cease.

Although consistency is important when it comes to consequences for wrongdoing, the severity of the punishment must also be considered. Common sense dictates that the more severe the penalty for committing the offense, the less chance there will be that someone will take that chance. Granted, without some consistency in enforcement, the severity doesn't matter at all, so a balance between the two is needed. Consider the results if every person who was caught shoplifting was immediately taken outside and executed on the spot. It would take just a few executions before all shoplifters would consider another line of work. If this penalty was enforced even sporadically, few would take the chance of being one of the few being put to death behind the mall by trigger-happy mall security guards. If that most severe penalty was combined with precise consistency in enforcement, I can guarantee you that all shoplifting would cease.

Now we all know that being executed for shoplifting a candy bar is excessive. So somewhere between killing the person and doing nothing there is a logical answer. I like Bob Reitman's mosquito analogy about this issue. Bob told the seminar audience about the couple who couldn't agree on how to handle the pesky insect. The woman argued that if they just waited long enough, it would eventually die of old age. It's just that they would have to put up with it biting them during the night, every night until it died. The husband, more aggressive than his wife, got out the shotgun, planning to shoot the pest. This plan would definitely eliminate the problem; they would just have to deal with the large hole in the wall. His point was that somewhere between doing nothing and destroying their home was a logical solution.

One night while patrolling on the graveyard shift, our station dispatched myself and several other cruisers to a trucking firm in our city. Someone had called the police to report that there was a suspicious man sneaking around the tractor trailers parked near the docks. As we pulled into the lot we killed our headlights and coasted to the area where the male had been reported. Exiting our police cars, we spotted a van parked with its lights out and the rear doors open. Inside the van were four truck tires. We soon located the man, very suspiciously kneeling down next to a trailer with a breaker bar in his hand. It was obvious he was trying to dislodge tire number five. The threat of a shotgun pointed at his head quickly convinced mister suspicious to drop his breaker bar and place his hands over his head. He was soon being booked in the booking room of our police station. A check of his criminal history uncovered the fact that he had been convicted eleven prior times for stealing truck tires. This, for him, was a way of life.

We soon noticed that the truck tire bandit was a bit skittish. He would flinch every time we moved near him. When I fingerprinted him, he cowered as though I was going to break his fingers. He kept covering up every time someone walked close to him. As he sat at the booking table answering questions, one of the officers asked him to sign the Miranda form advising him of his rights. As he pushed the piece of paper across the table, the prisoner flung his hands up in front of his face and moved backward. The officer, noticing the strange behavior of the arrested man, asked him, "What in the world is wrong with you?"

"Why don't you guys just go ahead and get it over with and beat the snot out of me!" he replied. We all looked at each other in amazement. The officer pursued the mystery. "What in the world do you mean?" the officer asked. "We're not going to beat the snot out of you!" The prisoner then relayed an incident in which he was involved in another city. (We'll call that city Hitsburgh for obvious reasons.)

"Well," mister breaker bar replied, "the cops in Hitsburgh did! They broke my jaw; they broke four of my ribs; and they broke my right arm. And they said I resisted arrest. And I didn't!" We all knew the reputation of the Hitsburgh boys in blue. We chuckled as we asked the thief for more information.

"Why did the Hitsburgh cops beat you up?" asked the booking officer.

"Because they caught me stealing truck tires for the fourth time," he answered.

"Well," the booking officer asked, "do you steal truck tires in Hitsburgh any more?"

The prisoner looked at him in amazement. "Are you kidding?" he answered. "I don't even drive through Hitsburgh!"

Although no one condones the police taking the law into their own hands, and certainly no one will defend police officers beating up a criminal without just cause, we all realized that the Hitsburgh cops had accomplished something that the courts had been unable to do. They were protecting the trucking businesses in their city against Billie breaker bar. Truck drivers could show up for work in the morning in Hitsburgh without worrying if their trucks were up on blocks. The penalty in Hitsburgh for stealing truck tires was too severe. So what did our dishonest, suspicious, skittish, breaker bar friend learn? Steal truck tires in other cities. Namely, ours!

The moral of this story should be evident to all. Punishment doesn't work if the recipient isn't afraid of it. Obviously, jail wasn't a deterrent for our thieving friend. He was willing to break the rule and take the chance of being sent back to the pokey. But he was afraid of the consequences in Hitsburgh. He was afraid of the pain. He didn't want to spend more time in the hospital. He didn't want his nose bent in the wrong direction. He had *fear* of the consequences in Hitsburgh.

It is never too late to train a person to react to certain stimuli. I have known eighteen-year-old punks who have signed up with the Marine Corps, only to emerge years later with a new respect for authority. Anyone who has served in the military can tell you that with structure, discipline, and reward, a person will soon react to an order or command as they have been trained to. A child is much easier to "train" and will tend to shy away from activity or behavior that has resulted in negative consequences while attempting to behave in such a manner that results in reward. Both are critical in "training up a child."

Bob Reitman refers to the technique used to "train" a child as "behavior modification." Although each child reacts differently to each technique, they all contain the same message—act proper and get rewarded, act improper and get punished. One of Reitman's analogies used in our seminar "How to Change Your Child's Behavior" that I found interesting was the "conditioned pigeon" story. "There was this guy named B. F. Skinner at Harvard," Reitman said "that claimed he could train a pigeon to turn to the right in a circle in eight minutes. Every time the pigeon turns to the right, I'm going to give it a food pellet. It took Skinner eight minutes to train the pigeon to turn in a circle to the right. Somebody else came along and claimed that they could get the pigeon to react sooner by giving the pigeon a shock every time it turned to the left. So every time the pigeon turned to the left, it got an electric shock. Sure enough, it only took four minutes to train the pigeon to turn to the right. It didn't take long to figure out that with a combination of food pellets when the pigeon turned to the right, and electric shocks when the pigeon turned to the left, it only took two minutes to train the pigeon to do what they wanted it to do." Reitman went on to say that although he didn't think it was appropriate to give children food pellets or electric shocks, he made his point that inappropriate behavior needs to be dealt with by disciplining the child and extraordinary behavior needs to be rewarded. These are the basic fundamentals of training.

3
THE BIBLE

"But I will shew thee that which is noted in the scripture of truth" *(Daniel 10:21).*

In August of 1997, my wife Nancy and I were invited to appear on the MS-NBC News Cable Channel on a program that addressed the issue of spanking. We appeared opposite Dr. Murray Straus, today's leader of the nonspanking movement. I began to understand, for the first time, the real mind-set of the nonspanking advocate. As the live debate on the air progressed, I was shocked by the hostile and confrontational attitude of Dr. Straus regarding the subject. I was experiencing my first dose of anger from a movement designed to completely eliminate corporal punishment in child rearing and to reduce the authority parents have over their own children. I began to understand the agenda that the nonspanking group represents.

Another thing that I realized during my on-the-air confrontation with Straus was that although the nonspanking advocates profess to be knowledgeable in biblical facts, they are not. When I quoted Proverbs 29:15 during our debate, "The rod and reproof give wisdom: but a child left to himself bringeth his mother to shame," Straus immediately attempted to discredit the Bible by stating, "It's interesting that you didn't quote Leviticus, which says that if a child talks back to his parents, he should be stoned to death." I'm sure that many Christians watching this program immediately recognized that Straus had referred to the wrong book of the Bible. The passage Straus meant to use as his argument that the Bible is unreliable is actually located in Deuteronomy chapter 21. From my experience, I have found the nonspanking advocate (from here on referred to as the NSA) as having

25

read very little of the Bible. In fact, many actually appear to have a working knowledge of God's word, but that knowledge eventually emerges as being of little depth. In addition, their limited research in the Scriptures does not seem born of any sincere interest in God's word. The NSA apparently attempts to discredit the Bible by confusing their followers with claims that the Bible is ambiguous and contradictory. In order to argue against the Bible, the NSA needs to know something about the Bible. But unlike the dedicated Christian who, like those in Acts 17:11 "received the word with all readiness of mind, and searched the scriptures daily, whether those things were so," the NSA is blind to the truth of God's word. In order for the Christian to effectively use the Bible as a reference to advocate corporal punishment, he must know exactly what the Bible says about spanking.

Many of the nonspanking books on the shelves of our nation's bookstores include inaccurate information about God's word. Many of the authors of antispanking rhetoric also attack the Bible. William Sears, M.D., and Martha Sears, R.N., are a husband and wife team who feel they can convince their readers that the Bible is unreliable as a source of information. In their latest publication, *The Discipline Book*, is a section which is titled "Hitting Is Actually Not Biblical." The first paragraph states, "Don't use the Bible as an excuse to spank. There is confusion among some people of Judeo-Christian heritage who, seeking help from the Bible in their effort to raise good children, believe that God commands them to spank."[1] The Sears go on to say that people who "love God" misunderstand the concept of "the rod." However, it is the Sears who misunderstand what the Bible teaches about "the rod."

All scripture is given by inspiration of God, and is profitable for doctrine, for reproof, for correction, for instruction in righteousness.

It was not until I accessed the internet that I discovered how large the antispanking movement is. There are numerous web pages that advocate the elimination of corporal punishment in America. Many are sponsored or compiled by doctors and psychologists who attempt to prove their theory by posting statistics and findings for the general public to read. Unfortunately, there are no "internet police" to investigate and confirm that the web page you are reading is actually constructed by the party claiming to be the expert, or to substantiate the facts and statistics shown. In fact, many web pages have been found to be inaccurate and even downright deceiving.

By activating a search engine and typing in "corporal punishment," a person will receive information on all of the addresses on the World Wide Web that deal with that subject. There are thousands of web sites that deal with spanking children. The overwhelming majority of them are designed by the antispanking crowd. There are some sites that deal with the biblical approach to spanking, but they are few in number. As I searched the many sites dealing with this subject, I found that most antispanking advocates boast of their large numbers and claim that the few prospanking studies available are funded or supported by "fundamental Christians." One web site, www.religioustolerance.com makes the statement, "We have been unable to find any non-Christian references which promote child spanking."[2] Although this claim is not one hundred percent accurate, it does appear that the majority of prospanking studies and web sites are actually based upon or at least refer to biblical principles.

One of the advantages to internet information is the ability to contact the parties responsible for the information that appears on your computer screen. Many web pages have electronic mail available to those visiting the web site. Many encourage the reader to leave opinions or comments. When I began leaving e-mail messages for those running the web sites, I discovered two very important things. One, the people responsible for posting information on the internet regarding corporal punishment are generally misinformed and lacking in knowledge of statistics and facts. Secondly, the nonspanking advocate engages in an argument about biblical principals, not with personal knowledge but with a series of "cut and paste" statements designed to answer the many questions posed by the biblical scholar. The Christian who decides to take on this bunch with biblical facts will soon be talking to themselves. Although the nonspanking crowd will attempt to argue their case with paragraphs alleging the Bible to be ambiguous and contradictory, they will eventually give up when the real facts are presented to them. Before they give up, they will state that they are correct, no matter what, and that you are wrong, no matter what. I have experienced that reaction and will try to demonstrate in this chapter the methods used by the NSA with actual e-mail correspondence. It will become clear that the agenda of the NSA is to eliminate the authority that a parent has over the child. The NSA movement is definitely of the "it takes a village" to rear a child mentality.

There is a much more ominous objective behind the nonspanking movement. I believe that this group falls into the same category as the American Civil Liberties Union and other atheistic groups that are attempting to completely eliminate God from our culture. Their purpose in using Holy Scripture to argue their position is not because they believe that the Bible is inspired by God. I am sure that the NSA would rather that the Bible did not exist. Because the Holy Scriptures are still revered today by a large portion of our society, the NSA is desperately trying to destroy its validity. By criticizing selected portions of Scripture, the NSA attempts to criticize all Scripture, claiming it is not applicable to present-day child rearing. I have seen the faces of parents light up when I quote Proverbs 29:15. Even though our culture is moving further and further from God, many still believe the Bible to be the inspired word of our Creator and trust the advice contained in its pages.

In August of 1998, I accessed a web site called "The No Spanking Page." This web site contains numerous links to other no-spanking web pages and advice from countless "experts" on the subject of spanking. The site is operated by Randy Cox, whose screen name is RCox. I decided to send Cox an e-mail message to express my viewpoint on the elimination of corporal punishment and the increase in juvenile crime. I received Cox's answer several days later. At first, it appeared that Cox had a limited knowledge of the Bible. It was not until several more e-mail messages were sent back and forth that I realized how limited that knowledge was and that Cox's agenda was much more complicated than at first suspected. After receiving several answers to my questions, I shared some of Cox's answers with my father. My dad has been in the Lord's work since I was twelve years old and spends many hours a day studying God's word. His knowledge of the Bible is surpassed by few, and his ability to recall particular passages from the Bible is uncanny. Dad agreed to answer some of Cox's feeble attempts to use the Bible as an argument against spanking. The answers that we received to this new set of questions were of a different flavor completely than the first response, and I am not sure that the same individual was sending the answers we were now receiving. I suspect that there are several individuals who are responsible for answering e-mail questions and gather their responses from one large document.

What we have tried to do here is to answer the arguments of the NSA from a biblical standpoint. From William and Martha Sears to the Randy Cox web page, the NSA attempts to use the Bible as an argument against spanking. In order to understand what God's word says about corporal punishment, we must understand exactly what the Bible is. My father sent the following message to RCox to set the stage.

> To understand and rightly discern the Holy Scriptures one must consider a few things. First of all, one must acknowledge that ALL contained in the Holy Bible is divinely inspired by God. In other words, it is God, not man, that wrote the Bible. 2 Timothy 3:16 states—"All Scripture is given by inspiration of God, and is profitable for doctrine, for reproof, for correction, for instruction in righteousness." God used holy men to accomplish His design in giving us His divine revelation, as 2 Peter 1:21 states—"For the prophecy came not in old time by the will of man: but holy men of God spake as they were moved by the Holy Ghost." The Lord Jesus placed great value on the Old Testament Scriptures and declared them to be the word of God. After His resurrection, we read in Luke 24:27, "And beginning at Moses and all the prophets, he expounded unto them in all the scriptures the things concerning himself." In the four gospels, Christ refers to the Scriptures no less than ten times. God inspired the apostle Paul to pen these words, found in Romans 15:4, "For whatsoever things were written aforetime were written for our learning, that we through patience and comfort of the scriptures might have hope."

> Thus Christians believe the Holy Scriptures to be the infallible guide for every circumstance in life. The psalmist uttered, "Thy word is a lamp unto my feet, and a light unto my path" (Psalms 119:105). However, to have the Scriptures act upon the Christian thus, they must be diligently read. It is a poor Christian that doesn't read their Bible completely through at least twice every year.

On the other end of the spectrum we have the unconverted who have never experienced the new spiritual birth found in trusting Christ as one's own personal Saviour. Such are termed by God as NATURAL. Regarding such, the Lord says, "But the natural man receiveth not (rejects) the things of the Spirit of God (the Scriptures): for they (the Scriptures) are foolishness unto him: neither can he know them, because they are spiritually discerned" (1 Corinthians 2:14). It takes a spiritual person to rightly discern the Holy Spirit's writings.

Explaining the Scriptures as such sets the stage for the responses to many of the claims made by the NSA that the Bible is ambiguous and contradictory. I have listed several arguments from the NSA, not only from books such as *The Discipline Book*, but also entries from many of the "antispanking" web pages found on the internet. When receiving e-mail messages from the different NSA web pages, I received answers to some of my questions *exactly the same*, word for word, as others I had already received. This leads me to believe that the answers sent to inquiring web page visitors have been "cut and pasted" and sent to the inquiring party. I have listed the argument by the NSA, then the actual Scripture the NSA is referring to, and finally the biblical answer to that argument.

NSA—Jeremiah 18:21 says, "Therefore deliver up their children to the famine and pour out their blood by the force of the sword; and let their wives be bereaved of their children and be widows." Nowadays, this is called "war crime" and "ethnic cleansing." (Few modern-day Christians feel compelled to obey verses like this one.) But if it is okay to ignore verses about murdering children, why is it not also okay to ignore verses about beating them? Psalms 137:9 which extols the joys of committing mass infanticide against non-Jews by bashing their skulls open on the pavement. Leviticus 25:44–46 which endorses slavery? How about Numbers 15:32–36 in which God commands that a person shall be stoned to death for picking up sticks on Saturday. Do you consider it your religious duty to defend slavery and baby-killing because they are defended by a few isolated verses in the Old Testament? If not, then how do you decide which Old Testament verses to ignore and which ones to take seriously?[3]

Answer—The apostle Paul cautioned Timothy in 2 Timothy 2:15, "Study to shew thyself approved unto God, a workman that needeth not to be ashamed, rightly dividing the word of truth." Thus we see, that the Holy Bible (the Scriptures) in order to be understood, not only requires the new spiritual birth, but also needs to be rightly divided. Seemingly in this area the NSA has failed. The consequence of their failure has caused them to criticize the violent actions of Moses and others against people. The Bible is pure and non-deceiving. It plainly reveals the sins of people such as Lot. In mentioning his sins, God is not condoning what Lot did, but He is rather exposing him as lessons for Christians today.

However, let us rightly divide the word of truth. There is a difference between God dealing in a national way and God dealing in a domestic way. There is a reason why the seeming atrocities took place in the Old Testament. When God sent Israel, as a nation, to inflict death upon their inhabitants, there was a divine reason. God was executing judgment upon those nations for their sins and abominations. He simply used the Nation of Israel as His weapon to accomplish His divine design and will. Failure to understand this shows a vague concept of what God really is. People today seem to think that God is all love. Certainly He is a God of love, and this tremendous love was revealed at Calvary.

However, all the attributes of God are extreme, so that His righteousness, holiness, judgment and anger are just as extreme as His love. Notice His attitude to the gay community in Sodom. Genesis 13:13, "But the men of Sodom were wicked and sinners before the Lord exceedingly." Now then, what did God do to them? Notice the divine account in Genesis chapter 19. "Then the Lord rained upon Sodom and upon Gomorrah brimstone and fire from the Lord out of heaven; And He overthrew those cities, and all the plain, and all the inhabitants of the cities, and that which grew upon the ground." Thus the righteousness of God against their sin was manifested. But that was not the end of those poor folks. We read in the New Testament in Jude 1:7, "Even as Sodom and Gomorrah, and the cities about them in like manner, giving themselves over to fornication, and going after strange flesh, are set forth for an example, suffering the vengeance of eternal fire." The word "suffering" is in the present tense, showing that these souls are now in hell, suffering the vengeance of eternal fire. Eternal simply means never ending. Christians accept, understand, and receive this truth. The natural man rejects it.

Notice also what God did to families in the Nation of Israel who rebelled against God's order. The sons of Korah sought to assume the priesthood, contrary to God's will and notice what, not Moses, but the Lord Himself did. Numbers 16:29–35 reads:

29. If these men die the common death of all men, or if they be visited after the visitation of all men; then the Lord hath not sent me.

30. But if the Lord make a new thing, and the earth open her mouth, and swallow them up, with all that appertain unto them, and they go down quick into the pit; then ye shall understand that these men have provoked the Lord.

31. And it came to pass, as he had made an end of speaking all these words, that the ground clave asunder that was under them:

32. And the earth opened her mouth, and swallowed them up, and their houses, and all the men that appertained unto Korah, and all their goods.

33. They, and all that appertained to them, went down alive into the pit, and the earth closed upon them: and they perished from among the congregation.

34. And all Israel that were round about them fled at the cry of them: for they said, Lest the earth swallow us up also.

35. And there came out a fire from the Lord, and consumed the two hundred and fifty men that offered incense.

16:49, Now they that died in the plague were fourteen thousand and seven hundred, beside them that died about the matter of Korah.

NSA—The Old Testament is full of cruelty to children. The handful of verses from Proverbs about beating children with the "rod" which religious prospankers love to quote over and over again are only the tip of the iceberg. Therefore, the Old Testament should not be taken literally as a source of child-rearing advice, (especially the Book of Proverbs, authorship of which is attributed to a tyrannical idolater with hundreds of wives whose children turned out badly).

Solomon was a terrible parent. He was a lousy leader. He was anything but a good example for those who would be devout followers of God. His son, who followed him to the throne, was a lousy leader too. King Solomon's harsh methods of discipline led his own son, Rehoboam, to become a tyrannical and oppressive dictator who only narrowly escaped being stoned to death for his cruelty.[4] [This last paragraph is one I have received numerous times from other nonspanking advocates.]

Answer—The NSA makes several statements here that cause me to doubt his knowledge of the Bible. First, he refers only to Solomon when he names the author of Proverbs. He fails to mention that the entire Bible is inspired by God, and that "All Scripture is given by inspiration of God, and is profitable for doctrine, for reproof, for correction, for instruction in righteousness" (2 Timothy 3:16). This fact is reiterated in 2 Peter 1:21 which states, "For the prophecy came not in old time by the will of man: but holy men of God spake as they were moved by the Holy Ghost." Another statement by Cox gave an indication of his ignorance concerning biblical facts. He refers to Solomon as a tyrannical idolater whose "children turned out badly." While there are implications in the Scriptures that Solomon probably had many children, none of them, other than Rehoboam, are ever even mentioned. The NSA is trying to make people believe that Solomon was a failure as a parent many times over with many children. That statement is totally false.

In addition, the NSA is missing one very important point with the argument that Solomon's son was a "tyrannical and oppressive dictator." First Kings 14:21 states, "And Rehoboam the son of Solomon reigned in Judah. Rehoboam was forty and one years old when he began to reign, and he reigned seventeen years in Jerusalem." Verse 15 states, "Wherefore the king hearkened not unto the people; for the cause was from the Lord, that he might perform his saying, which the Lord spake by Ahijah the Shilonite unto Jeroboam the son of Nebat." So the people tried to kill the king and ran him out of town. The Bible is pretty clear here. God Himself was controlling the actions of the king in order to establish his will ("for the cause was from the Lord"). The NSA is blaming Rehoboam when "God made him do it." An attempt is made by the NSA to portray Solomon as an abusive father who mistreated his son, who in turn mistreated his people. The people in turn attempted to assassinate him for his horrendous behavior. Nowhere in the Bible does it indicate that Solomon's "harsh methods of discipline led his own son, Rehoboam to become a tyrannical and oppressive dictator" as the NSA implies. In fact, the statement is completely without foundation.

NSA—The Bible says a parent may murder his child for deviating from Judaism.[5]

Deuteronomy 13:6–10

6. If thy brother, the son of thy mother, or thy son, or thy daughter, or the wife of thy bosom, or thy friend, which is as thine own soul, entice thee secretly, saying, Let us go and serve other gods, which thou hast not known, thou, nor thy fathers;

7. Namely, of the gods of the people which are round about you, nigh unto thee, or far off from thee, from the [one] end of the earth even unto the other end of the earth;

8. Thou shalt not consent unto him, nor hearken unto him; neither shall thine eye pity him, neither shalt thou spare, neither shalt thou conceal him:

9. But thou shalt surely kill him; thine hand shall be first upon him to put him to death, and afterwards the hand of all the people.

10. And thou shalt stone him with stones, that he die; because he hath sought to thrust thee away from the Lord thy God, which brought thee out of the land of Egypt, from the house of bondage.

Answer—The next verse is seldom mentioned by the NSA contending that this passage advocates killing children. Verse 11 states, "And all Israel shall hear, and fear, and shall do no more any such wickedness as this is among you." The crime is not as is stated by the antispanking crowd, but the fact that such sought to thrust away his kin from the Lord their God (verse 10). Thus God imposed the death penalty for what He termed "wickedness."

NSA—Examples of Old Testament child abuse abound. Deuteronomy 21:18–21 advocates stoning children to death for disobedience, or for having an alcohol problem or an eating disorder.[6]

Deuteronomy 21:18–21

18. If a man have a stubborn and rebellious son, which will not obey the voice of his father, or the voice of his mother, and that, when they have chastened him, will not hearken unto them:

19. Then shall his father and his mother lay hold on him, and bring him out unto the elders of his city, and unto the gate of his place;

20. And they shall say unto the elders of his city, This our son is stubborn and rebellious, he will not obey our voice; he is a glutton, and a drunkard.

21. And all the men of his city shall stone him with stones, that he die: so shalt thou put evil away from among you; and all Israel shall hear, and fear.

Answer—The word "glutton" is actually translated as "lazy," not one with an eating disorder. Many find fault with the action, but in doing so they find fault with God, for after all, God commanded the action through the law-giver Moses. Moses was only the mouthpiece for God. All that he imposed on the Nation was from God Himself. The reason for this severe action is that the *willful boy is no longer a family problem but a national government problem*. Thus God inflicts the death penalty to keep the Nation of Israel obedient to Himself.

NSA—Moses exhorts his soldiers to kill little boys while keeping virginal girls alive for their own uses.[7]

Numbers 31:17–18.

17. Now therefore kill every male among the little ones, and kill every woman that hath known man by lying with him.

18. But all the women children, that have not known a man by lying with him, keep alive for yourselves.

Answer—The punishment of God was to be inflicted on a nation that sought to turn Israel away from their God. They caused the children of Israel to sin, thus bringing down the wrath of God upon their own heads, and God used the Nation of Israel to inflict that wrath. The Lord Jesus Himself upholds the governmental action of God on this occasion, referring to it in His letter to the Church in Pergamos. "But I have a few things against thee, because thou hast there them that hold the doctrine of Balaam, who taught Balac to cast a stumbling block before the children of Israel, to eat things sacrificed unto idols, and to commit fornication" (Revelation 2:14). God was against Balac and his nation and executed judgment. Christ was against those in that church who were teaching the same thing and even threatened to fight against them with the sword of His mouth if they refused to repent (verse 16). To the Church at Thyatira, Christ threatens to kill her children if they continue on in their disobedience. Again we come to the fact that many of those that use Old Testament Scripture to argue against corporal punishment are ignorant of the actual ways of a God who is righteous and holy. In the early church God killed a couple that lied to the Holy Ghost (Acts 5:1–10). In the church at Corinth He put Christians on beds of sickness and some He removed their lives for not discerning in the emblems the body and blood of the Lord at His supper. (1 Corinthians 11:30, "For this cause many are weak and sickly among you, and many sleep.") The word sleep indicating a body "sleeping" in the grave but the departed spirit with Christ in heaven. Thus the Lord, who in love died to save sinners, is also a righteous God who will punish His own children. As for sinners who have never accepted Him as their own and their personal Savior, the Lord has much to say about their end. Matthew 25:41, "Then shall he say also unto them on the left hand, Depart from me, ye cursed, into everlasting fire, prepared for the devil and his angels: [verse 46] And these shall go away into everlasting punishment: but the righteous into life eternal." The final abode of the lost our Lord reveals in Revelation 20:15, "And whosoever was not found written in the book of life was cast into the lake of fire." Sinners would term this brutality. Saints would rightly term such action as righteous.

What the NSA has failed to realize is the fact that in all these Old Testament incidents we have a nation under law, a law given to them on Mount Sinai. Today we are in a different dispensation. Israel's position as the only chosen group has been set aside, and Jew and Gentile are now treated alike. God has now come out in grace and is offering salvation to all through the death and atoning work of His Son on the Cross. Thus God's national dealings with the Nation of Israel are suspended, and God is no longer executing immediate judgment upon nations as under the old economy of Old Testament times.

But please notice that the instructions of the Lord uttered through Solomon in the Book of Proverbs are not the national dealings of God with Israel and the nations, but rather God's instructions regarding a family's domestic behavior. This expected behavior from God never changes. Notice the history of Abraham and what God says of him. Genesis 18:19 says, "For I know him, that he will command his children and his household after him, and they shall keep the way of the Lord, to do justice and judgment." We are not told how Abraham accomplished such obedience, but he certainly would not disagree with God's way, which was put into writing years later through Solomon, for Abraham is spoken of as the friend of God.

NSA—Proverbs 8:33 says that we must "Listen to discipline." The verse does not say "feel discipline."[8]

Answer—Here the NSA is using Proverbs to prove their point, something they have just criticized the Christian for doing. Since the NSA is using this passage to argue against corporal punishment, we will use it to endorse corporal punishment. Here, children are instructed to "listen" to instruction. According to King Solomon, if the child does not heed the instruction, the parent is then instructed to use more severe methods (spanking) in order to modify improper behavior.

NSA—Christian-oriented apologists for spanking tacitly recognize that they have a problem citing NT Scripture to back up their claims that hitting their kids is some sort of religious duty. Hence, many of them attempt to argue that Hebrews 12 commands parents to hit their kids. However when read in context, this chapter is about the relationship between the Heavenly "Father" and his earthly "children," and is not parenting advice.[9]

Hebrews 12:5–8
5. And ye have forgotten the exhortation which speaketh unto you as unto children, My son, despise not thou the chastening of the Lord, nor faint when thou art rebuked of him:
6. For whom the Lord loveth he chasteneth, and scourgeth every son whom he receiveth.
7. If ye endure chastening, God dealeth with you as with sons; for what son is he whom the father chasteneth not?
8. But if ye be without chastisement, whereof all are partakers, then are ye bastards, and not sons.

(The word chastening in Hebrews 12:5, 7 and chastisement in verse 8 is the same Greek word nurture in Ephesians 6:4.)

Ephesians 6:4, "And, ye fathers, provoke not your children to wrath: but bring them up in the nurture and admonition of the Lord."

Answer—This word *paideia* means, "Discipline that regulates character." Christ said about His own spiritual children, "As many as I love, I rebuke and chasten" (Revelation 3:14). Christ's word chasten is in the Greek *paideuo* meaning to chastise with blows, to scourge. Hebrews 12:7 refers the reader back to the normal way children were reared—their fathers chastened them, just as God chastens his spiritual children.

NSA—The Old Testament does mention the word "rod," which is translated from the ancient Hebrew word "she'vet." To the Hebrews, she'vet meant a stick or a staff, such as that used by shepherds. In this context, the rod of authority suggests loving guidance, not harsh brutality.[10]

Answer—The NSA will attempt to refer to the rod meaning a stick or a staff, such as used by shepherds. The "context" would actually imply physical pain. "Thou shalt beat him with the rod" says the Lord in Proverbs 23. This is not pounding on the child like a wild man, but rather striking appropriately. Rose Kennedy severely spanked all of her children. Was J. F. Kennedy a violent man? J. C. Penney was spanked many times by his preaching father. Was he a violent man? He was one of the most gentle and honest men that walked this earth. God says in Proverbs 29:15, "The rod and reproof give wisdom: but a child left to himself bringeth his mother to shame." Now then, let's be fair. If the rod means loving guidance as the NSA suggests, where does the word reproof fit in? I'm afraid that the reproof is verbal and the rod is physical. God would not have mentioned both words in the same verse if they meant the same thing. Let us also be open-minded. God used the Assyrian nation to severely punish Israel, calling the punishing nation, "The rod of mine anger" (Isaiah 10:5). The word rod is also used for God smiting the earth (Isaiah 11:4). No, the rod means a physical means of bringing discipline to the disobedient child.

NSA—Much of what poses as biblical grounding for corporal punishment really is secular thinking wrapped up in religious language. It does not stand the test of what Jesus said and taught. Consider the following: Jesus was overwhelmingly committed to nonviolent response, even in situations of high stress and conflict. This is shown in the Beatitudes and his rebuke of the follower who brandished a sword during his arrest. Corporal punishment is a violent act against a child's body; it is not a response that is consistent with what Jesus demonstrated. Jesus was committed to love and forgiveness as both the means and the end of all human relationships. These two qualities form the very foundation of his ministry. An action such as spanking that is clearly intended to cause pain hardly qualifies for what Jesus would call an "act of love." Jesus advocated non-violent conflict resolution.[11]

Answer—Let's consider the actions of Christ described in John 2:15, "And when he had made a scourge of small cords, he drove them all out of the temple, and the sheep, and the oxen; and poured out the changers' money, and overthrew the tables." This certainly does not sound like a "nonviolent response." A scourge of cords was certainly not designed to tickle the armpits, and the act of spilling money on the floor and overturning tables certainly does not sound like "non-violent conflict resolution."

NSA—Can anyone imagine Jesus striking a child? If we are to act in a Christ like fashion, we should strongly consider the issue of corporal punishment and its correct use.[12]

Answer—Of course Jesus never spanked or hit children. He never had a family. I have no right to spank other people's children, but their parents not only have the right to do so, they are encouraged by the Lord to carry out this form of discipline.

NSA—Jesus admonished some adults once, saying that whatever they might do to children, they do to him. Spank Jesus?[13]

Answer—First, the NSA is totally misinformed about this issue. I am sure that the passage they are referring to is Matthew 25:40 which does not involve the subject of children at all. The verse reads, "And the King shall answer and say unto them, 'Verily I say onto you, inasmuch as ye have done it onto one of the least of my brethren, ye have done it onto me.'" Jesus here is referring to the future when he addresses those who have helped or harmed his believers (brethren). This has nothing to do with children. I believe the NSA may also be thinking of the verses in Matthew 18:6, Mark 9:42, and Luke 17:2, in which Jesus says, "And whosoever shall offend one of these little ones that believe in me, it is better for him that a millstone were hanged about his neck, and he were cast into the sea." In its original Greek context, this verse does not imply that anyone who spanks a child will die a horrible death. The word "offend" has no connection with spanking. Jesus was not prohibiting corporal punishment in this address.

This is an excellent example to demonstrate the ignorance of the NSA regarding biblical truths. If we continue with this line of thinking by the NSA, we have to conclude that all children are as God. Should parents correct children when they are wrong? Certainly. Would you dare attempt to correct God? No. Would you tell a child he is wrong? I would. Would you tell God he is wrong? Never. The concept is ridiculous.

Most people believe that the Ten Commandments were given to man as a guide to living. The Bible tells us differently. Romans 3:19–20 states, "Now we know that what things soever the law saith, it saith to them who are under the law: that every mouth may be stopped, and all the world may become guilty before God. Therefore by the deeds of the law there shall no flesh be justified in his sight: for by the law is the knowledge of sin." In effect, God's word is explaining that the Ten Commandments were given to show man how completely incapable he is to live up to God's standards. We simply cannot follow the law. Still, most of the secular world believes that the Ten Commandments are the "guide" to moral living.

The Ten Commandments are located in the Book of Exodus. Ask a nonspanking advocate if he/she believes in the Ten Commandments. Odds are that one would answer in the affirmative. Strange, since Exodus also advocates offering animal sacrifices. Most of the NSA will be unable to explain how they subscribe to the Ten Commandments and do not subscribe to animal sacrifices. Although this is not the best example to use, this is one way to show the NSA how God's word needs to be "rightly divided."

As I transmitted these messages back and forth to the unseen faces behind the nonspanking web pages on the information highway, I began to realize how incredibly shallow their arguments were. During our volley of electronic ideas, RCox had suggested that I read the studies of Irwin Hyman, a researcher at Temple University who is attempting to eliminate all corporal punishment in this country. In my last message to the nonspanking web page, I asked RCox to actually read the Bible to confirm the information that I had sent him. His answer to me confirmed what I had suspected about the mind-set of the NSA. The answer simply said, "I've read your bible. You go read Hyman. Randy Cox." This time the word Bible wasn't capitalized. RCox had indicated that the Bible wasn't his book; it was mine. RCox never contacted me again, and the e-mail voice from the nonspanking page became silent.

I thank my father for his help in answering some of these complex questions concerning the biblical approach to corporal punishment. I have also thanked my father for the manner in which he and my mother reared me. There is no one who could convince me that spanking is counterproductive and causes irreparable harm to children. I am living proof that this theory is dead wrong. I close this chapter with my father's "closing statement."

> I have written you at the request of my son. I love the Bible and read it for hours daily. In it I discover God's non-flexible and righteous ways. How wonderful that such a holy God would ever take an interest in us, so much so, as to send His beloved Son into this world to die on the behalf of our sins, that we may be cleansed from all of our sins through faith in His blood. I found this truth February the 10th, 1952 and obtained a peace that the world knows nothing about. I am saved from going to hell because of my sins and I am saved to be in heaven with Christ eternally—all because of the fact that He died for me. How wonderful! I do trust that you too will find the blessed Saviour as your very own. Let me say in closing, that as born again children of God, my wife and I diligently spanked our children when we thought it appropriate. How did they turn out? Our firstborn, Robert, seeks to help juveniles and is head of the juvenile unit in the police department. Our second son, David, is ultra mild with a unique sense of humor. Both are Christians and extremely honest and law-abiding citizens. When I hear that spanking produces violent children my sides actually hurt—from laughing.

There's nothing I can add to this . . . except "Amen!"

4

KIDS AND CRIME

"Whoso keepeth the law is a wise son: but he that is a companion of riotous men shameth his father" (Proverbs 28:7).

The most dramatic evidence to prove that the permissive method of rearing children is a dismal failure is the current crime rate in the United States. Modern crime statistics are compiled from monthly law enforcement reports that are forwarded directly to the Federal Bureau of Investigation in Washington D.C. The primary objective of the Uniform Crime Reporting Program (UCR) is to provide a reliable set of criminal justice statistics for law enforcement administration, operation, and management. At the same time, the yearly UCR reports are supposed to give us an indication of which direction the crime rate is headed. Unfortunately, since 1992, these figures are not as accurate as they would appear. Let me explain.

In 1992, many of the law enforcement agencies in the United States switched to another form of entering crime statistics. Prior to 1992, each department reviewed their crime incidents and entered that information on a form that was forwarded to the F.B.I. In 1992, an alternative was offered to police departments. It was called the National Incident Based Reporting System, or NIBRS, for short. It incorporated the use of computer data entry screens and special formats, making it extremely easy for records personnel to enter information and quickly retrieve crime statistics for their community. Departments were advised by the promoters of this product that it was compatible with the computer format used by the F.B.I., so there would be no further need to compile figures by hand. The department would be able to fire off the digital information from NIBRS directly to the F.B.I. There was only one problem. It wasn't compatible.

After an entire year of entering figures into the NIBRS program, many departments found that the information could not be sent to the F.B.I. In that year, my department found it impossible to recompile all of the figures as they had in years past, so they did not send any statistics to the F.B.I. for that year. In the years following 1992, we continued to use the NIBRS system because of its usefulness as a valuable database for local crime information, but we also paid an employee to record that information by hand to forward to the F.B.I. for the Uniform Crime Reports.

So there is one major factor to consider when looking at the F.B.I.'s Uniform Crime Reports. In the years following 1992, there were many departments that began utilizing NIBRS to enter their crime statistics and simply quit sending the figures to the F.B.I. This fact can easily be confirmed by comparing the UCR figures from 1991 to the present. For example, in the 1991 UCR, one can see the list of cities that reported to the F.B.I. from the state of Illinois. There are a total of 177 cities shown, from Addison to Zion. In fact, the list takes up four pages.

However, if one looks at the 1996 Uniform Crime Reports, the list of cities in the state of Illinois that are now reporting their statistics to the F.B.I. consists of six cities. As far as the F.B.I. is concerned, all of the crime that is occurring in Illinois is occurring in six cities. It's no wonder that the politicians are boasting that the crime rate is dropping. Little does the public know that the crime rate is exploding. It just isn't being reported. I have talked to many law enforcement officers about this apparent fraud being perpetrated on the public. We all agree that the population is being lulled into a false sense of security by the inaccurate figures being published by the F.B.I. I even went to the news media in my area and showed them the figures right from the UCR. The reporter found it hard to believe but researched the claim himself and did a story on the six o'clock news. The one thing to keep in mind when studying the F.B.I.'s Uniform Crime Reports is that after 1992, the overall crime figures are not accurate. One can, however, recognize the increase in juvenile crime over adult crime.

The preface to each yearly report states, "UCR crime statistics permit a study of the nature and movement of crime over time that allows researchers to theorize about the underlying changes and fluctuations and to hypothesize about possible effects on families and communities. For these reasons, UCR data are used not only by criminal justice agencies but by university researchers, sociologists, criminologists, community development organizations, tourism agencies, media and many others."[1]

The introduction to the yearly UCR report states, "Historically, the causes and origins of crime have been the subjects of investigation by varied disciplines. Some factors which are known to affect the volume and type of crime occurring from place to place are . . . " There are several reasons given for the causes of crime, such as climate, population density, and economic conditions. Also listed as a cause of crime is "family conditions with respect to divorce and family cohesiveness."[2]

When studying the trend in crime, one of the most obvious contrasts is between crimes committed by adults and crimes committed by children. The most recent overall trend shows that the increase in violent crime that has been prevalent over the past thirty years is slowing. The UCR released on September 28, 1997, shows that murder and nonnegligent manslaughter has been reduced by 3.7 percent over the past ten years. This reduction is in part due to the fewer numbers of law enforcement agencies reporting. It's when the category of murder is split into two separate groups, those committed by adults and those committed by children, that we become alarmed.

Although the UCR inaccurately shows that the rate of total murders has decreased over the past ten years, the rate of murders committed by children seventeen years of age and younger has increased during the same period by 50.5 percent. The 1995 UCR showed the most dramatic increase in murders committed by kids at any one time. Between 1985 and 1995, murders committed by children increased by 150 percent. This type of statistic should activate all kinds of alarms. There appears to be the same trend in other crime categories also. During the same ten-year period, robberies committed by adults has been reduced by 3.2 percent, while robberies committed by children has increased by 57.4 percent. Arson, the crime of intentionally setting fire to the property of others, has been reduced amongst adults by 17.1 percent, while it has increased amongst children by 35.9 percent. Carrying or possessing weapons amongst adults dropped by 9/10 of one percent, while increasing 69.5 percent amongst children. The simple crime of disorderly conduct, showing a slight increase amongst adults of 1.6 percent, jumped dramatically by 92.5

percent amongst children. Even some nonviolent crimes such as gambling, reduced amongst adults by 26.3 percent, jumped to a 213.3 percent increase amongst children.

One of the most disturbing figures from the Uniform Crime Report is the section on offenses against family, including domestic violence offenses committed by the youngsters in the family. Thirty years ago, arrests of children for assaulting their parents was almost unheard of. During the past fifteen years, there has been a steady increase in children abusing their parents. In 1983, the UCR showed a total of 1,120 arrests of juveniles for domestic violence. By 1985 it had risen to 2,177 cases. In 1991, there were a total of 2,523 children arrested for domestic violence. In 1994, it was 3,743 cases, and in 1996, it had increased to 4,400. Another tremendous jump occurred in 1997—up to 5,018 cases. In the short period of fifteen years, there has been a 348 percent increase in children committing domestic violence offenses. Remember, these are not cases of parents abusing children. These are cases of the children being the abusers. In my city alone during the past ten years, domestic violence attacks, child against parent, have increased 700 percent.

The number of juveniles being arrested for violent crime is rising dramatically.

There's a saying that "liars figure, but figures can't lie." To a certain extent that is true. But anyone with any intelligence at all knows that sometimes statistics can be manipulated to suit the manipulator's needs. During a recent Geraldo Rivera program, the host made the comment that juvenile crime was on the decrease. Geraldo referred to the UCR as his source of information and stated that his information was taken from the statistics released on September 28, 1997. That report included all of the crime statistics up through December 31, 1996. It is frustrating to watch a national broadcast supply inaccurate information to the public. It certainly is not Geraldo's fault. He has no idea why the F.B.I.'s figures are not reliable. Geraldo claimed that in several categories, such as robbery, murder, and felonious assaults, there was a slight drop in 1996, even amongst juveniles. The most recent UCR shows that there was a decrease in robberies committed by juveniles. However, there have also been other years during the past several decades when certain categories of crime have decreased for a year or two, only to skyrocket in the following years.

To give Geraldo the proper credit, in 1996 there were 36,569 robberies committed by juveniles as compared to 45,046 committed in 1994. The problem is that the 36,569 robberies committed by juveniles in 1996 was a tremendous increase over the 23,229 robberies committed by juveniles in 1987. In fact, that is a 57.4 percent increase in ten years. In 1987, the 23,229 robberies committed by juveniles was a decrease from 28,688 committed in 1985 and 29,018 committed in 1984. I can imagine the surprise of those who had concluded in 1987 that robberies committed by juveniles were on the decrease when the statistics were released for the following years.

My point is that most of the time, anyone can make figures work for them. If someone asks me if robberies committed by juveniles are presently decreasing, I would have to say that the Uniform Crime Report indicates that. Ask me if juvenile crime has decreased over the past thirty years, and I will be able to say emphatically that the UCR indicates the opposite, even with the smaller number of reporting agencies included. Almost every category of the report shows slight decreases during certain years. When looking at the long term picture, it's a different story. For instance, domestic violence offenses committed by children have shown a steady increase, year by year. Then there was a slight decrease in 1987. Anyone who was foolish enough to think that we had licked our juvenile domestic

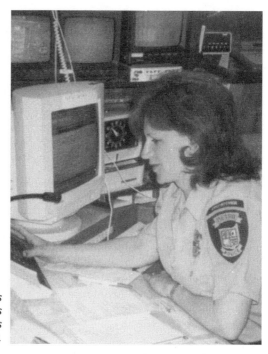

In the author's city, officers dispatched to calls of juveniles attacking their parents has increased by 700 percent.

violence problem certainly had their eyes opened in the following years. Is anyone going to argue that we have a serious problem with juveniles assaulting their parents? Aside from 1987, you would look foolish arguing that point.

In fact, the latest UCR released by the F.B.I. proves my point. When I receive the new UCR reports, one of the first categories I check is the domestic violence arrests. I believe one of the best gauges to determine the "no fear" attitude in our children is the incidents of assault, child against parent. As I located the statistics for offenses against family, the figure in the "Under 18 years of age" column jumped out from the page. In 1997, there were 5,018 children arrested for domestic violence, a 55 percent increase over 1996, and a 348 percent increase since I began my career with the police department in 1982. This statistic continues to increase in severity almost every year.

When detailing statistics from the UCR, it is very important not to look at a one year change. It is important to look at a pattern of increase, not just over several years, but over several decades.

Detention homes are becoming overcrowded due to the explosion in juvenile crime.

Without any doubt, there is a steady increase in crimes committed by juveniles over the past twenty years. The children and teenagers of the 1960s are now the parents of the children and teenagers of the 1990s. The kids that I grew up with in the 1960s are now rearing children of their own. Those who have fallen for the rhetoric of the peddlers of permissiveness have realized too late that eliminating corporal punishment in the upbringing of their child has resulted in a teenager with "no fear."

Crime Statistics 1983-1997

YEAR	1983	1984	1985	1986	1987	1988	1989	1990	1991	1992	1993	1994	1995	1996	1997
MURDER															
CHILDREN	1,175	1,154	1,193	1,255	1,355	1,610	1,854	2,331	2,465	2,680	3,092	2,982	2,383	2,039	1,545
ADULTS	14,260	13,972	13,195	13,042	12,611	13,022	13,001	14,220	14,601	15,484	15,764	14,675	13,001	11,407	9,930
ROBBERY															
CHILDREN	31,290	29,018	28,688	25,607	23,229	22,464	25,604	30,235	33,510	38,192	40,499	45,046	41,841	36,569	25,065
ADULTS	88,162	86,504	85,024	88,064	79,087	79,512	85,023	92,597	96,063	106,701	103,378	95,133	86,968	76,520	58,022
FELONIOUS ASSAULTS															
CHILDREN	29,917	31,315	32,809	32,598	29,705	33,992	39,395	45,534	47,013	58,383	62,039	64,648	58,113	50,560	46,072
ADULTS	199,903	210,349	204,790	227,853	211,793	236,989	256,782	287,257	284,680	337,957	346,109	350,422	341,301	295,084	282,628
MISDEMEANOR ASSAULTS															
CHILDREN	63,435	65,444	73,778	69,554	77,415	86,077	94,944	108,908	105,701	130,459	138,713	157,734	146,543	154,762	146,105
ADULTS	324,639	357,814	408,552	418,451	459,112	515,787	557,046	619,467	580,474	691,583	731,433	764,433	737,327	718,268	700,086
DOMESTIC VIOLENCE															
CHILDREN	1,120	1,439	2,177	2,287	2,063	2,021	1,849	2,066	2,523	3,493	3,034	3,743	4,077	4,400	5,018
ADULTS	35,160	36,403	38,833	36,768	34,467	40,509	45,356	53,924	55,094	62,930	68,085	78,056	80,560	76,171	83,444
VIOLENT CRIME															
CHILDREN	66,296	65,844	66,976	63,454	58,071	61,753	71,002	82,260	87,082	104,137	110,380	117,200	106,190	92,848	76,072
ADULTS	324,718	335,033	327,352	351,249	324,559	350,895	376,383	417,468	417,868	485,636	489,933	483,334	461,523	401,083	366,752
PROPERTY CRIME															
CHILDREN	496,688	486,427	513,522	473,437	445,458	456,744	488,868	503,900	482,224	550,746	534,415	568,841	511,497	480,772	435,370
ADULTS	965,252	945,385	988,143	986,086	933,719	991,129	1,054,031	1,059,446	1,025,732	1,122,660	1,077,417	1,051,463	961,813	881,983	808,140

Yearly Percentage Increase:
DOMESTIC VIOLENCE
1983 to 1997

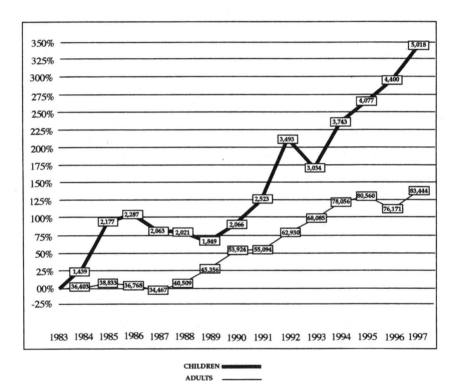

CHILDREN ▬▬▬▬▬
ADULTS ————

Between 1983 and 1997, domestic violence offenses committed by children increased 348.0 percent, as compared to an increase of only 137.3 percent by adults.

Yearly Percentage Increase:
MURDERS
1984 to 1994

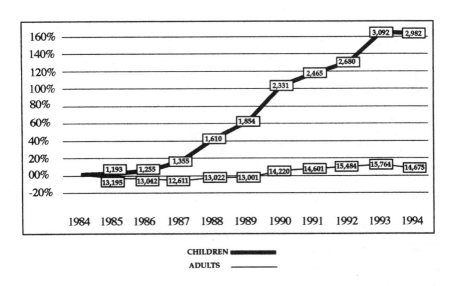

CHILDREN ▬▬▬▬

ADULTS ─────────

The largest increase in murders committed by children as compared to adults occurred between 1984 and 1994. Murders by children increased 158.4 percent during that time period, as compared to an increase of only 5.0 percent by adults.

Yearly Percentage Increase:
DISORDERLY CONDUCT
1990 to 1996

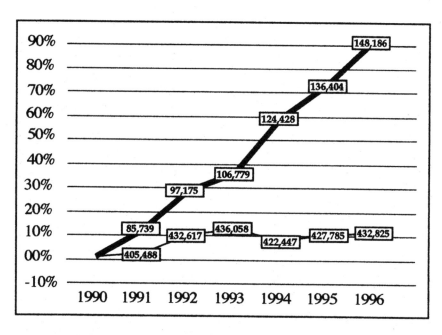

CHILDREN ▬▬▬▬

ADULTS ————

The largest increase in offenses of Disorderly Conduct committed by children as compared to adults occurred between 1990 and 1996. Disorderly Conduct offenses committed by children increased 88.4 percent during that time period, as compared to an increase of only 8.7 percent by adults.

Yearly Percentage Increase:
ARSON
1988 to 1994

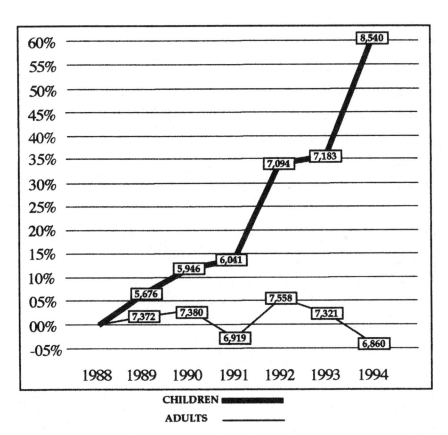

CHILDREN

ADULTS

The largest increase in offenses of Arson committed by children as compared to adults occurred between 1988 and 1994. Arson offenses committed by children increased 60.9 percent during that time period, as compared to a decrease of 4.4 percent by adults.

Yearly Percentage Increase:
VANDALISM
1988 to 1994

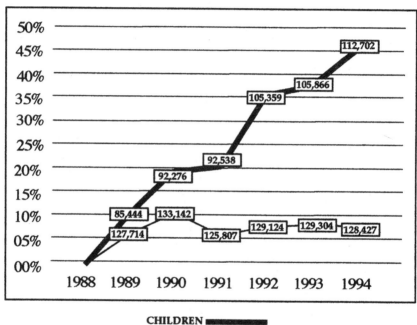

CHILDREN ▬▬▬

ADULTS ▬▬▬▬

The largest increase in offenses of Vandalism committed by children as compared to adults occurred between 1988 and 1994. Vandalism offenses committed by children increased 46.4 percent during that time period, as compared to an increase of only 8.2 percent by adults.

Yearly Percentage Increase:
WEAPONS POSSESSION
1987 to 1994

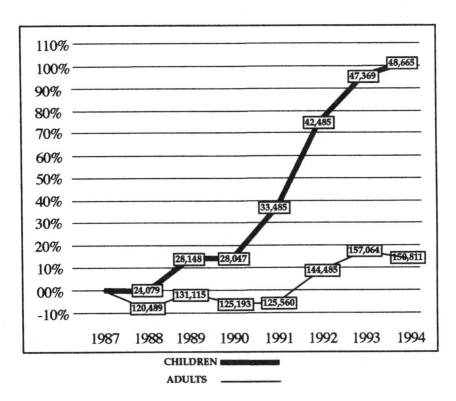

CHILDREN
ADULTS

The largest increase in offenses of Weapons Possession committed by children as compared to adults occurred between 1987 and 1994. Weapons offenses committed by children increased 101.4 percent during that time period, as compared to an increase of only 14.0 percent by adults.

THE LAW

"And thou shalt teach them ordinances and laws, and shalt shew them the way wherein they must walk, and the work that they must do"
(Exodus 18:20).

The laws concerning children in most states were designed to protect those who are unable to defend themselves against legitimate child abuse. Nobody is questioning the claim that child abuse is on the rise. Statistics prove it. The problem is that the restrictions placed on parental discipline by social services and the media has done nothing to solve that problem. At the same time our culture is being told "do not touch your kids," child abuse is increasing. The effort by liberals to convince parents to lay off their children has not solved the problem of some kids being abused by their parents. In fact, that attitude may be contributing to the problem.

Parents are at the end of their rope—afraid to spank their children when they know it should be done. The child becomes more and more defiant until the parent loses control and overreacts. When a simple slap on the bucket may have deterred future misbehavior, the parent endures weeks or months of frustration simply because they have been made to believe that tolerance is the best policy. Finally, the parent cannot tolerate any more misbehavior and combines months of discipline into one session. I have had parents in my office who admit that they have "stepped over the line" because of frustration which could have been prevented if they had taken the necessary steps earlier.

Most of us can relate to that feeling. We perhaps have had a situation which has angered us, and if left unaddressed, it festers to the point where we are ready to explode. When we finally address the issue with the person, it's like a load lifted off our shoulders. Our attitude toward our adversary improves and the frustration is gone. It's a natural process. I believe a portion of today's child abuse is caused by frustrated parents who are not only angry at their child for continually defying their authority, but also mad at themselves for not taking disciplinary action when they know they should have. Finally it's "enough is enough" and the last effort to control the child gets out of hand.

A good example of this frustration getting out of control is a family living in my city. The father, we'll call him Mr. Thomas, called my office one morning and asked if he could come in to talk to me. He indicated that he was having a "problem" with his fifteen-year-old son. Less than an hour later, Mr. Thomas was sitting in my office pouring out his soul. He was an extremely frustrated man, explaining that his son, Jason, was no longer following the rules. He had been easy to control when he was younger, but he was now swearing at his parents and refusing to do what he was told. The father explained that although he had been diligent as a parent, he had "never struck the boy." When I asked him what would have happened to him if he had acted in such a manner towards his father, Mr. Thomas admitted that his father would have "knocked him out." I then asked Mr. Thomas why his approach to discipline was so much different than his father's. Blaming everyone from his wife who wouldn't let him spank the child when he was young, to a fear of being arrested for child abuse, Mr. Thomas finally admitted that his permissive child-rearing technique had resulted in a son who was not afraid of authority.

I tried very hard to explain to Mr. Thomas that "knocking out" a fifteen-year-old boy was not the answer. I arranged for the Thomas family to see Bob Reitman, the family counselor who works with our police department. Within days, I learned that the family had stopped the counseling sessions because Jason refused to go.

It was about two weeks later that I received a call from Mr. Thomas. "I just thought I would let you know," he said, "that I took care of my problem." Mr. Thomas went on to explain how Jason had become enraged over being grounded and had swore at his father, shoving him in the chest. Mr. Thomas then explained how he "took care of things like they did in the Corps." When I nervously pursued the meaning of his last statement, Mr. Thomas advised me, "I knocked him out." Mr. Thomas then added, "I haven't had a lick of problem with him since!"

Unfortunately, the department of human services wasn't as impressed with the change in Jason's attitude. One week later I received a report that Mr. Thomas was being investigated for child abuse. Under the law, knocking a child unconscious is child abuse. The frustration in the father built up to a point where he exploded. If the proper discipline had been used on Jason as a child, the odds are that such drastic action would have never been necessary. Instead, we have another legitimate case of child abuse.

When the laws were written to protect children against excessive force used by a parent, legislators in most states were careful not to take parental authority away completely. Although we will attempt to cover the basic child abuse laws of each state, it is wise to obtain a copy of the law from the state in which you reside. You can obtain copies of the criminal code at your local library. If you have access to the internet, there are several Supreme Court web pages that have a browse feature. You simply type in the key words you are looking for and the information is quickly available.

When compiling this book, I requested the child abuse laws from every state in the country. Each attorney's general office was generous enough to forward the laws to me. Although the laws are similar from state to state, there are minor differences that will be addressed. I found that Ohio law is the most detailed and specific when it comes to "drawing the line" between discipline and abuse. Therefore, I am using the Ohio law as a gauge, occasionally referring to the laws in other states that are similar or that differ in some manner.

The laws in most states allow a parent to use corporal punishment. Most parents just don't realize it.

The law in Ohio that addresses child abuse specifically describes the line which the parent cannot cross. Section 2151.031 of the Ohio Revised Criminal Code is titled "Abused Child Defined." In order to make things easier to understand, I am including the entire section as it is written.

[§ 2151.03.1] § 2151.031 Abused child defined.

As used in this chapter, an "abused child" includes any child who:

(A) Is the victim of "sexual activity" as defined under Chapter 2907. of the Revised Code, where such activity would constitute an offense under that chapter, except that the court need not find that any person has been convicted of the offense in order to find that the child is an abused child.

(B) Is endangered as defined in section 2919.22 of the Revised Code, except that the court need not find that any person has been convicted under that section in order to find that the child is an abused child.

(C) Exhibits evidence of any physical or mental injury or death, inflicted other than by accidental means, or any injury or death which is at variance with the history given of it. Except as provided in section (D) of this section, a child exhibiting evidence of corporal punishment or other disciplinary measure by a parent, guardian, custodian, person having custody or control, or person in loca parentis of a child is not an abused child under this division if the measure is not prohibited under section 2919.22 of the Revised Code.

(D) Because of the acts of his parents, guardian, or custodian, suffers physical or mental injury that harms or threatens to harm the child's health or welfare.

(E) Is subjected to out-of-home care child abuse.[1]

Subsection (C) states, "Except as provided in section (D) of this section, a child exhibiting evidence of corporal punishment or other disciplinary measure by a parent, guardian, custodian, person having custody or control, or person in loco parentis of a child is not an abused child under this division if the measure is not prohibited under section 2919.22 of the Revised Code." Here is the exemption that allows the parent to incorporate physical force in the discipline of their children.

Again, it should be noted that this section begins by saying, "Except as provided in section (D) of this section." The section ends by saying, "if the measure is not prohibited under section 2919.22." These sections are used by nonspanking advocates when arguing whether the parent has the right to use force against the child. It is important to know what these sections mean when preparing an argument on the prospanking side.

Section (D) simply states, "Because of the acts of his parents, guardian, or custodian, suffers physical or mental injury that harms or threatens to harm the child's health or welfare." Taken out of context, this section could very well pose a problem when trying to prove in a court of law that spanking does not cause "mental injury" to the child. This section was designed to include other areas of abuse that are not covered by the rest of this section. For example, parents who would lie to their child and tell them that the child had a fatal disease and only had six months to live, would be an offense that is not covered under any other area of the abused child section. There is no doubt that this "act" by the parent is abusive to the child. Section (D) simply addresses situations such as this one and holds the parent accountable for those actions.

Why are we afraid to enforce those restrictions we have imposed on our children when we know what they are doing is harmful to their welfare? Is it because we have seen on the nightly news about a parent who was arrested for slapping his/her child? What we don't usually see are the results of those arrests. Most of those charges stem from law enforcement officers who themselves are not familiar with the law. Parents should be armed with a knowledge of what the law says and even keep a copy handy if need be to show anyone in authority who questions what actions they have taken. I usually use extreme examples to make a point. Let's look at this one.

There is a house near yours that is well-known as a haven for drugs and illegal activity. Numerous people, including children, have over-dosed while visiting that house in which a family lives, including several children. If your ten-year-old child had befriended one of those children and wished to play with his friend at that house, would you be within your rights to prohibit your ten-year-old child from visiting that house? Sure you would. What would you do if your ten-year-old child defied your instruction and went to visit his friend at that house? Would you use physical force in retrieving your child? Sure you would. Would you be within your rights to spank your child as a consequence for violating a clear-cut restriction? Would anyone argue with you about your use of force against your child? It is very doubtful under those circumstances. The police would support you. The courts would support you. It is very doubtful that any of the liberal supporters of children's rights would dare to argue with your authority as a parent under those circumstances. Why? Because there is a clear-cut danger to your child that is evident to all. Public sentiment would be the same if you used corporal punishment to keep your small child from constantly running out onto the interstate highway behind your house. A swat on the bucket is much less serious than a head-on meeting with a Peterbilt tractor trailer.

In fact, section 2919.22 of the Ohio Revised Criminal Code addresses that issue and should be used in the parents' favor when questioned about the use of corporal punishment. I am including the entire section as it is written.

§ 2919.22 Endangering children.

(A) No person, who is the parent, guardian, custodian, person having custody or control, or person in loco parentis of a child under eighteen years of age or a mentally or physically handicapped child under twenty-one years of age, shall create a substantial risk to the health or safety of the child, by violating a duty of care, protection, or support. It is not a violation of duty of care, protection, or support under this division when the parent, guardian, custodian, or person having custody or control of a child treats the physical or mental illness of defect of the child by spiritual means through prayer alone, in accordance with the tenets of a recognized religious body.

(B) No person shall do any of the following to a child under eighteen years of age or a mentally or physically handicapped child under twenty-one years of age.

(1) Abuse the child.

(2) Torture or cruelly abuse the child.

(3) Administer corporal punishment or other physical disciplinary measure, or physically restrain the child in a cruel manner for a prolonged period, which punishment, discipline, or restraint is excessive under the circumstances and creates a substantial risk of serious physical harm to the child.

(4) Repeatedly administer unwarranted disciplinary measures to the child, when there is a substantial risk that such conduct, if continued, will seriously impair or retard the child's mental health or development.

(5) Entice, coerce, permit, encourage, compel, hire, employ, use, or allow the child to act, model, or in any other way participate in, or be photographed for, the production, presentation, dissemination, or advertisement of any material or performance that the offender knows or reasonably should know is obscene, is sexually oriented matter, or is nudity-oriented matter.[2]

This section addresses situations that might place an innocent child at risk, either physically or mentally. The section begins by assigning the parent or person having control of the child as the party responsible for the welfare of the child. Section (A) deals with those guardians who violate a "duty of care, protection, or support." Suppose that a parent was aware that his/her ten-year-old child was frequenting a known drug house and took no action whatsoever to bring the child home or prevent the child from being in that atmosphere. If that child were to die of an overdose of drugs, and it was discovered that the parents condoned the child being in that environment, there would be a good chance that the parents would be arrested and charged with a violation of duty of protection. It is the parents' responsibility to protect their child from harm in this world. To ignore a dangerous situation and harm to the child results, the parent is guilty of the endangering children section. For example, Nebraska's law states, "A person commits child abuse if he or she knowingly, intentionally, or negligently causes or permits a minor child to be placed in a situation that endangers his or her life." North Dakota classifies a parent as abusive if the parent "permits the child to be in a disreputable place or associating with vagrants or vicious or immoral persons."

One exception to the "duty of care" provision that is present in every state's law is the First Church of Christ Scientist rule. Parents who belong to a recognized religious organization, who fail to treat their child for an illness in a conventional manner because of a religious belief, cannot be charged under this section. A court can order that the child be placed in the custody of someone other than the parents if it feels that serious physical harm to the child will occur as a result of the parents' failure to treat the illness medically. The parent, though, cannot be charged with endangering that child even if the child dies as a result of that neglect. If you look at the child abuse laws in your state, you will find this exemption. Every state has one.

There are several points that need to be made concerning section 2919.22 of the Ohio Revised Code. There are several key phrases, that if recognized, change the entire complexion of the law. First, section (A) states that no one "shall create a substantial risk to the health or safety of the child" by violating a duty of care, protection, or support. The definition of the term "substantial risk" is important when interpreting this law. According to subsection (H) of section 2901.01 of the Revised Code, which defines each term used in the section, "substantial risk" means a "strong possibility, as contrasted with a remote or significant possibility, that a certain result may occur or that certain circumstances may exist." In the same section of the Revised Code, simple "risk," a lesser degree, is defined as "a significant possibility, as contrasted with a remote possibility." The term "substantial risk" involves a much higher degree of risk than is normally required. Thus, when this term is used in this section, we must remember that it takes a more serious risk to satisfy the law than what would be required under normal "risk." This same term, "substantial risk," is used in the laws of Alaska, Illinois, New Jersey, New York, North Carolina, Oregon, Pennsylvania, Rhode Island, Virginia, and Wyoming. In the state of Arkansas, the term used is "substantial possibility." The South Carolina law uses the term "unreasonable risk." Tennessee's legislators decided to use the terminology "likely to cause great bodily harm." Texas law states "genuine threat of substantial harm." Although worded differently, these laws mean basically the same thing.

This term is used again in the Ohio law in subsection (3) and subsection (4) which deal specifically with corporal punishment. If you look closely at these two sections, you will see that section (3) deals with warranted discipline for a child's improper behavior. Section (4) deals with unwarranted physical punishment. We will first examine warranted discipline.

Section (3) states that no person who is a parent, guardian, etc., shall "Administer corporal punishment or other physical disciplinary measure, or physically restrain the child in a cruel manner for a prolonged period, which punishment . . . is excessive under the circumstances and creates a substantial risk of serious physical harm to the child." There are four main points to consider in this section.

First, the phrase "excessive under the circumstances" means that the punishment must in some manner fit the offense. There is a great deal of latitude in this phrase which has caused some child advocates to point it out as an argument against spanking. True, when taken out of context, this phrase could be interpreted in many ways, and one might argue that spanking is excessive under any circumstances. The next word in the sentence must be recognized as an inclusive term. The word "and," following the phrase "excessive under the circumstances," means that the phrase must be combined with the following phrase, "creates a substantial risk of serious physical harm to the child." Read in its entirety, the law states that no one may administer corporal punishment or restraint if it is "excessive under the circumstances *and* creates a substantial risk of serious physical harm to the child."

The next question is this. What is considered to be "serious physical harm" to the child? Again, the law is specific when defining the difference between simple physical harm to persons and property and serious physical harm to persons and property. In section 2901.01, we find the definition of simple "physical harm to persons." It states that it means "any injury, illness, or other physiological impairment, regardless of its gravity or duration." In Ohio, if this definition were applied to the endangering children section, then a parent would be severely restricted in the use of physical discipline. I have noticed in other states, such as New Mexico, there are restrictions on a parent causing "physical abuse," which includes "skin bruising" and "soft tissue swelling." But even in those instances, authorities must find that there "is not a justifiable explanation for the condition." In Ohio, "serious physical harm to persons" is much more defined and specific when describing the criteria needed to satisfy this section. There are five subsections to this definition. I will show the entire section in order to understand it better.

§ 2901.01 Definitions

(5) "Serious physical harm to persons" means any of the following:

(a) Any mental illness or condition of such gravity as would normally require hospitalization or prolonged psychiatric treatment;

(b) Any physical harm that carries a substantial risk of death;

(c) Any physical harm that involves some permanent incapacity, whether partial or total, or that involves some temporary, substantial incapacity;

(d) Any physical harm that involves some permanent disfigurement, or that involves some temporary, serious disfigurement;

(e) Any physical harm that involves acute pain of such duration as to result in substantial suffering, or that involves any degree of prolonged or intractable pain.[3]

By looking at the definition of serious physical harm in the Ohio law, it is easy to see how the law protects parents who have chosen to incorporate corporal punishment into their discipline. Serious physical harm would require a visit to the hospital, would carry a substantial risk of death, would involve some incapacity or disfigurement, or would cause acute pain resulting in substantial suffering. If the parent invokes corporal punishment as discipline for a violation of the rules, and none of the indicated results occur, then the punishment cannot be considered a violation of the endangering children statute. You will note that the phrase "substantial risk" is used in regards to death. Remember, this is a more serious definition than simple "risk" of death, which would be a significant possibility. This is a substantial risk of death, which means a strong possibility.

Sections (3) and (4), which address incapacity or disfigurement, are also specific about the degree of harm done. Both indicate that any permanent incapacity or disfigurement would satisfy this restriction. It goes a bit further to include temporary serious incapacity or disfigurement. If the damage is temporary, it must be serious in order to satisfy the law.

I once had an attorney argue with me that the word "and" in the endangering children statute could not be inclusive. His argument was that any action by a parent which created a substantial risk of serious physical harm to the child would be excessive under any circumstances. After some research, I realized that the word "and" was necessary in the statute. For example, if a child came charging at his mother with a chain saw, waving it wildly about trying to cut off the mother's head, and she grabbed a baseball bat and whacked him a good one on the arm to get him to drop the saw, would it be excessive force if she fractured his arm? Certainly not. She would have caused serious physical harm, but her efforts to protect her own life would not be considered excessive. She could not be prosecuted under the child abuse statute.

However, there are specific laws in other states that are much more restrictive. Arkansas statute 12-12-503 states, "Abuse shall not include physical discipline of a child when it is reasonable and moderate and is inflicted by a parent for purposes of restraining or correcting a child." The restriction is located in the definition of what is reasonable and moderate. Further on in the statute, it states, "The following actions are not reasonable or moderate when used to correct or restrain a child: (g) Striking a child in the face." Wow! Although I was never slapped in the face when I was a child, I know numerous parents who have used this form of discipline on a sassy youngster. Just don't do it in Arkansas.

So we have determined that if parents decide to impose a spanking as punishment for an offense their child has committed, they are protected under the law as long as they do not "step over the line" that has been drawn by our legislators. That line is in approximately the same place that it was when our parents were in charge. The problem is that parents today are not cognizant of the law and, therefore, are afraid of being charged with child abuse if they spank their child. Nothing could be further from the truth.

The next section in 2919.22 addresses unwarranted physical force used against a child. The law in other states also provides for this violation. Here's a theoretical situation to help make clear how the same amount of force could be considered warranted in one situation and unwarranted in another. Let's pretend that little five-year-old Susie hasn't been listening lately, and she has been running out into the street and dodging traffic as a form of entertainment. Mom, concerned about her daughter's safety, catches the girl running into the street for the fifth time today. Mom grabs the little girl, lifts her arms over her head, and slaps her on the bottom. Little Susie runs into the house crying. Was mom justified in spanking Susie? Sure she was.

The next day, little Susie is behaving herself, sitting in the living room watching Barney on TV. Mom enters the room and lifts Susie off of the couch, holding her hands over her head and swatting Susie once on the bottom. Susie runs into her room crying. Was mom justified in spanking Susie. Of course not. Although the same amount of force was used in each case, one was warranted and one was not.

The child advocates would quickly endorse this section as their argument against spanking if it were not also specific about certain criteria. Even though the law prohibits a parent from dealing unwarranted discipline, it still demands other criteria for the entire section to be satisfied. The section states, "Repeatedly administer unwarranted disciplinary measures to the child, when there is a substantial risk that such conduct, if continued, will seriously impair or retard the child's mental health or development."

Even when the punishment is unwarranted, it must be administered repeatedly, and even then, there must be a substantial risk that it will seriously harm the mental health of the child. If mom whacks Susie once for no reason, this statute is not violated. Even though that action is wrong, there must be a pattern of this type of behavior by a parent in order to be charged with this crime. When we examine the laws from around the nation, we find that California refers to this type of action as "unjustifiable punishment" which causes "unjustifiable physical pain." Minnesota law prohibits the parent from using "unreasonable force or cruel discipline that is excessive under the circumstances." New Jersey's law prohibits the parent from "inflicting unnecessary severe corporal punishment upon a child."

If the parent must be concerned with the responsibility of protecting the child, then the law must give the parent the authority to restrict the child's behavior and activities. When I talk to parents about their responsibility and authority, I use a theoretical situation to make my point. We all know that if a child walks into a china shop and starts smashing the Waterford crystal causing ten thousand dollars in damage, the store doesn't sue the juvenile. Juveniles are not responsible for the damage they cause, the parents are responsible. So the parents, under an order from a court, would be forced to pay the store for the damages that were incurred by their child. The parents then discover that the child is planning to again smash some Hummels down at the china shop. As he leaves the house, hammer in hand, the parents watch helplessly, wringing their hands and pleading with their out-of-control son to consider how he is ruining their financial future with his antics. "Ha ha," he laughs, "you can't touch me."

This scenario is ridiculous. Yet thousands of parents watch their children defy their instruction and go off on their own, placing the parents at risk with every bad decision they make. I find that most parents, who end up dealing with a defiant teenager whom they haven't properly disciplined when they were growing up, failed to use corporal punishment because they were afraid of getting into trouble with the law. Our society has been inundated by all types of influences that have made us believe that we can't touch our kids.

When a parent instructs a sixteen-year-old boy that he cannot use the car without permission, the son must comply with the rule. According to the law, he has no choice. In fact, a child who refuses to obey his parents is violating the law himself. The unruly child section of the Ohio Revised Code addresses this subject.

[§ 2151.02.2] § 2151.022 Unruly child defined.

As used in this chapter, "unruly child" includes any of the following:

(A) Any child who does not subject himself or herself to the reasonable control of his or her parents, teachers, guardian, or custodian, by reason of being wayward or habitually disobedient;

(B) Any child who is an habitual truant from home or school;

(C) Any child who so deports himself or herself as to injure or endanger his or her health or morals or the health or morals of others;. . . [4]

This section provides the criteria for determining an unruly child. Every state has a statute that defines what an "unruly" child is. The components necessary to declare a child unruly are pretty broad. Most courts have ruled that for a parent to demand that a child do chores is "reasonable" and a refusal to comply with that reasonable request is considered unruly. Parents must keep in mind that one of their major objectives in rearing that child is to instill some sense of responsibility in them. Honesty, respect for authority, and reliability are just a few of the qualities that parents hope their child has obtained once he/she reaches adulthood. There is only one way to instill those qualities into the child. The method best used is discipline and instruction, the "rod and reproof." Children aren't born with those qualities. They must be programmed in. That fact can be substantiated by watching a young teenager who has never been disciplined by his parents, one who has never been forced to respect any authority or to be honest or truthful. No one had to train this child to be undesirable. He was already like that when he was born.

The parent is the deciding factor when it comes to desirable attributes in a child. The parent is the one who "trains" the child to be a responsible person in society. Our lawmakers have always recognized that fact. It is not the responsibility of the police department, the schools, or anyone else to instill values and responsibility into a child. It is the parents' responsibility. Section 2151.41.1 of the Ohio Revised Criminal Code states just that. Other states have very similar laws.

[§ 2151.41.1] § 2151.411 Parent or custodian charged with control of child; liability and searches during probation period; order to exercise control.

(A) A parent of a child whose marriage to the other parent of the child has not been terminated by divorce, dissolution of marriage, or annulment, a parent who has parental rights and responsibilities for the care of a child and is the residential parent and legal custodian of the child, a guardian who has custody of a child, or any other custodian of a child is charged with the control of the child and shall have the power to exercise parental control and authority over the child.[5]

The law here is very specific. A parent of a child is charged with the control of the child. This means just what it says. The parent is charged, or held responsible, for the child's actions by the state. The parent is the one who must correct the child when he does something wrong. The parent must take the necessary steps to change the child's undesirable behavior. The statute continues to give the parent the authority to do just that. It states that the parent shall have the power to exercise parental control and authority over the child. There is no question here. The government expects parents to control their children. In order to do that, the same government empowers the parent with the authority to carry out that responsibility. With liability comes authority. Parents are liable and responsible for the actions of their children. They also have the power to control what their children do. It is written into law, and there is no one who can take it away.

Most states have instituted some sort of domestic violence laws to attempt to curb the problem of spousal abuse. Originally designed to protect battered women, the law places a blanket of protection over all of the members of the family and/or those living together. In Ohio, the law simply states that one member of a household or family member cannot commit or threaten to commit violence against another member of that household or family member. The law in Ohio is written as follows:

§ 2919.25 Domestic violence
(A) No person shall knowingly cause or attempt to cause physical harm to a family or household member.
(B) No person shall recklessly cause serious physical harm to a family or household member.
(C) No person, by threat of force, shall knowingly cause a family or household member to believe that the offender will cause imminent physical harm to the family or household member.[6]

In most states, the domestic violence law is not the most appropriate law in determining whether excessive force has been used against a minor child. If it did apply to parents who wished to use corporal discipline, it would contradict the child abuse law. The child abuse statute authorizes a parent to spank a minor child. However, if dad strikes mom with an open hand using the same force used to spank a child, dad goes to jail.

At the same time I was writing this chapter, an incident took place that convinced me that this type of information was needed by parents. Our city houses the municipal court that has jurisdiction over several other surrounding communities. On any one day, you will see police officers from four or five different communities, as well as the state highway patrol and the sheriff's office, conducting business at our municipal court. My son is a police officer with one of the adjoining communities. On this particular day, he called to tell me he was bringing in an adult male to be arraigned before the judge. He told me that his prisoner had been arrested the previous evening for domestic violence. When he arrived in court and I asked for the specifics in the case, he stated that the man had been arrested for committing a forceful act against his daughter. I guess it was the look of horror on my face that encouraged my son to indicate that he wasn't in agreement with the arrest. He went on to explain the circumstances surrounding the charge.

The man had gotten into an argument with his fifteen-year-old daughter, with whom he lived alone. The daughter, in a fit of rage, struck her father in the face with her hand. The father then grabbed the girl by the arm and led her out of the house to the car, where he placed her in the passenger seat. He then drove to the police station, where he again led the girl by the arm into the building. His intent was to have a police officer speak to his daughter about her striking him in the face. His daughter lifted her shirt sleeve to show the officer a red mark where the father had grabbed the girl's arm. Much to the father's dismay, the police officer placed the father under arrest for domestic violence and put him in a jail cell, where he spent the night. The daughter was able to call other relatives to stay with that night.

Everyone in the courtroom heard me say, "What?" I picked my jaw up off the floor and shook my head in amazement. I tried to tell my son that the domestic violence law does not apply to a parent correcting a child. Then an officer from another city who had been standing nearby piped up, "What do you mean? We arrest parents for domestic violence who hit their kids." I began to wonder what academy this officer had

Just a few of the many Cuyahoga County juvenile probation officers who deal with kids prosecuted by detective Surgenor.

attended. Then a middle-aged woman stood up and walked over to where we were standing. She introduced herself as a "court advocate" for abused family members. She questioned me about our conversation and asked me if I could prove what I was saying. "I certainly can," I answered. I ran back to my office and pulled out several copies of the child abuse and domestic violence laws, highlighted in the important areas. Running back to the courtroom, I provided everyone involved in our conversation with proof that a parent can spank his or her child. The court advocate indicated that she had been working with the courts for several years and was unaware that the law was worded as such. Good grief! It's no wonder parents are afraid to discipline their kids. Social workers, advocates of abused children, and even law enforcement officers are often uninformed and ignorant of the law. Parents who are armed with a copy of the statute and a reasonable understanding of the way the law works have a distinct advantage when questioned about the way they discipline their child.

Now consider that there are indeed cases where a parent has been charged with domestic violence against a child, but the case did not involve any kind of discipline. It was an unwarranted assault on the child. In 1989, *The State of Ohio v. Suchomski* addressed that type of case. A father came home late one night highly intoxicated, pulled his eight-year-old son out of bed, and started punching the boy in the stomach and pounding his head against the wall. The father, after being arrested for domestic violence, argued that he was allowed to discipline his son. Under normal circumstances, he was allowed. Putting his son's head through the plaster wall for no reason while in a drunken state was not allowed. That's just plain common sense. Although the laws in every state protect the parent under normal circumstances, there have also been cases when parents have experienced a nightmare defending themselves against unwarranted claims of child abuse.

I have explained in depth the child abuse laws in Ohio for two reasons. One, I am most familiar with that law and have discussed its meaning with those in the legal field. Second, because Ohio law is one of the most specific laws addressing child abuse in the country, by explaining each portion of the Ohio law, it will make the terms used in other states much clearer and easier to understand. At the end of this book, I have included the child abuse statutes from each state. You can see how your lawmakers feel about parental discipline by reading the law from your own state.

For those of you who find that the laws in your state are too restric-tive and hinder a parent's ability to effectively discipline a child, I would suggest that you do something about it. I truly believe that the overwhelming majority of people in this country feel as I do. One of the problems with conservatives is just that—we are conservative. We do not force our opinions on others. We tend to stand back while others get involved in changing laws. We are not activists when perhaps we should be. It's the "loudest hinge gets the oil" routine. If the First Church of Christ Scientists can get legislation passed in every state that allows them certain exemptions from the law, why can't we in the Christian community have the laws pertaining to corporal punishment reinforced to support our viewpoints? If we allow "experts" like Murray Straus to continue his attack on spanking without any resistance, we will find ourselves unable to bring up our children in the manner prescribed by God.

It's time for conservatives to stand up and loudly proclaim "enough is enough!" The liberal way has proven itself to be destructive. The evidence is overwhelming. We can sit around and do nothing, or we can make a concerted effort to address our legislators and keep the laws from ruining our children.

6

CHILDREN'S SERVICES

"But let none of you suffer as a . . . busybody in other men's matters" *(1 Peter 4:15).*

Both mom and dad sat in my office with their thirteen-year-old daughter. Recent problems with defiance had prompted them to make an appointment with me to discuss their rights and responsibilities as parents. The girl displayed a slight attitude as I spoke with them about the problems they were experiencing. The father indicated that the daughter had recently acquired new friends—the kind that wore black lipstick, nose rings, and purple hair. It seemed that the daughter felt that she was no longer subject to the authority of her parents and that she was able to do whatever she wanted.

Dad explained that the daughter would suddenly appear in the living room at eleven o'clock P.M. and head for the front door. When questioned, she would advise her father that she was going out with her friends. Even though it was a school night, the girl felt that she had the ability to carouse into the early morning hours and still perform in school. Perhaps she did not care if she did well in class. However the girl was thinking, dad informed her that she was not going out. The daughter advised the father otherwise and left the house.

When dad asked me what he should do under those circumstances, I was stunned. I asked him what his father would have done if he had acted in such a manner. His answer was indicative of the experience of most parents his age; his dad would have killed him. I explained that although he probably meant it figuratively, homicide at this point was out of the question. As the thirteen year old snickered in her seat, I mentioned that we just might leave that option open to discussion. I did explain to the father that if his daughter was arrested for a violation of the city's curfew law, he would be cited into court under the parental responsibility portion of the law and fined one hundred dollars for the offense. I suggested that the next time his daughter announces her departure at midnight, he simply state that she was to stay home and vocalize his intent on enforcing his order. If she defied him and attempted to leave the house, he should restrain her physically, using whatever force was necessary to keep her in the house. He agreed to try.

I heard from dad several days later. Dad told me that he didn't care how many times he was cited into court, he was never touching his daughter again. I realized as dad was talking that something had taken place to instill fear into this man. When I asked him why he had adopted this position, the anger in his voice was evident. He explained that he had taken my advice, and the next time his daughter's friends came to the door at midnight and the daughter announced her departure, dad said that he was vetoing the daughter's decision. He informed her that she was staying home. The daughter, obviously not believing the father's resolve in the matter, opened the front door and began to leave. Dad and mom, on the advice of the juvenile detective, grabbed hold of the daughter's arms and attempted to keep the girl from walking out the front door.

The girl immediately began an assault on her parents. She kicked her father violently between the legs. She struggled away from the mother and attempted to reach the front door. Dad grabbed the girl again by the arm and held on. Mom assisted and placed the girl in a big hug. Both parents were able to take the daughter to the ground where she was restrained while dad explained that she was not going anywhere that night. It was some time before the daughter was calm enough to be released from her father's grasp. Dad made it clear that he was not losing this battle. The daughter was staying in the house if mom and dad had to sit on her the entire night.

The following morning the girl went quietly to school. Dad stated that he felt like he had finally taken control of the situation. Perhaps his ability to make his daughter behave had been enhanced by the daughter's apparent loss of the battle. It appeared that she had been humbled when she walked out the door to catch the school bus. It appeared that way at first, until there was a knock on the door later that evening.

The young woman standing on their porch identified herself as a social worker from the department of children's services, a county agency designed to investigate child abuse. The father described her as a young girl "barely wet behind the ears." The social worker advised the parents that their daughter had gone to a school counselor earlier that day and had claimed that she was being abused by her parents. The social worker immediately took the side of the daughter and began an interrogation of the parents. During this investigative discussion, the daughter proudly displayed a bruise on her upper arm, a wound that no doubt occurred during the struggle with her parents. The social worker declined the father's invitation to see the large bruise on his crotch and pointed her finger under his nose, "If you ever touch this girl again," she said, "I will personally see that you are thrown in jail." Neither parent said anything more as the social worker concluded her investigation and pronounced that the daughter was "abused." She encouraged the girl to call the abuse hotline if she were ever again touched by her parents.

I couldn't blame the parents for taking a cautious position under the circumstances. I advised the father that the social worker was wrong, but my words fell on deaf ears. Both parents had been told point blank by a county official that if they used any physical force against their daughter for any reason, they would go to jail. When I indicated to them that I wished to call the social worker, they eagerly supplied me with her business card.

The moment I was connected to Ms. Smith and identified myself, I could feel the hostility over the telephone. I informed Ms. Smith that I was calling in regard to the Jones case and asked her what conclusion she had drawn from her visit with the family. She replied by asking me what interest I had in the case. When I informed her that the parents had contacted me in regard to their daughter's refusal to obey, I was interrupted by Ms. Smith who asked me if I had observed the bruise on the daughter's arm. I told her that I had not personally observed the bruise, but I understood that the mark had occurred as a result of the daughter trying to pull away from her father, who was simply trying to keep the girl in the house. Ms. Smith interrupted me again to tell me that the father was "not allowed" to hold onto his daughter's arm to restrain her. I asked Ms. Smith what action the father was supposed to take under those circumstances. "Call the police," she replied. It was obvious that Ms. Smith also held the "it takes a village" mentality.

"Wait a minute," I said, "if the daughter goes out and gets arrested, the father gets cited for a curfew violation. Are you going to pay the one-hundred-dollar fine for the father?" Ms. Smith insisted that if the father called the police, he should be exempt from any penalty involved with a curfew arrest. "Alright" I argued, "how many police departments should the father call to exempt himself from any curfew ordinances that might exist in the surrounding communities." Ms. Smith continued to argue police department policy, assuring me that she knew more than I did about the way police departments operated.

My next question to Ms. Smith was concerning the amount of force that should be used to effect the arrest of the thirteen-year-old girl. "What happens if she decides that she is not going to listen to the police either?" I asked.

She insisted, "It's the police's responsibility to take custody of the girl." She became very irate when I asked her if she would throw the policeman in jail who tried to hold on to the girl's arm and caused a bruise. She also couldn't explain to me how a police officer would have any more authority to use force to make a juvenile comply with the rules than the child's own parents.

Ms. Smith's constant interruptions got to the point where I was unable to convey my thoughts to the young social worker. She finally blurted, "Officer, you don't know what you are talking about." The silence that followed that outburst gave me the opportunity to tell Ms. Smith that there was something I wanted to read to her. In front of me on my desk was a copy of page eighteen of the department of human services handbook. This particular page quoted verbatim section 2151.031 of the Ohio Revised Criminal Code, which describes an "abused child." I read to Ms. Smith subsection C which says, "A child exhibiting evidence of corporal punishment or other disciplinary measure by a parent . . . is not an abused child under this division." I was interrupted again by Ms. Smith who demanded "And where did you find that?" When I informed her that I was reading from her own department's handbook, Ms. Smith quickly referred me to her supervisors. I was quickly disconnected, and repeated efforts to recontact those supervisors were met with futility.

Stories like this one are more common than one would want to believe. One of the problems that we have in our society is the general public's ignorance of the law. Now, I realize that we can't expect everyone to know every ordinance or statute. If that were the case, we wouldn't need attorneys. But if an individual is having difficulty in one area of the legal system, it's wise to become versed in that area.

In my line of work, I have encountered three main categories of parents. There are those on one extreme end of the spectrum who do not care about their children at all. When their kid gets arrested, they get mad at the police. When their kid gets in trouble in school, they get mad at the teacher and principal. When their child is out gallivanting around at two o'clock A.M., they could care less. The child is an inconvenience, and the parent would be happy if the kid ran away and never came back.

Then there are those parents on the opposite end of the spectrum. These parents love their children and would give their lives for them if necessary. They are diligent in the supervision of their child and keep track of what the child is doing and the friends they have. They set limitations on the child's freedom and carry out the consequences that they have made clear if the rules are violated. These types of parents I very seldom see in my office. I'm not saying that these types of parents never encounter problems with their children's behavior. I am saying that it is rare to find their children committing severe crimes.

Then there is the third class of parent. I would estimate that the parents in this category make up the largest portion of those I deal with on a daily basis. These are loving parents who want the best for their child. They want to provide everything that is needed for the child to grow into a responsible individual and a productive member in our society. But for one reason or another, they have lost control of their child. They are confused about how they should handle adversity with the youngster. They are afraid to take strong action when the child flagrantly disobeys the rules. These are the types of parents who, when I tell them what they are legally allowed to do, say, "I didn't know I could do that!"

So what has caused the confusion in child rearing that parents today are experiencing? A quick digression from social workers will help to make this clear. If you pay attention to everything around you, it won't take you long to spot it. Hollywood is one reason. I have turned a television show off in disgust in front of my children when the actors start to convey that the child in the imaginary household is much wiser than his stupid parents. Any child whose mind is filled with this garbage certainly feels empowered. I have watched TV shows and movies that portray incredible miracles in child rearing performed by parents who treat their children as equals. Any young parent watching this slop is being deceived by actors who spend their entire lives pretending they are someone else. They are following a script written by someone whose ideas are being projected onto the screen. It's not real life!

If you watch the news on a regular basis, you've probably seen several news stories that have made it to the national level. Almost everyone that I have talked to has seen the news story on the mother who spanked her four-year-old child in the grocery store and was arrested on the spot by the police. Although millions saw that story on the evening news, not one was made aware of the results of that arrest. No one realizes that the charges against the mother were thrown out and the mother released. Parents all over the country remember seeing the arrest, a real deterrent when they feel like spanking their child in public.

But no doubt, the strongest influences on this group of confused parents are the numerous publications that claim spanking is harmful to children. From Dr. Spock to Dr. Murray A. Straus, there have been a plethora of psychologists who feel that their "theory" should be considered as fact. A closer investigation of these studies uncover faulty information and statistics. Engrained in every one of the "no-spank" studies are subtle tricks designed to deceive those who read them. As

Newspapers, magazines, and books. The three most common types of media that promotes the nonspanking agenda.

will be discussed in greater detail in upcoming chapters, some studies use ridiculous examples of when to punish a child and then point out how harmful the spanking would be to the child at that moment, when any type of discipline under those circumstances would be improper. Some of these studies use data that is faulty to begin with, not comparable at all with normal families living under normal living conditions. Whether in books, magazines, or in the daily newspaper, parents interpret the information as proven fact. Most of it has never been proven, and little of it is fact. But parents have come to believe that their instincts are wrong, and that others, who know nothing about their child, can make wiser decisions about their upbringing than they can.

Returning to the topic of social services, early one morning, I received a telephone call in my office from a father with whom I had previously dealt on several occasions. His thirteen-year-old daughter had reached a stage of defiance that the entire family had found difficult to deal with. When the father filed unruly charges against the daughter in juvenile court, the judge assigned the case to Pro-Kids, an organization originally designed to protect abused children. In recent years, they have gained the reputation of protecting all kids, even the bad ones.

The tone of Mr. Wilson's voice indicated that he was extremely upset. "Detective Surgenor," he said, "I have just about had it with Pro-Kids." Further prompting of the father uncovered why he was so upset. The father went on to explain, "My daughter went berserk last night and started smashing everything in the living room." The father explained that in an effort not to use any type of physical force against the girl to keep from upsetting the caseworkers from Pro-Kids, he called them on the telephone. When the caseworker came to the phone, Mr. Wilson began to explain that his daughter was smashing the figurines in the living room. "Detective Surgenor," he stammered, "you won't believe what she said!"

"Try me," I coaxed.

You could hear the anger in Mr. Wilson's voice as he continued. "She told me 'You are the adult in the household, you go to your room until your daughter cools off.'"

"You have to be kidding," I said. I was picturing in my mind the chaotic scene at the Wilson household as the thirteen-year-old girl was smashing expensive knickknacks, and the father, afraid to even touch the out-of-control brat, being told to go to his room. "Well," I asked, "did you go to your room?" The answer I got from Mr. Wilson is a prime example of how easy it is for "experts" to convince the layman that they know best. "Sure I did," he said. "I figured she knew what she was doing!" By the time Mr. Wilson ventured out of his bedroom, his thirteen-year-old daughter had left the house. Our department ended up taking another runaway juvenile report.

We have to remember that in our present environment, most organizations designed to protect children, such as the department of children and family services, are coming under an intense amount of pressure for not protecting the kids who are really being abused. Not all social service workers are as inexperienced as Ms. Smith or as ridiculous as Pro-Kids Patsy. There are many compassionate county workers who have a great deal of common sense. But parents must be prepared to defend their actions if the unreasonable investigator is encountered. It is wise for parents to do their homework and investigate the law and what it says about parental authority and corporal punishment.

One morning I received a call in my office from the local high school. The principal and one of the counselors indicated that there was a fifteen-year-old girl in her office who was being abused by her parents. When the counselor gave me the girl's name, I immediately recognized it as one of several juveniles who had been involved in a recent arson of a local motel, the result of a drug party that got out of hand. The girl, along with several of her friends, were being charged with numerous offenses including drug and alcohol possession. The girl had never been in trouble before; it appeared as though the fifteen year old was just beginning to stick her toe over the line. I conveyed this information to the counselor who requested that an officer respond anyway to take the child abuse report.

There is one advantage that our police department has over many of the surrounding departments. Our officers have been well versed in the area of child abuse and domestic violence. The officer who was dispatched to this call came to my office shortly after taking the information from the fifteen year old girl. The girl had written out a statement, which the reporting officer forwarded to me. The officer indicated that nothing that the girl said indicated a violation of the child abuse law. According to the girl's written statement, the punishment dealt out by the parents was totally within the guidelines of the law and appeared to have resulted from her involvement in the arson and drug bust.

Later that day, I received a telephone call from the girl's father. The frustration in his voice was evident as he asked me for some advice.

The father stated that he had just received a call from the department of children's services, who advised him that his daughter had been removed from his custody based on an abuse charge and had been taken from school to a safe place. The father went on to explain to me that his daughter was not really a "bad girl," she had just recently started to hang around with an "undesirable" crowd. The father suspected that his daughter had recently experimented with drugs and was aware that she was involved in the motel arson a few weeks earlier. Dad insisted that he had never abused his daughter, but since her arrest he had instituted stricter rules. The dad felt that the report his daughter had given to children's services was an effort to force him to relax his grip on her activities.

I advised the father to gather as much information as possible about the case. I instructed him to call the abuse hotline and identify himself. He should ask under whose authority the child was removed from the custody of her parents. When he received that information, he should ask for a schedule of events. When was the case being heard by a judge or magistrate? When are the social workers going to interview the parents? What kind of probable cause did the social worker have to take the child from her parents? Each one of those questions should have an answer, and the department of children's services should be able to provide them. The father thanked me for the advice and hung up.

The following day, I received another call from the father. He expressed his thanks for my encouragement to pursue the "abduction" of his daughter. He advised me that his daughter was home again and seemed to be under control. He indicated that what he was about to tell me was almost unbelievable. His voice quivered in anger as he related the events following his call to children's services.

The father stated that soon after his call to the county agency, a female social worker appeared at his door. She asked to talk to the parents and was allowed into the home. The young lady indicated that the agency was willing to relinquish control of the daughter and return her to her home if the parents would sign an agreement stating they would seek family counseling. A bit suspicious of the social worker's mannerisms, the father attempted to read the document that the woman was encouraging them to sign. Insisting that the form simply stated that the parents would promise to get counseling, she tried to cover up the paper. The father finally was able to read the form he was being asked to sign. It turned out to be a confession that the parents had indeed abused their daughter. The father promptly kicked the social worker out of his house, advising her that she could expect to be named in the lawsuit he was about to file. Within a couple of hours, the department of children's services delivered the daughter back to her parents.

Parents have to understand that in order to be formally charged with child abuse, there has to be probable cause that some type of abuse has occurred. This probable cause must come in the form of some type of evidence. There must be some type of physical evidence or eyewitness accounts in order to substantiate the allegation. It doesn't matter what the child says. The accusation must be backed up with evidence. If there is no evidence against the parent, the charge cannot go forward. Although the parent feels helpless at the time, if there is no history of abuse, there is light at the end of the tunnel.

Child abuse investigators are by no means totally exempt from liability. Parents have every right to question the actions of the investigator if it appears to be unreasonable. A Supreme Court case which occurred in 1989 is an example of how, at times, a child abuse investigator can be held accountable for unreasonable action. In *Good v. Dauphin County Social Services (1989) 891 F 2d 1097*, an investigation was initiated by social services. The female investigator advised school officials that the two children involved in her investigation, a teenage girl and her twelve-year-old brother, were possibly being abused. The bases of her report were bruises that were observed on the children's bodies.

The principal of the school was familiar with the family and the alleged victims of the abuse. The principal's opinion concerning the origin of the bruises differed. The principal advised the child abuse investigator that the children played sports—the boy was on the school's rugby team. Additionally, the relationship between the parents and the two children was well-known and had never indicated that there was a problem. When the investigator interviewed the children, they denied that they were being abused by their parents. The children asked the investigator permission to call their parents. The investigator refused. The two children were ordered to strip to their underwear in the presence of the principal, the investigator, and each other.

The parents were understandably upset and filed a lawsuit against the county department of social services. Although the investigator had the authority under the state abuse statute to perform a strip search and was absolutely immune under the law, the federal court ruled that no common sense interpretation of that authority would lead a reasonable person to do what the investigator did. The court ruled against the investigator and she was denied federal immunity on the grounds that her actions were reckless.

We must remember that most child protection agencies are organizations controlled and funded by the county. The area of jurisdiction is a very large one. The agency usually has one central location where the office is located. The distance the social worker has to travel to investigate an abuse report is usually long. The agency is probably understaffed and overworked. The salaries for most county employees leave something to be desired. I have yet to find a county agency that runs as effectively and efficiently as it could. All of those factors combined place the effectiveness of the county department of children's services in question.

Another factor to consider is the difference of ideals between child abuse investigators. I have encountered few investigators who believe children should be spanked. Most county social workers are against corporal punishment of any kind. Most are on the other end of the spectrum, to what extent depends on the worker. You can get as many opinions as there are social workers. Some believe parents should never touch their child at all, not even to guide the child by the arm. Some, like social worker Smith, believe that a parent has no authority to restrain a child who is about to violate the law. I have only encountered a few social workers who have admitted to me that they have felt a spanking was in order, but even then, they have jokingly stated that they would deny it if I repeated them.

I would suggest to parents who are concerned about an investigation by children's services to contact the county agency and ask for information. Document each contact that you have with the agency and record the conversation or make detailed notes and list the people you talk to. Ask several questions and don't quit until you receive answers. If you don't receive the answer you are looking for, call back and talk to a different person. You will find that you will collect numerous opinions about the same subject. If you are advised that you are prohibited from performing certain tasks, ask why. If you are armed with the law pertaining to child abuse in your state, read the law and ask the social worker for an interpretation. You may want to talk to your state legislator first to get the real meaning of the law.

A parent's best defense against an overzealous county child abuse investigator is a working knowledge of the child abuse law. In my area, I receive child abuse investigation reports on a daily basis, forwarded to me from the Cuyahoga County Department of Children's Services. The page, titled "Cuyahoga County Department of Human Services and Law Enforcement Agency Child Abuse/Neglect Report—Response Form,"[1] contains all of the information about an initial abuse investigation by the county social worker. The subject of the abuse report is listed, along with the alleged perpetrator, nature of the complaint, and a disposition section. The disposition section indicates if the complaint is substantiated, unsubstantiated, or indicated. At the bottom of the page, the worker checks the most appropriate space. One of those selections is "Complaint is unjustified. Further involvement not indicated." Another selection states, "Providing protective supervision—parents are cooperating," and "Seeking custody in Juvenile Court." There is a selection that, in the past, has seldom been marked by the social worker, but one that I have noticed recently has been more frequently selected. This selection states, "Unable to obtain cooperation of parents. Court action premature." When I see this selection marked by the social worker, I know that the parents have told the child abuse investigator to take a hike, and the worker did not have any evidence to pursue the allegation in court. With parents becoming more educated and aware of child abuse laws, I should be seeing this selection marked more often.

When parents stand up for their rights, good things do happen. What it takes is a loud voice. If enough parents make enough noise, lawmakers will sit up and take notice. It may take pushing to change the legislation in your state, but persistence pays off.

In the May 30, 1998, edition of the *Cleveland Plain Dealer,* the headlines read "Welfare agency agrees to ask court before taking children."[2] The story was the result of pressure applied to the department of children's services for overstepping their bounds. The article pointed out that child welfare workers in Cuyahoga County would no longer act alone in deciding whether children should be removed from homes on an emergency basis. The article states that "Court and child welfare officials say they hope the procedure will protect children's and parent's rights."[3] The article confirms what I have been trying to point out to parents for years. "The new policy," the article says, "is nothing more than existing state law, from which the court and department had strayed in the last decade."[4] The article explains how, in violation of state law, "child welfare workers, usually in consultation with their supervisors, decided whether to remove a child and only later sought approval from the court."[5]

The article goes on to say that the new administrative judge rescinded that authority, claiming that it had been abused. The judge stated, "A lot of the kids were taken into emergency custody without reason."[6] The judge is not telling us anything that we didn't already know. The judge went on to state that in the future, the information about the case would be taken to the court, where a judge or magistrate would decide if there was enough evidence of abuse to remove the child from the custody of the parents. The county commissioner stated that she predicted that the court would usually agree with the child welfare workers on child removal. If they do, it will be for one reason. With the court looking over their shoulders, child welfare workers will be much more careful about which children they attempt to take from their parents. If there is no evidence, and the child is just trying to get mom and dad in trouble, the child is out of luck. Things are looking up.

7

STUDIES

"Ever learning, and never able to come to the knowledge of truth" (2 Timothy 3:7).

In August of 1997, Dr. Murray A. Straus and the Family Research Laboratory released a study that indicated "when parents use corporal punishment to reduce [antisocial behavior], the long term effect tends to be the opposite."[1] This study, conducted by Murray Straus and Nancy Asdigian, contends that corporal punishment is counterproductive and causes irreparable damage to children. In fact, the researchers suggest that if parents were to quit spanking their children altogether, the overall level of violence in our society would be reduced.

Straus could be considered the leader of the current nonspanking movement in the United States. He is the codirector of the University of New Hampshire's Family Research Laboratory. His book, *Beating the Devil Out of Them: Corporal Punishment in American Families* is his most famous work and is referred to by many other NSA members. He has conducted studies through his Family Research Laboratory that he claims proves corporal punishment is counterproductive and damaging to children. Straus has received much publicity by the media and appears to be the spokesman for the nonspanking advocate (or NSA) when the subject of corporal punishment hits the headlines.

Because of my outspoken viewpoint in favor of spanking as a form of discipline, my name was also becoming familiar within the news media. As previously mentioned, my wife and I were invited by the MS-NBC cable network to appear on a program opposite Straus to discuss

the subject of spanking. The program was slanted '
view that spanking was harmful, but we were given ͺ
some of the many concerns we have had over the past severa͏ͺ ͺ
about out-of-control children.

What amazed me the most was the confrontational attitude displayed by Dr. Straus during the live broadcast on national television. His reaction was one of indignation that someone would question his findings. I explained to the moderator that as a police officer who worked with the youthful criminal element, I had discovered that most of the juveniles I saw in court in front of a judge had experienced little or no discipline as they were growing up. Straus insisted that his study showed that children who had been spanked by their parents went on to a life of crime. I argued that point and stated that if Dr. Straus's study was accurate, all of the juveniles I was seeing in juvenile court should be the ones that have been spanked as children. Straus's answer was, "That is the case, without exception." My answer was, "That's not what I'm seeing out here where the rubber meets the road."

I believe Dr. Straus is wrong. In the years I have been a police officer working with kids, I have discovered one glaring correlation. There is a connection between kids who have never been spanked, and those who are now out of control, those who now have no fear of consequences, those who are not afraid to commit crimes, and those who are not afraid of their parents, the police, or the judge. I believe Dr. Murray A. Straus is one of the leading causes of parental confusion and one of the reasons our youth are now out of control.

The problem with the study conducted by Straus is the data that was used to reach such a conclusion. According to Dr. Den Trumbull a Montgomery, Alabama, pediatrician who is very vocal and supportive of corporal punishment, the findings in Straus's study are questionable. To begin with, the information was gathered over the telephone by the U.S. Bureau of Labor Statistics, starting in 1979. A total of 807 mothers were asked questions about their methods of disciplining their children. The ages of the mothers who participated in this survey ranged from fourteen to twenty-one years. As Michael Lemonick states in the August 25, 1997, *Time* magazine article "Spare the Rod? Maybe," "[t]hat is hardly a representative slice of American motherhood."[2]

The article also points out that the children involved in this telephone survey ranged in ages from six to nine. According to Trumbull, "More sophisticated studies have consistently shown that corporal punishment is effective and not harmful to long-term development as it is confined to youngsters between eighteen months and six years."[3] We have no idea in Straus's study if the nine-year-old children surveyed had been disciplined from the toddler stage or whether a young confused mother just occasionally smacked her child out of frustration. The same mothers were contacted two years later to determine how the children had fared since the last contact. According to Straus, the children who were spanked by their parents had become increasingly antisocial.

Straus also left out other very important factors in his study. In an article in the August 1997 *Archives of Pediatrics and Adolescent Medicine*, it is revealed, "Because many of the children were living with both parents, a more complete measure would require obtaining the same data from fathers. However, the NLSY-CS did not conduct interviews with the fathers, nor did it ask the mothers about spanking by the father or other caregivers."[4] In other words, if there was a father in the family who was the primary disciplinarian, that factor was not taken into consideration. A child could be spanked by dad but because mom was not the parent who actually performed the discipline, the child was counted as a nonspanked child. Dad may have spanked the child, resulting in a positive change in the child's behavior. Straus's research shows the child not spanked by mom, yet better behaved. The fact that Straus eliminated this very important factor from his study places doubt on the accuracy of his findings.

Without realizing it, our society is becoming conditioned to believe the teachings of a few dangerous men. When Sigmund Freud, an atheist and the father of psychoanalysis, introduced his theory that man is motivated by pleasure, he began laying the groundwork for our modern-day permissive society. When Dr. Spock introduced many of Freud's thoughts into his writings and teachings, trusting parents hopped on the permissive bandwagon, allowing their children to behave in a manner that their very instincts told them was socially unacceptable. Instead of following the traditional Judeo-Christian values that have been so successful for several thousand years, parents began listening to men whose theories had not yet withstood the test of time. The resulting damage is irreparable—the child's computer-brain programmed with faulty input. That faulty program will be passed down to the next generation, and the next, and the next. The saying "As the twig is bent, so grows the tree" gives an accurate picture of the damage done to a small child if not properly trained. If you damage the attitude while one is young, like a tree, it is almost impossible to correct once full grown.

I have my own laboratory. It consists of thousands of people from all walks of life. Included in my laboratory are rich people living in large elaborate homes, welfare recipients living in squalor, white people, black people, doctors, lawyers, nurses, secretaries, factory workers, janitors, policemen, firemen, and every other profession imaginable. They all come from diverse backgrounds, some who had loving parents, some who did not. Some were reared sternly with structure and discipline; some had no guidance at all. Some were loved by their parents; some were abused. Many of my subjects are now rearing children of their own. With a large sample of our society for me to observe in a very private, special way, I contend that "cause and effect" is more accurate in my laboratory than in the psychologist's little world where a small sample of human nature is used to conclude such astounding discoveries.

Some of the most glaring evidence that spanking does *not* contribute to an increase in juvenile delinquency is the present trend in juvenile crime. We must admit that parents today spank their children less than even thirty or forty years ago. Yet juvenile crime is increasing by leaps and bounds. If spanking causes all of the problems that Straus is proclaiming, the opposite should be true. According to the U.S. Department of Justice, and the Federal Bureau of Investigation's Uniform Crime Reports, juvenile crime is increasing rapidly. Over the period of 1985 through 1994, murders committed by persons under the age of eighteen years increased by 150 percent. Murders committed by adults during the same period increased by only 11.2 percent. (See chapter 4 for more detailed statistics of juveniles and crime.) Why are so many more children committing murders than in the past? Is it because more children are being spanked? I think not. In fact, of those juveniles arrested for committing assaults against their own parents, only 1.9 percent were spanked as they were growing up. Are the modern-day psychologists correct in assuming that spanking a child makes them violent? No. The opposite is true.

There are numerous professionals who are realizing that spanking is a necessary part of child discipline. William Kilpatrick, a Boston College education professor and author of *Why Johnny Can't Tell Right From Wrong* says, "In our therapeutic society, we've paralyzed parents into believing that any kind of punishment will indelibly mark a child for the worse. Because of all the stress on egalitarianism, adults have lost confidence that they have the right to subject a child to the normal consequences of their behavior."[5] I couldn't have said it better myself.

A study by Dr. Diana Baumrind of the Institute of Human Development at the University of California, Berkeley, published in the October issue of *Family Relations* magazine, finds that "mild disciplinary spanking . . . used rationally on children between eighteen months and six years old and in the context of a warm and engaged parent-child relationship—can be effective in shaping socially constructive behavior and does not necessarily lead to delinquency."[6] The study by Dr. Baumrind concludes that rational spankings may even be "a necessary tool in the disciplinary encounter with young children."[7]

Then there is the research of Dr. Henry Harbin and Dr. Denis Madden which contradicts what liberal psychology is teaching. These two psychiatrists studied the circumstances surrounding vicious attacks on parents by their own children. Working at the University of Maryland's Medical School, they found that "parent battering" usually occurs when one or both parents have abdicated the executive position and when the parents are not in charge. They concluded that permissiveness and appeasement are related to violence in youth— exactly what I have been saying for years.

Another study is now being conducted by a former gang member who is gathering research on why kids join gangs. Among the elements of attraction offered to kids by gangs, power is not one of them. When one joins a gang, he/she is subject to the authority of many other gang members. Most people assume that kids join gangs to get a sense of "family." In part, that is true. But what causes that sense of family?

There are two things that a real gang, such as the Bloods or the Crips, offers to a child. One is a strict set of rules. The child is told, "You are allowed to do this, you are not allowed to do this." There is no gray area. The rules are black and white. The second thing a gang offers to a kid is severe punishment for violating the rules, up to and including death. So why would a kid join an organization like this?

I believe it's inherent in children to interpret structure and discipline as love. When someone in charge tells a child "You cannot do this; it is harmful to you," the child knows the restriction is being placed on his/her behavior for his/her own good. That love is reinforced when the authority punishes the child for stepping over those boundaries. That is how the child knows he or she is loved. This particular study indicates that kids who join gangs do not receive that structure and discipline at home. None of the kids who belong to the Crips, Bloods, or Folks are receiving discipline from their parents. They are floundering in life, looking for someone to place restrictions on their

The popularity of juvenile gangs is due in part to the lack of discipline in the child's home.

behavior and to impose consequences when they disobey. Their parents don't do that. The gang does.

But what about the "researchers" who are telling us that spanking a child causes harm to the child? Are these peddlers of permissiveness and telltalers of tolerance doing our society a favor or a disservice? For thousands of years, parents have been using corporal punishment as a form of discipline. For thousands of years, we have observed children who were spanked by their parents grow up to be productive members of society who respect authority and the rights of others. It was when the "no spanking" mentality began to permeate our culture that we began to experience the "no fear" attitude of rebellious youth. It's getting worse, and unless something is done to educate parents, we are headed for trouble.

In my research, I came across a book published by Free Spirit Publishing called *What Kids Need To Succeed*.[8] What first caught my eye was the top of the front cover that states that the study's results were "based on a nationwide survey of over 270,000 young people in 600 communities." Since I have always felt that the larger the number of individuals surveyed, the more accurate the findings, I felt that a quarter of a million kids would give a pretty accurate idea of what kids today are feeling. Written by Peter L. Benson, Ph.D, Judy Galbraith, M.A., and Pamela Espeland, the book is written for adults and children alike. The authors indicate that from September 1989 through March 1990, students in grades six through twelve were given a 152-item inventory called "Profiles of Student Life: Attitudes and Behaviors." The inventory was developed by Search Institute, a nonprofit organization that specializes in research on children and youth. To date, over 273,000 young people in six hundred communities and thirty-three states have taken the Search Institute inventory. They live in small towns, suburbs, and big cities; in traditional, single-parent, and adoptive families; in poverty, the middle class, and affluence. (My first thought was that this group was very similar to the people in my own laboratory.)

The results of the survey conducted by Search Institute showed that the difference between troubled teens and those leading healthy productive lives was strongly affected by the presence of what they called developmental assets. These were defined as thirty "good things" that every person needs in his or her life. There were sixteen external assets listed, such as family support, parental standards, parental discipline, and positive peer influence. Amongst the internal assets listed were achievement motivation, sexual restraint, and decision-making skills.

I must say that as I read this survey, I was impressed. The children surveyed were asked to fill out a Checklist for Kids. Some of the questions they were asked to answer are listed below.

I feel loved and supported in my family.

My parents clearly express their standards for my behavior.

The number of nights I can spend out of the house for fun and recreation is limited.

I do six or more hours of homework a week.

My friends are a good influence on me.

I attend a religious program or service at least once a month.[9]

Following the Checklist for Kids, was a Checklist for Parents. As I read the questions, I realized that these were the same questions that I asked parents who sat in my office asking for direction.

I talk with my child about school, sometimes help my child with schoolwork, and attend school events.

I clearly express my standards for my child's behavior.

I set rules for my child and enforce the consequences when rules are broken

When my child goes out, I check on where he or she is going, who with, to do what, and for how long.

My child's friends are a good influence.[10]

As I studied this book, I realized that many parents could benefit from this information, not because it contained any startling developments in child rearing but because it reinforced many of the important parenting ideas that I had found to be successful. For example, asset number eight is titled "Parental Standards." One of those listed is to clarify your standards to yourself and your spouse. Make sure that you agree on your expectations for your child's behavior. Kids need parents to stand together on important issues.

Asset number nine is titled "Parental Discipline." It states, "Work with your spouse to determine the rules and consequences for your children. Each parent should have the authority to set rules and carry out the consequences for breaking the rules."[11] It also suggests that the parent should "be consistent in communicating and enforcing the rules." This asset states that "Parents set rules for kids with fair and reasonable consequences. They enforce the consequences when rules are broken."[12]

What bothered me most about this survey was the opinions of the kids surveyed about their own parents. When the question "Parents set rules for their kids with fair and reasonable consequences and they enforce the consequences when the rules are broken," was asked to kids on the survey, only 58 percent of the youth surveyed indicated that they had this asset in their lives. That means that 42 percent of the youth surveyed did *not* feel that their parents provided structure and discipline in their lives. When asked if their parents "monitor their children's whereabouts and when the kids go out, the parents check on where they are going, who they will be with, what they will be doing, and how long they will be gone," 24 percent of the youth surveyed stated that they did not have this asset in their lives. One of the most disturbing answers was to the question of whether the parents took an active interest in the child's friends. Only 31 percent of the kids surveyed felt that their parents encouraged them to keep friends that were a good influence and that stayed away from risky behavior such as alcohol and other drug abuse.

I found this survey to be extremely enlightening. Not only does this survey indicate the feeling of many of today's youth, it offers suggestions for improving one's circumstances. These suggestions, called "Tips for Teens: Build Your Own Assets," utilize many of the time-tested methods to build character in one's self. Teens and young adults reading this survey cannot help but be impressed with the contents and, hopefully, will adopt some of the recommendations contained in its pages. I highly recommend this book to any parent attempting to change his/her child's behavior.

On April 7, 1998, I was again contacted in my office by the producer of MS-NBC. I knew immediately why they were calling. I had seen the headlines in the newspaper that morning, "Pediatricians Oppose Spanking." The papers hadn't hit the presses before the media started planning its daily programs around this news. I hadn't even had time to read the entire article before I was being asked to appear on a live broadcast that day opposite a member of the American Academy of Pediatrics. I gladly agreed to give my views on the subject in front of a national audience.

In 1983, the American Academy of Pediatrics took a much vaguer position on the subject of spanking. The academy suggested alternative forms of discipline to parents but did not go as far as to oppose spanking altogether. Following the lead of the August 1997 issue of the *Archives of Pediatrics and Adolescent Medicine*, the academy evidently felt it to be in their best interest to follow the "no spanking" crowd and publicly oppose it.

According to this study, released in the April issue of *Pediatrics* magazine, spanking teaches children aggression and is no more effective than other forms of punishment. The 53,000-member academy admits that it doesn't expect to eliminate the popular punishment overnight. According to a recent survey, about 90 percent of parents in this country use spanking as a form of discipline. In a 1992 survey, 59 percent of pediatricians in the United States said they support the practice. Dr. Mark L. Wolraich, who headed the committee that worked on the academy's recommendations states, "We would rather have pediatricians teach parents more effective techniques rather than teaching them to be better spankers."[13]

I found out after I went on the air that the academy may not have changed its opinion that much, just its public statement. Dr. Heidi Feldman was the academy's representative on the broadcast. I expected a confrontation similar to the one I experienced with Dr. Murray Straus. What I got was a pediatrician who agreed with me. Dr. Feldman began the program by stating her position on disciplining children. Surprisingly, her position was not much different than mine. She began by stating that there were many elements to discipline, and without excluding spanking, indicated that there were other forms of discipline that could be used. She stated that there are three main components to an effective discipline strategy. She advocated a strong supportive and nurturing environment for the child, something I believe is as important as discipline. She also suggested that parents encourage positive behavior. She certainly won't get any argument from me. Her third component was to discourage negative behavior. Dr. Feldman encouraged parents at that point to adopt "a series of strategies and techniques, of which only one is spanking."

When Dr. Feldman made that statement, I almost fell off my studio stool. In fact, when I was introduced I was a bit confused as to what I was supposed to argue about. Dr. Feldman had included spanking in her discipline plan, and I had expected a blanket restriction on the practice. When the camera light came on, I seized the opportunity to convey my thoughts on the "no fear" factor, indicating that I felt today's youth had no fear of authority because of the lack of spanking in their upbringing. I acknowledged that there was a problem with child abuse in this country, but I did not feel that the elimination of spanking had alleviated that problem at all.

Dr. Feldman responded by stating, "Sometimes parents who want to use spanking are so reluctant to do it that they wait, and then their children get away with things in the beginning. When the parents want to go and offer discipline later on, it's way late into the sequence and things are out of hand." She went on to explain that by the time things are out of control, the parent overreacts and the child cannot connect the consequence with the original offense. At this point I was not sure whose side the doctor was on. I decided to throw in my favorite argument for corporal punishment—King Solomon. I quoted my favorite spanking verse, Proverbs 29:15, "The rod and reproof give wisdom: but a child left to himself bringeth his mother to shame." I then stated that I felt it was difficult to argue with the wisdom of Solomon.

Dr. Feldman responded by saying "I would like to agree with the detective!" I have fun watching the videotape of the program. The look on my face is one of total confusion. My intent was to go into this interview with both barrels blazing. My plan of attack was slowly being deflated. I was looking forward to a good argument and was ending up being part of a combined effort. Dr. Feldman continued, "I think discipline is very very important, and I really shudder when I see children who haven't gotten good discipline from their parents." Dr. Feldman finished up the interview by stating, "I think strong discipline is important. I think parents should use every method of discipline available to them."

I walked out of the studio with a light step. "There's still hope," I thought to myself. Perhaps the "professionals" aren't really against spanking. Perhaps the American Academy of Pediatrics is just trying to be politically correct. According to the 1992 survey, almost 60 percent of pediatricians support spanking as a form of discipline. It was obvious on national television that the antispanking group is still in the minority. Let's hope it stays that way.

8

THE INTERNET

"And they shall wander from sea to sea, and from the north even to the east, they shall run to and fro to seek the word of the Lord, and shall not find it" (Amos 8:12).

As previously mentioned, Randy Cox runs "The No Spanking Page" on the Web. His e-mail address is RCox@cei.net. This web page has numerous links to other no-spanking web pages, such as "Ten Reasons Not to Hit Your Kids" by Jan Hunt; "Plain Talk About Spanking" by Jordan Riak, the executive director of Parents and Teachers Against Violence in Education; and "Hitting is wrong—and children are people too" by the organization EPOCH, otherwise called End Physical Punishment of Children. Randy Cox also maintains his own web link, called "Alternatives to Spanking?"

In his web site, Randy Cox encourages parents to eliminate corporal punishment from their itinerary of discipline. He states, "The alternative to spanking is . . . everything else you already use, honed and polished, without the spanking. What do you do when everything else has failed? You do the same thing that you're doing now, but instead of spanking, as you have more than once, you do all of the other things more and better." What Cox is advocating here is to continue to try the forms of discipline that have failed in the past. He continues to try to convince the parent that "Confidence in your mind, your heart, and your children's capacity and motivation for learning" will eventually overcome the obstacles you will encounter. This must also mean that confidence in your "mind" and your "heart" that you are a bird will enable you to fly.

The No Spanking Page encourages readers to communicate with Randy Cox. As previously mentioned, I decided to engage in an e-mail

The internet is loaded with antispanking web sites, all containing misinformation and deceit to promote the agenda of the NSA.

conversation with RCox (see chapter 3). This chapter will focus mainly on his responses to my experiences in juvenile crime. My first e-mail message to Randy Cox was as follows:

> FROM: BPDpolice@aol.com—TO: RCox@cei.net "I am a police officer in charge of our city's juvenile crime unit. I have but one thing to say. The elimination of corporal punishment results in a child who has no fear of consequences, no fear of their parents, no fear of their teachers, no fear of the police, no fear of the judge, and no fear of God."

Cox's reply indicates the mind-set of the NSA. He replies,

> Nonspanked children can turn out as fine or finer than spanked children. While parental warmth, positive reinforcement, active listening, setting clear limits, and maintaining realistic expectations have demonstrated positive effects, spanking has never been shown to add anything beneficial for the child. Certainly, "benefit" is in the mind of the spanking parent, but there is really NO objective evidence that hitting children results in ANY measurable long-term benefit. Since nonspanked children who enjoy the positive parenting methods I mention above, can turn out as well or better than spanked children who enjoy the same positive influences, spanking can not be logically credited for a good outcome.

Cox goes on to question my credentials and then makes a statement that has been proven to be false. He continues,

If you know anything about the work you claim to do, you know that most of the people who make your job necessary have NOT escaped physical punishment. They make up the best argument AGAINST physical punishment. Violence begets violence.

As you will see further on in this chapter, Cox is misinformed of the facts involving kids who have been spanked and those involved in criminal activity. In direct contrast with Cox's claim, kids who have *not* been spanked make up the best argument *for* corporal punishment. It was obvious that Cox was unhappy with my next claim, "The peddlers of permissiveness have turned the job of parenting into a nightmare for confused parents." His reply was clear in meaning. Cox wrote,

> Parents, struggling to achieve that "fear" you think is important by hitting harder and more frequent, IS a problem. Permissiveness is NOT advocated in anything you read at my web site. Fair, firm, consistent and decisive parenting is advocated. Hitting children is what we would eliminate . . . not parenting. Hitting children can not be declared safe, effective, or more effective and safer than several parenting methods that CAN be declared safe and more effective.

My next move was to interject Scripture into the conversation. I wrote,

> Obviously, all these experts consider themselves wiser than one of the wisest men who ever lived on the face of the earth, King Solomon, who wrote in Proverbs 29:15 "The rod and reproof give wisdom, but a child left to himself bringeth his mother to shame." Are you wiser than Solomon? I doubt it.

Randy's answer stated,

> But certainly hope so! Solomon was a terrible parent. He was a lousy leader. He was anything but a good example for those who would be devout followers of God. His son, who followed him to the throne, was a lousy leader too. . . . Proverbs is okay, as far as poetry goes, and it provides for us some nice things to repeat in worshipping God. However, no law abiding person would do EVERYTHING the Bible says to do. There's quite a lot of cruel and inhumane vigilante behavior there.

It was apparent from this reply that Randy Cox was ready to argue Scripture. RCox continued with his reply.

> Do you know Jesus? Solomon was no Jesus. The New Testament says nothing good about hitting children. Jesus supposedly admonished some adults once, saying that whatever they might do to children, they do to him. Spank Jesus?

This was my first clue that Cox's knowledge of the Bible was lacking. His use of the term "supposedly" indicated that he was unsure. Cox ended his message with another incorrect statement. "Jesus advocated non-violent conflict resolution," he wrote.

> Tested more than the vast majority of parents, Jesus refused to raise his hand even in defense of his life. It wasn't his way and it shouldn't be our way either. They're CHILDREN for Heaven's sake! We must do no harm. Thanks for visiting my page and offering your comments.

Cox had opened a door that allowed me to stick my foot in. His comments about Solomon, his son Rehoboam, and Jesus, had opened up a whole new can of worms. I began formulating my reply to Cox's comments, knowing that there was a good chance he would eventually retract his appreciation for me visiting his web page.

To address his doubts about my credentials, my reply was simple and to the point.

> The county juvenile court that I work with has the highest juvenile crime rate in the state. If YOU know anything about the juvenile justice system, you know the overwhelming majority of judges, prosecutors, probation officers and police officers are recognizing the correlation of children who have NEVER been spanked and children who have NO FEAR of authority and end up in trouble with the authorities. In my city alone during the past ten years, we have experienced a 700 percent increase in domestic violence attacks committed by children against their parents. I am responsible for collecting the information on each case that occurs in my jurisdiction. In my detailed report, the parents are asked about their family history and prior behavioral problems with the youth. Of all the kids who attack

their parents in my city, ONLY 1.9 percent were raised with any type of corporal punishment. And you are going to try to tell me that kids that are spanked are the ones who get in trouble with the law? You obviously have not talked to many police officers or juvenile court officials!

For those of you who intend to confront the NSA on-line, the following is typical of the response you should expect. Cox denied my claim that almost all cops and court officials recognize that kids who get in trouble with the law needed to be spanked. He wrote,

They may all be wrong, BPDpolice, at least about what is actually "correlating." However, I'd be interested in a citation. Where and how can I find the published research data supporting such a conclusion? I should be able to either "recognize" along with you guys or continue to presume that there is NO science in your method. At this point, however, I doubt that there is any published research that will confirm your claim.

In response to my comment "You obviously have not talked to many police officers or juvenile court officials," Cox replied,

What I think is in the best interests of the children and our society, now and in the future, will not be based on an opinion survey. Right and wrong, beneficial and harmful are not determined in an election. What we have learned about how children develop and learn and why they behave the way they do has not been generated by checking with Joe cop, Clarence jailer or Humphrey judge. Judges are supposed to know the law, but are more often much more ignorant of child development and behavior management then they are even of the law. Those who have a familiarity with the "state-of-the-art," have developed it by reading peer-reviewed published research, which leads most to devalue corporal punishment and to rank higher more positive prevention methods.

Here, the true colors of the NSA are beginning to bleed through. His arrogant references to "Joe cop, Clarence jailer and Humphrey judge" indicate his attitude toward authority. He refers to judges as "ignorant" of both the law and child development. As far as the NSA is concerned, they are better equipped to deal with your child than anyone else. He states that he has developed his "state-of-the-art" by reading "peer-reviewed published research." His peers just happen to be other nonspanking advocates.

Cox then begins an attack on my claim that statistics are showing that kids who are not spanked are assaulting their parents and getting in trouble with the law. He wrote,

> I will gladly cite data supporting any of my conclusions and consider it fair for you to do the same. As is typical for most people, however, attitudes precede reasoning and much of what we hold as truth is NOT and is based solely in myth and superstition. Personal bias is the number one reason to doubt "self" evaluation.

I assume that Cox does not apply this philosophy to himself. This advice is directed at me. Apparently, he and those who are likeminded are the only ones who are able to look at things logically and compassionately.

Cox then continues in his e-mail to convince me that the elimination of corporal punishment has resulted in a kinder, gentler society. What follows is a lot of information that is simply not true. Cox did not seem to care that I have the resources available to counter his claim. Cox wrote,

> The homicide rate has decreased 2 1/2 fold in those American states that have abolished corporal punishment in their schools. Statistics also prove that vandalism is less at schools in America where corporal punishment is banned.

What Cox has presented here is false propaganda used by the NSA to convince the public that the elimination of spanking has a positive effect on children. The problem is, none of it is true. Any person can look at the F.B.I.'s Uniform Crime Reports to determine what the murder rate is in the states that have restricted corporal punishment in the public schools. After receiving this e-mail, I double checked the statistics in the area that Cox gave and found absolutely no truth to it at all. Besides, Cox is claiming that the elimination of spanking at the school level makes a difference. The parent has been eliminated from this formula. I decided to send a message to Cox indicating that I was unable to substantiate his claim. I wrote, "I have looked diligently for the statistics you gave regarding the homicide rate reduction in states that have eliminated corporal punishment in their schools, and am unable to come to any such conclusion." Cox replied with,

> Ever read anything by Irwin Hyman? He is an educator/researcher at Temple University and his many published articles and books are easy to find. See *School Discipline and School Violence*, *Reading, Writing, and the Hickory Stick*, or *The Case Against Spanking*.

What Cox encourages people to do is read books written by "researchers." I felt that it was time to hit Cox with some cold, hard statistics.

My answer to Cox simply repeated some of those cold, hard facts that I have already presented to the reader. I listed some of the current trends that indicate without question that juvenile crime is on the rise. I began by stating, "You stated that you do not believe that the juvenile crime rate is skyrocketing." I then listed the figures that prove otherwise. (Incidentally, the figures I supplied to him and those given in this book are not inaccessible. Anyone can go to the local library and open up the UCR to check them out.)

Cox's answer is one of total denial, "I do not," he replied. "The most recent data suggests otherwise. The reason is unknown. Glad we should be that it has dropped, but we have no reason to think we know why or for how long that could be a trend." Cox is unaware of the fact that the F.B.I.'s crime reports are extremely inaccurate since 1992. He states that the recent data shows that juvenile crime is on the decrease. Although that is true in some categories, a comparison of the juvenile and adult crime rate indicates a very serious juvenile crime problem. And how does Cox explain the explosion of domestic violence offenses committed by children against their parents? Yet there are thousands of people who are being deceived by the nonspanking rhetoric.

When I indicated to Cox that I considered my entire city a "laboratory," where my data comes unsolicited from all walks of life and that I felt my findings were more accurate than those generated in a "controlled environment," Cox replied,

> You are entitled to have an opinion. It does not appear to be founded in *scientific* research, however; seeming to have

more in common with a really big pile of anecdotes . . . interesting, perhaps, but not representative, not replicable, and not valuable to the prediction of behaviors or any strategy for prevention. Your idea of a 'controlled environment' escapes me. Perhaps you are not very familiar with research methods in social science or perhaps I just don't understand what you mean to describe.

I attempted to show Cox that people in the juvenile justice system were beginning to observe a pattern that kids who have never been spanked were ending up in trouble with the law. I wrote, "When I see something 'correlating' over and over again, and find that other professionals working with kids see the same 'correlating,' I have to trust my research results."
Cox replied with more "scientific" jargon. He wrote,

I see. You seem to be using correlation non-scientifically. You are, perhaps, describing a process of visually scanning data and conjuring up guesses. To be fair, what IS your definition of correlation and what statistical formula are you using?

When I tried to present my figures that indicated that almost all children who assault their parents have never been spanked, Cox replied, "That is ONLY a possible factor. No one has shown either the presence or the absence of CP to be causative." (I'm not sure what Cox means by this statement, as he has been trying to convince parents that the presence of corporal punishment is causative in a negative way.) He continued,

However, several researchers over the past thirty years have shown that spanked children are more likely [to] engage in undesirable violent or aggressive behaviors than are non-spanked children. Spanking children is NOT safe. It is no more effective than several nonphysical alternatives. It is a popular method partly because it is quick and it doesn't require very much thinking. It provides the spanker with the illusion that behavior has changed. Any interruption in unwanted behavior is temporary at best and very likely is repeated outside the awareness of the spanker.

Cox tried to convince his audience that spanking is a tradition that continued with man after he evolved from the uncivilized creature he was in years past. He wrote,

Agricultural societies tend to use CP much more than hunter/gatherer societies. Field workers require force to do that kind of work. I believe that the evidence supports the contention that hitting children for the purpose of correction and control evolved as part of people's moving from small, nomadic, hunting/gathering life styles to larger, stationary, agrarian types. What our world needs today are people who have developed superior communication and negotiation skills, who think independently and are adept at cooperation and collaborative efforts. Hitting people, children or other, does not enhance these skills, but more likely results in a person who is prepared for brute labor, subordinate to others and their will and direction.

Notice the last sentence in Cox's statement. "Hitting . . . children . . . more likely results in a person who is . . . subordinate to others and their will and direction." Unwittingly, Randy Cox has very clearly stated what I have been contending since I began my drive to expose this movement. Children will act towards their parents in one of two ways. They will either be subordinate or insubordinate. Let me ask all of the parents who are reading these words, would you rather have your fifteen-year-old teenager be subordinate to you or insubordinate to you? Would you rather have your teenager obey your orders and be subject to your authority, or would you rather your teenager tell you to take a hike? Randy Cox is making my point for me. Insubordination is not tolerated in our society. Not in school, not in the workplace, and not in the military. It should not be tolerated in the home. If spanking a child causes him to be subordinate, I will choose that form of discipline over other forms that have no effect. God instructs us in Titus 3:1 "to be subject to principalities and powers, to obey magistrates, to be ready to every good work." Romans 13:1–2 states, "Let every soul be subject unto the higher powers. For there is no power but of God: the powers that be are ordained of God. Whosoever therefore resisteth the power, resisteth the ordinance of God: and they that resist shall receive to themselves damnation." When we teach our children to be subordinate, we are teaching them one of the most fundamental lessons in civilization—respect for authority. Romans 13:4 just happens to be my favorite "law enforcement" verse. There is a large poster in the lobby of my police station. It is a photograph of me sitting in a police car in the dark of night. I am looking out over the empty streets of the north end of our city in the shadows of the street-lights. (I have the same poster at home also.) At the bottom of the poster is Romans 13:4, "But if thou do that which is evil, be afraid; for he beareth not the sword in vain: for he is the minister of God, a revenger to execute wrath upon him that doeth evil." To be subordi-nate is vital in our society. If we are not, we will feel the wrath executed upon us by those who have authority over us.

RELIGION

"For they that are such serve not our Lord Jesus Christ, but their own belly; and by good words and fair speeches deceive the hearts of the simple" (Romans 16:18).

In late November of 1998, I received a telephone call from a friend, excitedly asking me if I had seen the advertisements now posted on the sides of the regional passenger bus line. Knowing my position on spanking, he went on to exclaim that I "wouldn't believe" what he had just seen. When he explained that the signs were being sponsored by the Inter Church Council of Greater Cleveland, I immediately assumed that for once, there was finally some public advocacy of corporal punishment from the biblical standpoint. I was wrong.

The sign my friend George had seen stated in large black letters, "It's Never Right To Hit A Child." Under the message was a phone number with the encouraging words, "We Can Help." The church council's formal title was at the bottom of the billboard. Now mind you, George was not one who frequented church often and was definitely not a Bible scholar. Yet even he knew instinctively that there was something wrong about an organization of churches joining the nonspanking crowd. "Do you believe this?" he exclaimed. "Now we even have the churches telling us we shouldn't spank our kids! What is the world coming to?"

The true Christian realizes that not all religions organizations are part of the true Church. There are millions of people on this earth who belong to a "church" who are not on their way to heaven. There are also countless leaders within these organizations like those described in Matthew chapter 15. When the disciples told Jesus that the Pharisees

Even some "religious" organizations have joined the nonspanking movement, displaying their message to millions in public advertising.

were offended by his message, Jesus answered them, "Let them alone: they be blind leaders of the blind. And if the blind lead the blind, both shall fall into the ditch." (verse 14). There is no difference between those righteous Pharisees and many of today's leaders in many of our religious organizations. They themselves are blind to biblical truths. Therefore, they are unable to teach others what God instructs us in our daily lives. They are teaching that spanking is wrong simply because they themselves do not know that the Bible teaches that spanking is right.

A few days after I was advised of the Inter Church Counsel's drive to eliminate spanking, I opened the religion section of a Cleveland newspaper to be greeted by a picture of a large billboard containing the no-spanking message. The headline read "Opening door to woodshed." The article refers to the campaign as "The absolute message carried on billboards and posters sponsored by the Protestant church umbrella group the Inter Church Council of Greater Cleveland." The article refers to the saying plastered on billboards all over the city as "Such a simple statement. Such a complicated issue."[1] The following day I traveled to one of the areas indicated in the article where a large lighted billboard was located. As I gazed up at the large sign, I wondered how many people would be influenced by this message loudly proclaimed by the "religious" organization.

Nonspanking rhetoric by the "religious" community is not limited to billboards and newspaper articles. Found within the no-spanking web pages is a person who claims to be the senior pastor of a church in Bexley, Ohio. The Rev. Thomas E. Sagendorf has decided to join the NSA to argue against corporal punishment, using the Bible as his tool. When I saw the title on the web page, it immediately sparked my interest. The title was "Corporal Punishment. What Does The Bible Say?" Considering the fact that this

This message placed strategically near main roadways helps to confuse millions of parents about the use of corporal punishment.

commentary was located on the antispanking section of the Web, the title "Reverend" attached to the author's name stirred my curiosity.

At the risk of being repetitive, I am including much of the Rev.'s comments that I found on his web page. He begins by writing,

> As a pastor, I'm often asked about biblical authority as it pertains to daily practice. What does the Bible say about the way we should live? How, for example, should we discipline our children? What about spanking? Whenever this question is raised, my answer is clear. I can find no sanction in the teaching of Jesus or the witness of the New Testament to encourage the practice of corporal punishment—at home, school or anywhere else.[2]

At this point, I immediately recognized the last sentence as one I had seen numerous times before on other web pages, word for word. Now I was wondering if the Rev. was actually the author of the text I was reading, or if he had "cut and pasted" it from that suspected large database that all of the NSA got their information from. I read on.

> "A number of popular voices take a different view," writes the Rev., "often quoting Old Testament scriptures to prove their point. Those who subscribe to this argument misunderstand and misuse Scripture. A similar method of selective reading

could just as well be used to justify slavery, suppression of women, polygamy, incest and infanticide."[3]

Uh-oh. Here were those same words again. They were identical to others spewing forth misinformation on the internet. I had read the same words on Randy Cox's web page, Jan Hunt's web page, and others, all purporting to be the authors of these same words. I knew exactly what to expect next. I knew the Rev. was going to attack "secular thinking wrapped in religious language." I read on.

"Much of what poses as biblical grounding for corporal punishment," the Rev. writes, "really is secular thinking wrapped up in religious language."[4] Ah-ha! I patted myself on the back. I was getting really good at this. I knew that the Rev. was about to point out how Jesus taught nonviolent responses to situations of high stress and conflict. I was right.

The Rev. continued with his dissertation.

It does not stand the test of what Jesus said and taught. Consider the following: Jesus was overwhelmingly committed to nonviolent response, even in situations of high stress and conflict. This is shown in the Beatitudes and his rebuke of the follower who brandished a sword during his arrest. Corporal punishment is a violent act against a child's body. It is not a response that is consistent with what Jesus demonstrated.[5]

At this time I pulled out a hard copy of the Randy Cox response I had received weeks ago. I compared the two documents side by side. There it was, identical, word for word. I thought that perhaps Randy Cox was the initial author of this gibberish. Now I was wondering if the Rev. had written this page and everyone else in the NSA was copying it. I read the next paragraph, identical to Cox's next paragraph.

Jesus was committed to the beauty, sanctity, innocence, and life-giving character of children. "Unless you become like a child," he said, "you will never enter the kingdom of heaven." When children were pushed aside by his impatient disciples, Jesus rebuked them, saying, "Let the children come to me and do not hinder them, for to such belongs the kingdom of heaven." It is hard to imagine that Jesus would sanction the practice of hitting those in whose very presence the kingdom is made real.[6]

The Rev. continued on his document.

Jesus was committed to love and forgiveness as both the means and the end of all human relationships. These two qualities form the very foundation of his ministry. An action such as spanking that is clearly intended to cause pain hardly qualifies for what Jesus would call an "act of love." For these reasons, I am convinced that corporal punishment is opposed to biblical teaching. People of faith are encouraged to find different methods to provide structure and direction for their children's lives. Discipline is important! Children must learn how to be accountable. But when parents hit children, no matter what the pretext, the opposite usually happens. Instead of learning values, children simply observe the capacity to be mean and harmful. Fear and resentment follow. Parents who work to establish a gentle and nonviolent environment will find good results. Nurtured in an atmosphere free from fear and threat, children will be able to better learn and embody the values that are most important.[7]

The document was signed "The Rev. Thomas E. Sagendorf, Senior Pastor, Bexley, Ohio." The Rev. had added an invitation at the bottom of the web page. "If you have any questions or comments about this site, please send mail to: nblock@infinet.com."

Ah yes, another opportunity for me to engage in a volley of e-mail messages with a member of the NSA. I decided to accept the challenge. I formulated a reply to the Rev.'s statements, beginning with,

For seventeen years, I have worked with kids as a police officer, most recently as a police detective in charge of our bureau's juvenile crime unit. I have seen firsthand the results of the "antispanking" movement on our culture. In eliminating corporal punishment from the discipline plan, we are eliminating the "fear" factor that a child should develop during their upbringing. Kids are growing up with no fear of their parents, no fear of their teachers, no fear of the policeman or the judge, and no fear of God. The correlation between kids who have never been spanked and kids who get in trouble with the law is blatantly obvious to us who work in law enforcement.

I felt that I had condensed my thoughts from the law enforcement standpoint into a fairly concise paragraph. Now it was time to address the Rev.'s statement from the biblical standpoint.

I wrote in the second paragraph, "I am also a Christian, and I will take you to task on your interpretation of what Scripture says about spanking." I went on to mention to the Rev. that I had noticed the information that he placed on his web site was identical, word for word, with other quotes I had read on the nonspanking web pages, such as Randy Cox's "The No Spanking Page." I indicated to the Rev. that I was not sure who was the author and who was the borrower. I stated that I did hope that he would consider my thoughts on the subject as a pastor of a church, whose congregation is thirsting for truth from God.

I mentioned that we must acknowledge that all contained in the Holy Bible is divinely inspired by God. I quoted 2 Timothy 3:16. I referred to Romans 15:4 that says, "For whatsoever things were written aforetime were written for our learning, that we through patience and comfort of the scriptures might have hope."

I mentioned the unconverted to the Rev., who "receiveth not the things of the Spirit of God: for they are foolishness unto him: neither can he know them, because they are spiritually discerned." I reminded the Rev. that it was easy to see that the Holy Bible, in order to be understood, not only requires the new spiritual birth, but also needs to be rightly divided. I did mention that if he believed what he was saying on his web page, it was apparent that he had failed to "rightly divide" the Scriptures. I was hoping that I was not being too judgmental.

I tried to explain to the Rev. the difference between God dealing with Israel in a national way and God dealing with Israel in a domestic way. I reminded the Rev. that all the attributes of God are extreme, so that His righteousness, holiness, judgment, and anger are just as extreme as His love. I asked the Rev. if he really accepted, understood, and received this truth.

I went on to state that what the Rev. had failed to realize was the fact that in all of the Old Testament incidents that he referred to that justify slavery, suppression of women, polygamy, incest and infanticide, we have a Nation of Israel under *law*. I reminded the Rev. that today we are in a different dispensation. God's national dealings with the Nation of Israel are now suspended, and God is no longer executing immediate judgment upon nations as He did under the old economy of Old Testament times.

I then asked the Rev. to notice that the instructions of the Lord uttered through Solomon in the Book of Proverbs are not the national dealings of God with Israel and the nations, but rather God's instructions regarding a family's domestic behavior. This expected behavior from God never changes and is applicable as much today as it was then.

I reminded the Rev. of his statement on his web page concerning Jesus and the way the Lord responded to conflict. I asked the Rev. what he thought of the fact that Jesus Himself scourged certain ones in the temple? I asked the Rev. to consider the actions of Christ described in John 2:15, "And when he had made a scourge of small cords, he drove them all out of the temple, and the sheep, and the oxen; and poured out the changers' money, and overthrew the tables"; I suggested that it certainly did not sound like a "nonviolent response." I mentioned the scourge of cords not being designed to tickle the armpits and the act of spilling money on the floor and overturning tables not sounding like "non-violent conflict resolution." Finally, I mentioned what God says in Proverbs 29:15.

I felt that I had successfully given viable answers to the subjects that the Rev. Sagendorf had addressed. I sent it off to him at the e-mail address indicated on his web page. Then I waited. The following day, as I accessed my server, I noticed that I had e-mail. As I opened up the mail, I recognized the address "nblock." With anxious anticipation I clicked on the icon, waiting to see what the Rev. had to say about my biblical response. I was disappointed. The answer was not from the Reverend at all, but from someone named Nadine Block, (the reason for the e-mail address "nblock") who claimed to be the executive director for the "Center for Effective Discipline" in Columbus, Ohio. Her answer to my quite lengthy message was a single paragraph. Her message read,

> It is interesting that we often get just the opposite point of view from people in law enforcement. Police tell us that almost every juvenile in prison has been hit, many have been beaten to the point of abuse. This obviously did not put fear in them. I think we would better place our efforts on teaching young people respect . . . respect for schools, for teachers, for public institutions and for themselves. That has to be done primarily by parents . . . who are, hopefully, good models for their children in their own deportment and attitudes. Kids need more discipline . . . more teaching, guiding, correcting . . . without hitting.

I agreed with nblock on one point. It was very interesting that people from law enforcement were advising her that children who are spanked end up in prison. That is certainly not the opinion I am getting from my law enforcement colleagues. But wait a minute. She didn't really say that, did she? What she said was, "Police tell us that almost every juvenile in prison has been hit, many have been beaten to the point of abuse." Is nblock stating that children who are spanked by their parents end up in jail? What she is saying is not even close. She is referring to abused children, not spanked children. I was invited to visit another web site listed at the bottom of this e-mail message. It read "http://www.stophitting.com." Here we go! Another web site to check out. I put the address on my list.

The very next day, I received my reply from Rev. Thomas Sagendorf. His attitude was similar to others in the nonspanking movement. It was also apparent that the Rev. had some problems with our biblical answers to some of his statements. I believe he was angry that some very logical theology had cast some doubt on his biblical argument against corporal punishment. His reply was at best, lame. Some of his reply is as follows:

> TO: BPDPolice@aol.com. I have just read your e-mailed reply to the Center for More Effective Discipline. I am appalled. Your communication reinforces the addage [sic] that a little biblical knowledge can be a dangerous thing.

> No matter how much prooftexting one employs (and your mumbo-jumbo takes the prize), there's no basis for hitting kids in the life and ministry of Jesus of Nazareth. When you engage in such a convoluted scriptural exercise, you're really taking a cultural practice and dressing it up in religious garb. It cannot stand the test of one simple Bible verse: "Let the children come to me and do not hinder them for to such belongs the kingdom of heaven."

> Your view of human nature in general, and children in particular, is tragic. Children are inherently evil, according to your view, and have to be beaten into control with pain and fear. Such a distorted view of God's most precious creatures hardly coincides with the Jesus I know!

It frightens me to know that you are a police officer. With your distorted view of children, your obvious need for control, and your wholehearted defense of violence under the guise of Christian teaching, I hate to think of the consequences for the community where you live.

I will hold you in prayer: that you may yet discover the magnificent gift God has given us in children; may learn to deal with your need to dominate; and may give up your attachment to violence (another false god). I'll pray also that, as a police officer, you are far removed from the children I know and love.

Yours truly, The Rev. Thomas E. Sagendorf[8]

In his reply, the Rev. attempts to make Jesus a part of the NSA. He claims that the concept of spanking cannot "stand the test" of one Bible verse. He states, "When you engage in such a convoluted scriptural exercise, you're really taking a cultural practice and dressing it up in religious garb. It cannot stand the test of one simple Bible verse: 'Let the children come to me and do not hinder them for to such belongs the kingdom of heaven.'" The Rev. is referring to either Mark 10:14 or Luke 18:16, which states, "Suffer the little children to come unto me, and forbid them not: for of such is the kingdom of God."

I decided to send the Rev. one more message. I quickly typed out "one simple Bible verse." The verse that I sent back to Rev. Sagendorf is from Matthew 15:4 and Mark 7:10. When questioned by the Scribes and Pharisees, Jesus reminded them of one of God's laws. He states, "For God commanded, saying, Honour thy father and mother: and, He that curseth father or mother, let him die the death." I titled the e-mail message to the Rev. "One simple Bible verse." I figured if the Rev. could play that game, so could I.

We read what God thinks of this type of individual in Romans 16:17–18,

> Now I beseech you, brethren, mark them which cause divisions and offenses contrary to the doctrine which ye have learned; and avoid them. For they that are such serve not our Lord Jesus Christ, but their own belly; and by good words and fair speeches deceive the hearts of the simple.

10

DECEIT

"They conceive mischief, and bring forth vanity, and their belly prepareth deceit" (Job 15:35).

"That we henceforth be no more children, tossed to and fro, and carried about with every wind of doctrine, by the sleight of men, and cunning craftiness, whereby they lie in wait to deceive," (Ephesians 4:14).

I believe that parents are instilled with an instinctive ability to know when their discipline is appropriate or excessive. Even abusive parents know when they step over the line and use inappropriate or excessive force against their child. Most parents know instinctively that a spanking is appropriate under certain circumstances. And yet something they have heard or read has convinced them that spanking is wrong. We have evolved from a society that universally accepted spanking as a form of discipline to a confused group of parents who question its effectiveness. Why?

There are several subtle but effective methods used by the nonspanking advocate to brainwash society into believing that spanking a child is harmful and counterproductive. Since most of this antispanking advice is in written form, most of this propaganda is obtained in books, magazines, and newspapers. The newspaper is the most effective medium to reach the masses. Many articles have been written for print in the family section of the Sunday newspaper that advise parents that spanking is harmful. Parenting magazines, purchased mainly by adults who are presently rearing children, often include antispanking advice. For those parents who are looking for more specific help in rearing their child, the parenting section of the bookstore is the answer. Unfortunately, mom or dad is more likely to pick up a book that encourages the elimination of corporal punishment. The prospanking books are outnumbered about twenty to one.

The most evident method of deceit used by the NSA is to illustrate an example or situation which makes the spanking given to the child appear to be extremely unfair. This method is fairly simple and is used over and over again by most of the "experts" who argue against corporal punishment. The NSA begins by creating an example where a child has done something of a negative nature but not an act where a spanking would be appropriate. Then, expounding on this negative act, usually a mistake or accident by the child, the NSA proclaims how unhealthy it is that this poor child has been spanked by his parents. In all of the examples that I have seen given by the NSA, I would have to agree with them that spanking a child under the given circumstances would be wrong. By convincing the parent that it is possible to wrongly spank a child, they have made the first step in their effort to convince the parent that *all* spanking is wrong. I call this method of deceit the "all inclusive abusive" method.

Two of the most popular nonspanking advocates today are William Sears, M.D., and Martha Sears, R.N. These two attack and attempt to discredit the Bible, using deceit to convince our society to eliminate corporal punishment in child rearing. It is obvious that they are intelligent people, which makes me think that their efforts in this area are not accidental. An excellent example of the "all inclusive abusive" method is used by the Sears in the March 1995 *Redbook* magazine. Titled "You and your child," the article includes 8 Reasons Spanking Doesn't Work . . . And 5 Hands-Off Techniques That Do. Reason number two of the eight states,

> For a child to act right, he has to feel right. If he breaks a glass and you spank him, he feels, I must be bad. He also concludes that the glass he broke is more valuable than he is. Even a guilt-relieving hug following a spanking doesn't remove the sting: The child feels hit, inside and out, long after.[1]

Imagine, a small child sitting at the dinner table reaches for the potatoes and knocks his glass to the floor, breaking it. He looks at dad with pain on his face and says, "Oops, I'm sorry." The parent tears him from his chair and whips him with a belt. Or imagine the ten-year-old daughter helping mom wash the dishes. She drops a slippery glass, resulting in the drinking utensil breaking into pieces on the floor. Mom races for the razor strap as the girl cringes in self-defense, knowing she is going to be beaten without mercy for her mistake.

This is the image that the NSA is trying to portray. To the parent who is trying to decide whether to follow the traditional methods of discipline that were so effective for their parents or to listen to the present-day rhetoric of the nonspanking crowd, this deceitful way of presenting examples of how spanking is wrong works. The offense surrounding the reason for the spanking is not one that warrants that form of discipline. Spanking the child was wrong. Therefore, spanking children is wrong. Deceitful, but effective.

Kathryn Kvols is another NSA who uses this method of deceit. Kvols is the president of the International Network for Children and Families and the author of *Redirecting Children's Behavior*. Kvols also maintains a web page on the internet. Her web page is titled "9 Things to Do Instead of Spanking." I would encourage readers to investigate this web site. Some of the most ridiculous advice can be found here. To think that anyone with any common sense would believe this rubbish is beyond me.

Kathryn Kvols utilizes the "all inclusive abusive" method in her article with the same title as her web site. She states,

> Consequences that are logically related to the behavior help teach children responsibility. For example, your child breaks a neighbor's window and you punish him by spanking him. What does he learn about the situation? He may learn to never do that again, but he also learns that he needs to hide his mistakes, blame it on someone else, lie, or simply not get caught. He may decide that he is bad or feel anger and revenge toward the parent who spanked him. When you spank a child, he may behave because he is afraid to get hit again. However, do you want your child to behave because he is afraid of you or because he respects you?[2]

Here Kathryn Kvols is using the "all inclusive abusive" method to convince her readers that this child was wrongly spanked. Without knowing the circumstances surrounding the breaking of the window, I would have to agree with her. So am I agreeing that spanking children is wrong? No. I am agreeing that the circumstances that this child was involved in probably did not warrant a spanking. However, we do not know all of the facts. Had the parent repeatedly instructed the child not to throw the ball in the backyard? Had he broken other windows in the past and been warned of a more severe consequence if he defied his parent's instruction and kept throwing the ball near the neighbor's house? I'm not sure.

But let's assume that junior simply was playing baseball in the backyard and one of his fastballs got away from him. Crash, the neighbor's window shatters. Kvols suggests in her example that the parents spank the child. The reader instinctively knows that something about this situation is wrong. Kvols has successfully convinced the reader that this spanking is wrong. Therefore, all spanking is wrong. But Kvols doesn't stop there. She goes on to give an example of the proper form of discipline under these conditions. The type of discipline that I would have imposed on my own children. She states,

> Compare that situation to a child who breaks a neighbor's window and his parent says, "I see you've broken the window, what will you do to repair it?" using a kind but firm tone of voice. The child decides to mow the neighbor's lawn and wash his car several times to repay the cost of breaking the window. What does the child learn in this situation? That mistakes are an inevitable part of life and it isn't so important that he made the mistake but that he takes responsibility to repair the mistake. The focus is taken off the mistake and put on taking responsibility for repairing it. The child feels no anger or revenge toward his parent. And most importantly the child's self-esteem is not damaged.[3]

Here, Kvols convinces the reader that the proper thing to do under these circumstances is *not* to spank. The reader has to agree. Therefore, *not spanking* is right. Mistakes in life are inevitable. Children tend to make many mistakes. Spanking a child because they made a legitimate mistake is wrong. But because a spanking under these conditions is wrong, does not mean that spanking under other conditions is wrong. Kvols last comment is also an indication of her inability to understand human nature. She asks, "Do you want your child to behave because he is afraid of you or because he respects you?" Kvols does not understand that without fear, children will do as they please. The reason I do not exceed the speed limit is because I fear the consequences that can be imposed on me by the police officer and the judge.

A child will not respect his parents without fearing them. A child with "no fear" is a child headed for disaster.

Penelope Leach is a psychologist who proclaims, "I am a part of that nonspanking group." She claims that spanking makes it much more difficult to teach children how to behave. In an article titled "Spanking: a shortcut to nowhere . . ." Leach uses the "all inclusive abusive" method in her advice to parents. She states, "A couple with a tired four year old are shopping. She whines, clings to her mother's coat and gets in her father's way. The third time he trips over her she bursts into tears and her mother's patience snaps. She grabs the child's arm and slaps her legs."[4] Notice that the small girl is very tired, she is stepped on by the father, and she cries. The mother "snaps" and strikes the child. Leach has very effectively demonstrated how wrong this spanking is. Leach is trying desperately to convince the reader that all spanking is wrong.

There are countless examples of this "all inclusive abusive" method used by numerous members of the nonspanking group. To list them all would completely fill another book. I would encourage those who read this advice to remember that spanking is not appropriate under all circumstances. There are situations when a grounding or a loss of privileges is a more appropriate form of discipline. But there are times when a spanking is the most effective form of discipline to deter future negative behavior. When a child flagrantly defies his parent's authority or commits a criminal act, corporal punishment instills the fear that is needed to prevent another offense.

Another unfair and deceitful method used by the NSA to prevent parents from using corporal punishment is to scare them into believing that serious harm will come to those children who are spanked. Some of the claims are ridiculous, and one wonders how they could be believed. Some claims are more believable, and to the average person who is ignorant of the actual facts, they are swallowed hook line and sinker.

One of the most ridiculous claims I have encountered is one made by Dr. Dennis Embry of the University of Kansas in a letter to *Children Magazine*. In this article, Dr. Embry writes,

> Since 1977 I have been heading up the only long-term project designed to counteract pedestrian accidents to preschool-aged children. Actual observation of parents and children shows that spanking, scolding, reprimanding and nagging INCREASES the rate of street entries by children. Children use going into the street as a near-perfect way to gain parents' attention.[5]

Did you catch that? This doctor is stating that if you spank your child, he is more likely to run out into traffic to play amongst the tractor trailers. Does anyone really believe this?

Let's consider what Jan Hunt, M.Sc. writes in her antispanking web page "The Natural Child Project." Some of her medical advice contains the following information. She states,

> Even relatively moderate spanking can be physically dangerous. Blows to the lower end of the spinal column send shock waves along the length of the spine, and may injure the child. The prevalence of lower back pain among adults in our society may well have its origins in childhood punishment.[6]

Wow! Is this a revelation, or what? Lower back pain in this country is caused by spanking. I searched and searched for some type of documented evidence to back up Hunt's claim but have been unable to uncover any medical proof that spanking is the cause of lower back pain in the United States. And then I started thinking. I gave very few spankings to my children when they were growing up, but I recall them constantly falling backward on their rear ends as little toddlers. Boom, they would hit the carpet with a jolt. They would then roll over and struggle to their feet, only to fall backward on their derriere again. To demonstrate how deceitful Hunt's claim is, if a child who experiences shock waves to their spine ends up with back problems, almost everyone living would be invalids.

Hunt also claims that spanking as a form of discipline causes sexual perversions. She states,

> Spanking on the buttocks, an erogenous zone in childhood, can create in the child's mind an association between pain and sexual pleasure, and lead to difficulties in adulthood. "Spanking wanted" ads in alternative newspapers attest to the sad consequences of this confusion of pain and pleasure.

Again, without any medical research that shows such a correlation, Hunt is making claims that may frighten parents into a no-spanking mode, fearful that they will harm their child if they strike his/her bottom.

The most blatant method used by the NSA to deceive the public is the use of lies to support their claims. This type of information is easy to dispel by simply researching the allegation. When I began to correspond through e-mail with RCox of the antispanking web page, Cox began sending me information that I knew to be false. In one of his messages, Cox included the statistic about the homicide rate having decreased 2 1/2 fold in states where corporal punishment was abolished in their schools.

I have researched the subject of corporal punishment enough to know that this information was totally inaccurate. Just to be sure, I again checked the states that had outlawed corporal punishment in the public schools. In addition, I listed the states where corporal punishment in the schools was still legal but was not utilized. I found that there was no basis at all for Cox's claim. In fact, any correlation between corporal punishment in the public schools and a decrease in the murder or vandalism rate was nonexistent. What Cox had presented to me was false propaganda used by the NSA to convince the public that the elimination of spanking has a positive effect on children. In addition, as mentioned previously, Cox's claim here refers only to the elimination of spanking at school.

Cox could not substantiate his claim with cold, hard facts. Instead, he encourages people to read books written by "researchers," such as Irwin Hyman. The NSA refuses to acknowledge any statistics that imply that corporal punishment *deters* criminal behavior in children. Because statistics overwhelmingly support the claim that kids who aren't spanked turn out to be in trouble with the law, the NSA simply fabricates their own statistics to meet their needs. It is pure and simple deceit.

Examples of false claims by the NSA abound. It seems that everyone involved in the movement against corporal punishment is jumping on the false information bandwagon. In a recent publication by the National PTA titled *Discipline: A Parent's Guide*, it states, "Studies have shown that physical punishment, such as hitting and slapping and verbal abuse, are not effective. While such punishment may seem to get fast results, in the long term it is more harmful than helpful."[7] Notice that the PTA has grouped together "verbal abuse" with hitting and slapping. They have included an abusive act with spanking (hitting), resulting in the entire package being questionable. The PTA has then made the assumption that hitting (spanking) is *not* effective and is more harmful than helpful. Do we dispute the PTA? Many parents would not question this information, although the PTA is neither a medical organization nor a research group. The PTA is simply repeating something they have been told by an "expert" on child rearing. Something that cannot be proven.

In the publication *Violence Against Children*, Murray Straus and Anita Mathur claim to have documented "Social Change and Trends in Approval of Corporal Punishment by Parents from 1968 to 1994." The study was conducted at Straus's Family Research Laboratory at the University of New Hampshire. Straus writes, "Kohn (1969) suggests that parents who hope or expect their child to attend college and be employed in nonmanual work occupations tend to avoid using corporal punishment."[8] Straus makes the statement, "Less educated and older people are now more approving of corporal punishment than better educated or younger persons." I myself know this to be false. The attitude towards corporal punishment is consistent across all lines of race, religion, and income. To state that only "educated" people understand that spanking is harmful, or that children that are not spanked turn out to be "better educated" than other children is the ultimate scare tactic. The Scripture that comes to mind is located in Romans 1:22, "Professing themselves to be wise, they became fools." As man becomes more "educated" and reliant on his own wisdom rather than the wisdom of God, even his common sense becomes clouded. Thus, the "better educated" person in today's culture does not approve of corporal punishment. Thinking that they are wise, they have actually become fools.

Because of the movement's lack of organization, facts and figures given by the NSA are often conflicting. The www. religious tolerance.org web page states, "A survey of U.S. parents shows a drop in the use of spanking as the main disciplinary method from 59 percent in 1962 to 19 percent in 1993. Parents now prefer using time-outs (38 percent) and lecturing (24 percent)." Compare this figure with a study conducted recently by Murray Straus, combining NSA rhetoric with conflicting statistics. It reads,

> Despite studies by Straus and others that corporal punishment can have long-term adverse effects on children (its use has been linked to an increased risk of delinquency as a child, and, as an adult, spousal abuse, crime, marital conflict and other societal ills) the vast majority of parents continue to spank their children. In fact, four national surveys by Straus and others show more than 90 percent of parents say they had used corporal punishment.[9]

The reason for this conflicting information is simple. On the one hand, some in the NSA feel it is important to convince parents that they are on the minority end of the spectrum if they spank their child. It is important to convince the spanking parent that they are part of a dying breed. Our modern society looks upon spanking as ancient and barbaric. Therefore, statistics are used that prove there is less corporal punishment in our society. On the other hand, Murray Straus is intelligent enough and possesses enough foresight to realize that this approach can be used against the NSA. If we are spanking our children less since 1962 as the first study indicates, then why are we not improving as a society? I have no problem proving that the crime rate in this county since 1962 has shown a steady increase. Child abuse is increasing. Spousal abuse is increasing. Juvenile crime is skyrocketing. The NSA then has a problem with "correlating." Straus realizes this. Others in the NSA seem to have forgotten this important fact.

11
THE FUTURE

"This know also, that in the last days, perilous times shall come. For men shall be lovers of their own selves, covetous, boasters, proud, blasphemers, disobedient to parents . . ."
(2 Timothy 3:2).

Since as early as I can remember, growing up in a Christian home, I was fascinated with the subject of biblical prophesy. I recall as a young child sitting in gospel meetings listening to the preacher warn sinners and Christians alike of the impending rise of the Antichrist and the formation of the ten nation union that would be under his control. I shuddered when I was reminded of the rapture and listened with interest to the signs that would signal the return of Christ to this earth in power and glory. Signs— predictors of things to come. Before I was saved, I dreaded the very thought of living long enough to see those things come to pass. Since my salvation, it has been exciting to observe the stage being set for the future fulfillment of those predictions spoken of by the Bible prophets.

The attitude of the civilization on earth during the last days is an important part of those predictors. In addition to the alignment of the nations and the rise of certain world rulers, there is an attitudinal transformation that years ago would not have been imagined. There will be an attitude of "no fear."

As I studied Bible prophesy, I learned that much of the information provided by the prophets could not be understood until current events shed light on the meaning of the prophesy. In Daniel 12:9 we read, "Go your way Daniel; for the words are shut up and sealed till the time of the end." The "words" refer to prophetic statements made to Daniel by God. The "time of the end" refers to the last days of man's history on this earth. I believe that the key that unlocks the prophetic statement is the current event that begins to fit into the predicted pattern. Many years ago, few people could understand how a large portion of the earth's population would bow to the Antichrist and allow a mark to be placed on their hand or forehead in order for them to purchase or sell any product or merchandise.

Revelation 13:16–17 states, "And he [the Antichrist] causeth all, both small and great, rich and poor, free and bond, to receive a mark in their right hand, or in their foreheads: And that no man might buy or sell, save that he had the mark, or the name of the beast, or the number of his name." We all know the familiar 666, the number of the beast. We just didn't understand years ago how the human race would be forced to receive a mark on their hand or forehead. We didn't understand, until bar codes became popular. With all of us using our debit cards at the grocery checkout, it's easy to understand how the public would concede

Soon there will be an entire generation of kids with no fear of authority.

to a computer chip being implanted under the skin that would contain all of the bank account information needed to purchase groceries. The public will not have to be forced to receive the mark of the beast, they will gladly accept the credit/debit system to safeguard their assets, never really understanding that they are fulfilling the words of the ancient prophets.

There are prophesies that refer to children and the mind-set of the younger generation in the last days. Second Timothy 3:1 states, "This know also, that in the last days perilous times shall come. For men shall be lovers of their own selves, covetous, proud, blasphemers, disobedient to parents . . ." Along with all of the other changes in attitude is the predicted change in the attitude of children toward their parents.

I believe that the antispanking movement has, and will continue to have, a hand in the fulfillment of biblical prophesy. Unbeknownst to the nonspanking advocates, they are helping to cause children to be "disobedient to parents," something that was predicted in 2 Timothy in the year A.D. 66.

I once argued with my father about a prophesy in the Book of Revelation. In chapter 19 and verse 19, we read about the Antichrist gathering the armies of the word together to do battle with Christ and his returning saints. The verse reads, "And I saw the beast and the kings of the earth, and their armies, gathered together to make war against Him that sat on the horse, and against His army." Here we see the Antichrist (the beast) and the world leaders (the kings of the earth) and the military (and their armies) gathering together to fight against Christ (Him that sat on the horse) upon his return. There was one problem with this picture. I did not believe that anyone would want to try to fight God. I was convinced that the masses on earth were gathering to fight an unidentified object, something that they would interpret as a threat, perhaps a UFO. My father insisted that the earth's population will knowingly try to defeat God.

As usual, I now think dad is right. I reached this conclusion when I noticed the defiant "in-your-face" attitude of many of today's special interest groups. The gay community doesn't care if the majority of people disdain their lifestyle. The militant feminist isn't worried about public opinion. Neither group is concerned that its agenda is in direct conflict with God's plan. The defiant attitude of these groups is obvious. The same goes for our younger generation. More and more, we are encountering kids with no fear of authority. Soon, we will have an entire generation of children who have never been spanked—out of control and defying authority as they grow into adulthood. An entire generation of people with no fear. Not afraid of their parents, not afraid of the police, not afraid of God.

Another factor I had failed to take into consideration is the lack of moral training in much of that generation. Not knowing the true Gospel, most children will grow up with little or no moral fiber. Although there will be a so-called worldwide "religion" in the last days, it will be a false hope, generated by the beast and his sidekick, the false prophet. After the rapture of the Church, the Holy Spirit's influence through the Church will be removed, making way for this religion to flourish. Once removed, that influence will cease to stem the tide of evil that will permeate the world. That generation will look at the true God in a whole different light. A hundred years ago, we would never have thought this possible, yet I am seeing the results of that moral vacuum in the kids I deal with on a daily basis. In the fall of 1998, our department made an arrest of a male who belonged to a group of "taggers," those who spray paint graffiti on the sides of buildings and vehicles. One of his last works of art was an upside down cross. Below the cross, he detailed unspeakable acts committed against Christ. Even the most hardened officers on the department were stunned at the lack of fear in the juvenile suspect. Our officers stated that they would "never think" of committing such an act. Yet today's youth think nothing of God's power and authority. Many of today's youth have no fear of God.

It will be easy for that generation to gather together under the direction of the Antichrist in an attempt to defeat the coming Christ. Without God in their upbringing and without the fear of authority that is instilled in a child with the use of corporal discipline, millions of people will gather in that last day in the valley of Megiddo in the final battle of Armageddon. They will realize that their "freedom of choice" is about to come to an end unless they can defeat the very God who created them. There will be a conscious effort to win the battle over Christ. On that day, they will learn a lesson that their parents never taught them. They will learn that there is an authority to which they must answer—One who is about to defeat them. An authority about to sentence them to death—an eternal death in hell and the lake of fire. Forever.

How do we, as Christians, prevent our children from adopting the attitude of the "no fear" generation? It's simple. We follow God's instructions in the rearing of our children. We trust God to know what is best. We rely on His infinite wisdom and what He tells us in His word. Do we subscribe to a group of so-called experts who contradict God's word? Of course not. Do we follow the advice of those who scoff at the Bible? Absolutely not. Do we allow ourselves to be brainwashed into believing that these men are wiser than God? Emphatically not.

The NSA is mounting an attack against parental authority. I believe Satan is using this group to accomplish his objective to eliminate the fear of authority from the coming generations. Never before in the history of the human race has this subject been such a volatile issue. There has never been a period in man's history when such effort has been made to prevent parents from spanking their children. Since man was created, there has never been such an effort by the medical profession, the mental health field, and the government, to interfere with parents' rights to rear their children in the manner prescribed by God.

We discussed the prophecy in Revelation 13:16–17 referring to the Antichrist. Many previously believed that the use of force would be necessary to convince people to receive this mark of the beast. One major factor makes me believe that force will not be necessary to "cause" the population to receive the mark. At the time this proposal is made, it will be the answer to a complex problem. By accepting the mark of the beast, it will improve a situation that needs improving.

I am sure that most readers have noticed lately that more and more bar code laser systems are being installed in stores nationwide. In my neighborhood during the last year, I have seen the installation of bar code laser systems in a hardware store, a drug store, and small family owned shops. It's just not the large retail companies that are equipped with the computer connected credit/debit system. Just last fall, my police department announced that now it would be possible to have our paychecks deposited into the savings facility of our choice through direct deposit. Soon, there will be no need to carry cash at all. From gas stations to department stores, the cost of our purchases will be deducted from the account in which our wages are deposited.

In the same manner that this system will be accepted as the answer to a problematic monetary system, the acceptance of a child rearing method void of corporal punishment will be widespread. There will be no need to legislate laws against spanking. Although the elimination of corporal punishment will at first seem to cause behavioral problems with the child, there will be solutions given by "experts" that will appear to solve the defiance problem encountered by the parent. Naturally, the media will have a hand in this brainwashing scheme. How do I know this? Because it has already begun.

In October of 1998, the NBC Network broadcast a story on its *Dateline NBC* program that made it perfectly clear to me how this will be accomplished. I wish the reader could view the videotape of that show because I do not believe I can convey the concept of the theory addressed on this program effectively with the written word. But I will try.

The program begins with interviewer Jane Pauley introducing the Cormier family, normal in almost every way, with the exception of their six-year-old son Christian. The young boy is described by his parents, Cindy and Kevin, as having two separate personalities. Unlike the schizophrenic who is totally unpredictable when it comes to mood changes, the cause of Christian's personality changes were very apparent. He was a "good kid" until he was told what to do. At that point, he slips into what his mother describes as his "zone." Mom explains to the interviewer while looking at the camera, "If he doesn't get what he wants, he gets locked into his zone until he gets what he wants. And there is no give." Mom goes on to say that this is a process the family goes through every time Christian doesn't get his way. In order to demonstrate Christian in his "zone," NBC was allowed to install hidden cameras in the Cormier household that captured Christian's antics, from the temper tantrums, to the physical assault of his parents, to the spitting in the face of his mother. In glorious color and stereo sound, we are treated to the brattish actions of a very spoiled child. From refusing to eat what is set in front of him, to refusing to go to bed when told, Christian was running his parents ragged.

Naturally, the "experts" have concluded that Christian's behavior is not his fault. According to an early diagnosis by the medical community, he is suffering from Attention Deficit Disorder, or ADD, a malady which is somehow connected to misbehavior. The name of this "disorder" appears to label it as one of forgetfulness or a tendency to daydream. A deficit in the area of attention would convey one's inability to keeps one's mind on a particular subject for any length of time. I admit there were times when I was forgetful as a kid, but that didn't result in me kicking my dad in the shins when I didn't get my way. I don't believe Attention Deficit Disorder can completely rationalize this portion of the problem. The psychiatric community would argue with this conclusion, since they contend that one of the manifestations of ADD is aggression and anger.

No matter what diagnosis the family had received, there was one major problem. The Cormiers were becoming walking zombies. Christian was refusing to go to sleep at night and would physically fight with his parents when they attempted to force him into bed. He would kick them and punch them and spit in their faces, but he would not go to bed. At one point during this twenty-minute broadcast, the camera showed Christian's father attempting to restrain the small boy in what they called "the wrap," a form of physical restraint accomplished by the father wrapping his arms and legs around Christian in order to prevent him from destroying any of the property nearby. The narrator explains that this is the method of discipline used when Christian's parents are "desperate." While the viewers are treated to Christian swearing at his father, the NBC reporter narrating the story states, "Kevin says at times, he's gotten so upset, so pushed to his limit, that he's thought of striking back in anger, but he never has." It is apparent that spanking is not on the Cormier's list of options. When the reporter asks the parents if they feel like Christian is in the driver's seat, the parents reply, "Yes, and we are under the tires."

So the Cormiers try one more doctor. Enter Dr. Ross Green, a child psychologist who has the answer to the problems the Cormiers are encountering with Christian. While watching this program, my wife decided that it was time for her to leave the room. She stated, "I know what's coming, and I don't want to be here when you see it!" She was right. What I saw next convinced me that the inmates are running the asylum and the whole world has "done gone crazy." On the more serious side, I realized how dangerous this propaganda was as it was being broadcast to millions of viewers.

The reporter referred to Dr. Green as an "expert in explosive children." What this "expert" advocated was the opposite of what God's word teaches. This expert's diagnosis was that Christian had "Oppositional Defiance Disorder," a psychological problem that resulted in the child refusing to do what he was told. What the child psychologist suggested was a temporary solution to the head-to-head confrontations that the Cormiers were experiencing with Christian, but in the long run it would help shape the personality of a human being with no fear of authority. You see, the doctor's solution to the problem was to let Christian do whatever he wanted to do whenever he wanted to do it.

As I watched the remaining portion of the program, I realized that my wife was much wiser than I had given her credit for. I'm sure she heard me yelling, "Do you believe this?" from the other room as I watched in disbelief. The good doctor, obviously not one who has reared any children through the teenage years, stated, "Battles over food are not battles that I think are worth having." He went on to say that Christian should be allowed to eat whatever he wants whenever he wants. The reporter, apparently doubting that the good doctor really meant what he was saying, asked if he didn't feel that good nutrition was important, and that one of the parental responsibilities was to ensure that the child ate a balanced diet. The doctor replied, "Ice cream has nutrients. Pizza has nutrients. So I don't think we're sacrificing too much to have him eat foods that he likes." The solution to the feeding confrontation was to allow Christian to pick what he wanted to eat at whatever time was convenient for him to chow down, and to provide him with his wish. Problem solved. Christian no longer has any temper tantrums about having to eat nutritional foods.

What about the sleep confrontations? Simple. Christian is never told to go to bed. The doc explains, "It certainly doesn't look like making him stay in his bed is calming to him." The doctor explains that since Christian likes to watch television, he should be allowed to watch television instead of going to bed. The camera then zooms in on mom, who expresses her concerns about the evils of television and Christian not receiving enough sleep. She asks the doc, "Shouldn't there be some limit on the amount of television that Christian watches?" The doctor, in his "wisdom" states, "You can go on pretending there's a set bedtime forever, OK? There is no set bedtime." Another major problem solved. Christian no longer has any temper tantrums about having to go to bed.

The third part of this broadcast put the icing on the cake. The narrator explains how they returned to the Cormier household three months later. As the camera shows a much happier Christian smiling and playing with mom and dad, the reporter states, "You can clearly see the results." The parents are interviewed again and dad states, "There's really not too many times we say no." Mom describes Christian getting his own way as a newfound "partnership." The cameras then capture the dinner table, with the rest of the family enjoying salads, vegetables, and meat, while Christian scarfs down a pizza. The narrator explains how Christian is allowed to do what he wishes whenever he wishes. The reporter states, "It is the hardest thing for his parents to let go of, but they say, well worth it."

The living room camera then captures bedtime. Christian, who is in full command of the television remote control, is perched on the couch watching his favorite program while mom and dad sit peacefully nearby. The time-lapse camera catches Christian falling asleep in the living room, and after reaching a deep slumber, is carried off to bed by a tired dad who has waited patiently for the right moment to avoid any confrontation. The Cormier household has turned into a nonconfrontational antiviolent conflict resolution family by never demanding anything of a six-year-old child. The report concludes by portraying the parents as a happy couple—happy that the conflict with their young son is now nonexistent.

Perhaps we should visit the Cormiers in ten years with the NBC hidden cameras. I would like to be there when the father tells Christian, "No, no, please, you can't take the car. You don't have your driver's license yet and you are not covered under our insurance policy!" Or how about, "Son, please, I've asked you a hundred times not to bring your criminal friends home with you when we are not here. More of your mother's jewelry is missing!" Or how about this scene in ten years. The telephone rings. The hidden camera catches dad saying, "I'm sorry, son, but I have no money left to bail you out of jail again. I keep telling you that the policeman expects you to do what he says. I don't know why you don't understand that!"

I know what will happen in eight or ten years to the little boy who was never told no. But millions of young parents who watched this program who are presently experiencing problems with a defiant child may apply this type of solution to their problem. They have already been told by the "experts" that spanking a child will cause behavioral problems. Now they are experiencing defiance in their four, five or six year old. Here's the solution. A whole generation of new parents watching a worldwide broadcast that solves their problem. Is it hard to imagine how easy it will be in the future for the "experts" to convince parents to not only eliminate corporal punishment from their child rearing, but also all parental authority? Parents will relinquish control of their children willingly. They won't have to be forced by some anti-spanking law. Parents will help fulfill the prophesy that children will become "disobedient to parents."

Today's "experts" continue to assault the time-tested methods of discipline that have been used by parents for thousands of years. We are being told that we should use "positive discipline" instead of spanking. We are told that "self-esteem" is worth more than a conscience. If parents are not careful, this humanistic approach will be introduced to their own children and they will be taught that spanking is wrong, and as long as you feel good, your actions don't matter. In early 1999, I received a list of classes being offered by the high school in the city in which I reside. My stepson was going to move into the ninth grade, and my wife and I were planning his schedule for the following year. While looking through the list of classes offered, I noticed near the back of the book, a class being offered to students in grade nine through twelve titled "Parenting Matters." The class description includes how the student (and very possibly the soon to be parent) can build a relationship with his/her child by using "positive guidance and discipline," and how to use parenting techniques that "promote self-esteem." Our fourteen-year-old children are being taught in the public schools the very ideals that have created a society of children with "no fear."

While discussing this future "no fear" attitude with my father, he reminded me of another very important point. Even Old Testament prophecies predict the "no fear" attitude in the last days. There are at least sixteen messianic psalms in the Bible. A messianic psalm is a psalm that refers to Christ and is quoted in the New Testament. The first of these psalms is Psalm 2, which deals with the official glory of the eternal Son of God. This psalm describes the "no fear" attitude of the generation alive during the last days.

Prior to the return of the Lord in power to this "no fear" earth, we have an amazing and accurate description of the "no fear" and antagonistic attitude of the nations against God. Psalm 2:1–3 states, "Why do the heathen rage, and the people imagine a vain thing? The kings of the earth set themselves, and the rulers take counsel together, against the Lord, and against his anointed, saying, Let us break their bands asunder, and cast away their cords from us." Verse one tells us that the nations (the heathen) will throng together (rage) and meditate (imagine) a vain (empty) thing. Verse two discloses that the kings of the earth will deliberately assume a hostile attitude ("set" present tense) against God (the Lord) and Christ (His Anointed), due to the fact that the rulers have already taken counsel together against God, the conspiracy and confederacy thus preceding the mustering of their hosts.

Because of their "no fear" character, they will declare, "Let us break their [God and Christ] bands asunder and cast away their cords from us" (verse 3). God has bands which fasten the yoke to the neck, and cords, or reins, which guide and keep society under control. In other words, the psalmist is telling us that the day will come when mankind will act upon the lie of the serpent (Genesis 3:5) and seek to actually dethrone God and do away with His authority in their society.

The shadows of this horrible "no fear" attitude are upon us today. However, if you think that things are bad now, just wait. Again we refer to what the apostle Paul warned Timothy, "This know also, that in the last days perilous times shall come." Those days are here, but things will get progressively worse. A "no spank, no discipline" society produces children who are self-centered (lovers of their own selves); arrogant, with contempt for everyone else (proud); abusive in their language (blasphemers); disobedient to parents; without self-control (incontinent); brutal, savage (fierce); despisers of those who are good; and swell-headed (high-minded). What a list!

The Bible that exhorts parents to spank their disobedient children is the same Bible that warns us of the results of not obeying God's word in the last days. Many children not reared by God's word are now adults, and many of those adults are in government. It is easy to see how Psalm 2, which depicts governments against God, will be fulfilled to the very letter.

Fortunately today, the law still protects parents who wish to use corporal punishment in the training of their children. Most parents just don't realize it. As Christians move forward in these last days, it is important for them to know not only what God says about child discipline, but what the law of the land says about spanking. With the Bible in one hand and a copy of the Criminal Code in the other, parents can reasonably argue with those who wish to strip them of their parental authority.

12

THE NONSPANKING ADVOCATE

"Professing themselves to be wise, they became fools"
(Proverbs 1:22).

In an August 25, 1997, *Time* magazine article "Spare the Rod? Maybe," Dr. Murray Straus received some criticism from other professionals who don't believe that spanking is as harmful as the NSA is making it out to be. Straus has defined corporal punishment as, "An act by a parent or other caretaker which is intended to cause physical pain, but not injury, for purposes of correction or control."[1] Although Straus believes this action to be damaging to kids, others do not. Dr. Den Trumbull, a Montgomery, Alabama, pediatrician is one of those who do not agree with Straus. But I believe even Dr. Trumbull fails to understand the motivation behind the antispanking movement.

According to the *Time* article, "It is the legitimate fear of child abuse that Trumbull believes is largely behind the antispanking movement."[2] I strongly disagree. I do not believe that the antispanking movement's agenda is based on the fear that spanking is abusive to children. I believe that there is enough overwhelming evidence to prove otherwise. Much of the "evidence" given by the NSA to prove their theory has been fabricated. Some of the statistics given by the NSA have been altered in order to support their theory. As previously mentioned, these statistics need only be confirmed by checking the F.B.I.'s Uniform Crime Reports; the differences between the actual figures and those given by the NSA are so blatantly obvious. I believe that the NSA is attempting to convince the public that spanking is harmful when the evidence proves otherwise.

While waiting to go on the air at the NBC studios in Cleveland, Ohio, to debate Murray Straus on the subject of spanking, I was introduced to Dr. Sylvia B. Rimm, a child psychologist who is the director of the Family Achievement Clinic at the MetroHealth Medical Center in Cleveland and a professor at Case Western Reserve University School of Medicine. I had the opportunity to speak with Rimm before and after the live broadcast. As we walked to the elevator together after the program, I seized the opportunity to ask her a few questions about her research and her conclusions. Rimm also feels that spanking is counterproductive and causes harm to children. I asked Dr. Rimm, "If spanking causes harm to children and results in antisocial behavior later in a person's life, why did I turn out okay?" Dr. Rimm stated that she felt that there had been other positive influences in my life that overshadowed the negative effects of my spankings. In other words, my mom and dad were such great parents, even though they made the mistake of spanking me, I turned out alright. I asked Dr. Rimm if that held true for other adults that I knew that had been spanked as a child. She insisted that was the case. I asked her opinion of my sergeant who was in charge of the detective bureau, who was a kind, considerate, honest, compassionate man, whose family comes first and whose children are the apples of his eye. He was spanked as a child. Why did he turn out to be such an exemplary person? Her reply was the same. It was obvious that his parents did such a great job in other areas of child rearing, that it balanced out the negative effects of the spankings they inflicted upon him. She simply would not admit that good parenting includes spanking when necessary.

In the January 24, 1998, issue of the *Cleveland Plain Dealer*, an article appeared written by Dr. Sylvia B. Rimm. The article was called "Spanking no solution to discipline problem," and was no doubt prompted by a letter written to the doctor by a concerned parent. The letter is a perfect example of how parents have been brainwashed by what they have heard and will believe the theory of some "professional" rather than learning from their own experiences. The letter read as follows:

> I am the proud father of three girls, ages seven, five, and three, and one boy, age two. We do not know what to do about discipline around the house. The main problem is our kids do not seem to realize that "no" means "no" until they are spanked. We try our hardest to divide our attention equally among each of

our children, and we treat them as individuals, but I do not want to have to spank my kids to get them to behave. It's just that we have tried following all of the books, and we have tried numerous methods of discipline, yet none of them work. My kids usually only quit offensive behavior after they are put over my knee and spanked. After that they seem to understand. We always reassure them that they are loved before and after spanking, and they seem to understand. It's just that we don't want it to have to be spanking after spanking. What are we doing wrong? Can you help?[3]

Here we have a parent who has read "all of the books" and tried "numerous methods" of discipline other than spanking, and "none of them work." The father's major concern is that he is causing damage to his children by spanking them more than once or twice. What caused dad to come to this conclusion? Is it the books written by the "experts" that he has read? Dad admits that he has discovered an effective discipline tool that changes his child's behavior in a very positive way. When he spanks his children, they "understand."

Dr. Rimm's answer is unbelievable. "If you tell your children how much you love them every time you spank them, they will learn that love and violence go together, which is likely to cause your daughters to be attracted to abusive men, and your son to abuse the woman he loves."[4] The doctor also states in her answer that if these parents spank their children, that "Eventually, during their teens, they will turn on you with violence of their own."[5] Dr. Rimm could not be further from the truth. For those of us who were spanked as children, the last thing we would ever think of doing would be to hit mom or dad. In fact, with the children that I deal with in my office, the exact opposite is true. The majority of teens who end up assaulting their parents have never been spanked. They are not afraid of their parents. There is no fear of consequences. In the overwhelming number of cases, kids who attack their parents have *never* been spanked. The correlation is blatantly obvious to those of us in law enforcement who deal with out-of-control children.

William Sears, M.D., and Martha Sears, R.N., have written several books on child rearing, including *The Baby Book*, *The Birth Book*, and *The Discipline Book*. My first encounter with the Sears' philosophy was through the article they wrote in the March 1995 *Redbook*, which I referred to previously. This article included the 8 Reasons Spanking Doesn't Work . . . And 5 Hands-Off Techniques That Do. The article states,

Even parents who don't believe in spanking may occasionally find themselves swatting the rear of a willful toddler or fresh preschooler. And when the child does put down your glasses or stop the back talk, it's easy to think that spanking is a useful disciplinary tool after all. It's not. Hundreds of studies show that in the long run, spanking harms, rather than helps behavior.[6]

I am a bit skeptical that there have been "hundreds" of studies that show spanking harms a child's behavior. It doesn't say one hundred, it says "hundreds," indicating that there have been at least two hundred official studies conducted that prove that spanking is harmful to children. The authors have made a claim that they cannot prove. The rest of the article is as hard to believe.

Reason number one of 8 Reasons Spanking Doesn't Work states, "Children from families that spank are more likely to use aggression to handle conflicts."[7] I will reiterate over and over again that the kids who are ending up in trouble for assaulting others, including their parents, have never been spanked. It is obvious that these two researchers have never stood in juvenile court and watched the parade of out-of-control children who are unbelievably aggressive, all of which have had no discipline in their lives at all. With the exception of those kids who have a genuine mental illness, every child I have ever dealt with who has physically assaulted his/her parents has never been spanked growing up. What these two "experts" have written is a statement that cannot be substantiated with facts or statistics.

Notice in this first paragraph how the author refers to the child being disciplined as a "willful" toddler or "fresh" preschooler. Yet further on in the article, in reason number two, the author states,

For a child to act right, he has to feel right. If he breaks a glass and you spank him, he feels, I must be bad. He also concludes that the glass he broke is more valuable than he is. Even a guilt-relieving hug following a spank doesn't remove the sting: The child feels hit, inside and out, long after.[8]

We have previously discussed this quote and can easily recognize the trick of the authors. By making the reason the child is being spanked absurd, the spanking itself seems absurd.

Reason number three states,

Deep down, parents who control their children through spanking don't feel right about it. Often, they've spanked in desperation—but afterward, when they see it doesn't work, they feel more powerless. Spanking also diminishes the role of the parent. Being an authority figure means you are trusted and respected, not that you're feared.[9]

The authors have included a subtle trick in this "reason" also. They are making a statement that parents who spank "don't feel right about it." This statement is made to make the reader conclude that such a result is factual. If there is any doubt in any parent's mind about whether spanking is proper, that doubt was planted by "researchers" like Mr. and Mrs. Sears, whose theories cannot even be proven to be accurate. The couple also claim that in order to be an authority figure, you cannot be feared. I would bet that neither of these two ever spent a minute in the military. The fear factor is what is missing today in our out-of-control youth. That factor must be restored to parents if any positive changes are to be made.

Reason number eight states that Hitting Has Bad Long-Term Effects. The article states,

The research is overwhelming. The more physical punishment children receive, the more aggressive they'll become as adults, the more likely they'll be harsh with their own children, and, for boys, the greater chance they'll be abusive husbands. Conversely, not one study shows the usefulness of spanking.[10]

Again, the authors are using flagrant untruths in order to promote their theory. The research is not overwhelming. There are studies that show spanking is useful. Dr. Sears and his wife are making a gallant effort to convince the public that the case against spanking is over-whelming. This type of proclamation is simply irresponsible. Yet "researchers" like the Sears keep getting away with it, unchallenged and unchecked.

But the most bizarre part of this instructional article are the Hands-Off Techniques That Do work. Naturally they have included the "time-out," not to be thought of a punishment, mind you, but rather, "the child should be taught to view it as a way of getting herself under control."[11] One of the problems with the modern approach to child rearing is the lack of punishment for negative behavior. Researchers like the Sears would like to make us believe that punishing a child causes low self-esteem. We need to quit emphasizing high self-esteem at the expense of respect for authority and respect for others.

The technique titled Disarming Your Child, And Yourself is a gem. Try to think of this technique when the child has gone berserk, has grabbed the kitchen knife, and has threatened to cut your throat. Warning everyone to stay away, the child begins destroying the china cabinet. This technique should work. The author writes, "Humor can defuse a willful child. It catches her off guard, sparking instant attention. You don't have to be a brilliant comic: Simply putting a toy on your head as your child starts to protest can change the mood."[12] For those of us in the law enforcement field who respond to domestics where the child is attacking the parent, we know what we have to do. It's the old rubber duck on the head routine.

The William and Martha Sears juvenile domestic violence response team.

The Sears' view on child rearing prompted me to search the bookstores for their latest effort, *The Discipline Book*. The book addressing the subject of discipline states on its cover, "Everything you need to know to have a better-behaved child—from birth to age ten."[13]

Much of the child-rearing advice by the Sears is common sense and applicable to today's children. Several of the discipline concepts are effective and have been used by loving parents for thousands of years. But the underlying theme in the Sears' method of discipline is the same as that of most of the NSA. Children are basically good, and the parent will make them bad if improper disciplinary measures are used.

The Sears are dead set against spanking. Their reasons are explained in this chapter along with some examples from their book. The Sears also go that extra step and make a valiant attempt to discredit the Bible as a source of information regarding corporal punishment. The Sears claim that Christians are "devoted parents who love God and love their children, but they misunderstand the concept of the rod."[14] We will show in this chapter that it is the Sears who "misunderstand" the concept of the rod. It is very doubtful that the Sears have studied God's word to the extent that they understand its true meaning. I believe these "experts" have swallowed the rhetoric of others in the NSA that have attempted to discredit the Bible. The Sears are not arguing their case with any genuine insight into Scripture. They are simply repeating information told to them by others totally ignorant of the meaning of God's instruction.

Chapter 1 is titled "Our approach to discipline." Amongst the information contained in this chapter are suggestions on how to Nurture Your Child's Self-Confidence, Talk And Listen, and Get Connected Early. Suggestion number three is titled Help your Child to Respect Authority. What the Sears advocate here is more of the rhetoric that is causing a generation of teenagers with "no fear." This suggestion claims, "The child who is told he must obey 'or else' may behave, but he does so out of fear, not respect. 'Honor thy father and mother' is the wise and time-honored teaching; not fear them."[15]

Millions of people who have successfully reared children of their own disagree with this theory. I would be unable to count the number of people who, when they were growing up, refrained from talking back to dad because they were *afraid* of him. My dad was a big man who, up to when I was twelve years old, made a living working in the steel mill. When I was a youngster, he expected me to do what I was told, when I was told to do it. I don't recall ever giving my dad any lip. I would guess that I received a few spankings that I don't remember. I also received some I remember clearly, but I do know that by the time I was entering puberty, I knew better than to "disrespect" my dad's authority. My mother, on the other hand, was a much more patient parent. Yet, when I defied her authority, she had no trouble grabbing the belt and whacking me a good one on my rear end. But through my entire childhood, I never felt that my parents didn't love me. In addition to the punishment when I misbehaved, I was showered with love and rewards when I acted properly.

The Sears suggest that children should obey their parents out of respect, not fear. They attempt to use God's word to substantiate their claim that children should not fear their parents. They quote a passage from the Bible which is repeated in several areas of the Old and New Testament. First mentioned in Exodus 20:12, it is one of the Ten

Commandments given to Moses on Mount Sinai. It states, "Honour thy father and thy mother: that thy days may be long upon the land which the Lord thy God giveth thee." According to the Sears, this verse implies that children should not "fear" their parents; they should "honor" them.

What is more interesting is that the Sears are using biblical instruction to convince their readers that God prefers that our children have no fear. This is one of the major problems the NSA encounters. They are aware that most people consider the Bible to be the inspired word of God. They will take portions of Scripture out of context and attempt to make it fit into their argument against spanking.

I am doubtful that the Sears have any idea that Jesus expounded on this commandment as he addressed the scribes and Pharisees in Matthew 15:4. Jesus said, "For God commanded, saying, Honour thy father and mother: and, He that curseth father or mother, let him die the death." Jesus went on to explain how the commandments of God were without effect due to the traditions of men. Jesus called those scribes and Pharisees "hypocrites." But the Sears would not dare add these words of Jesus, "He that curseth father or mother, let him die the death." They would contend that Jesus was being too brutal.

I would not mind hearing the foolishness spoken by the Sears if it were not for the fact that most of the secular world knows very little about the Bible and will fall for their interpretations. The Sears have attempted to use Scripture in their effort to convince parents not to spank their children. Chapter 12 of *The Discipline Book* is devoted entirely to the subject of spanking. It is titled "Spanking—No? Yes? Sometimes?" It doesn't take long reading this chapter to realize that the answer expected by the Sears is "No." It is in this chapter that the author attacks the credibility of the Bible.

Of the ten reasons the Sears list not to spank your children, number six grabbed my attention. It is titled Hitting Is Actually Not Biblical. The Sears begin this section with a command, "Don't use the Bible as an excuse to spank."[16] The following paragraphs explain the Sears' viewpoint on the use of the Bible as a reference tool for daily living. I have included most of the text from this section.

> There is confusion among some people of Judeo-Christian heritage who, seeking help from the Bible in their effort to raise good children, believe that God commands them to spank. They take "spare the rod and spoil the child" (which is not found in the Bible) seriously and fear that if they don't spank,

they will commit the sin of losing control of their child. In our counseling experience, we have found that these people are devoted parents who love God and love their children, but they misunderstand the concept of the rod.

Rod verses—what they really mean. The following are the biblical verses that have caused the greatest confusion:

Folly is bound up in the heart of a child, but the rod of discipline will drive it far from him. (Prov. 22:15)

He who spares the rod hates his son, but he who loves him is careful to discipline him. (Prov. 13:24)

Do not withhold discipline from the child; if you punish him with the rod, he will not die. Punish him with the rod and save his soul from death. (Prov. 23:13–14)

The rod of correction imparts wisdom, but a child left to himself disgraces his mother. (Prov. 29:15)

At first glance these verses may sound prospanking. But you might consider a different interpretation of these teachings. "Rod" (shebet) means different things in different parts of the Bible. Our Hebrew dictionary defines it as a stick, whether for punishment, writing, fighting, ruling, walking or other activities. While the rod can be used for hitting, it is also used to protect vulnerable sheep. Shepherds don't use the rod to beat their sheep—and children are certainly more valuable than sheep.

The book of Proverbs is one of poetry. It is logical that the writer would have used a well-known tool to form an image of authority. We believe that this is the point made about the rod in the Psalms: Parents, take charge of your children. When you reread the "rod verses," use the concept of parental authority, rather than the concept of beating or spanking, when you come to the word "rod." It rings true in every instance.[17]

Let's consider the claim by the Sears that the word rod does not mean "spanking," but instead means "nurturing" or "teaching." Let's consider that this concept "rings true in every instance." Even people with limited Bible knowledge can conclude that this theory is wrong, as long as the Sears give the readers all of the information they need to draw their own conclusion. But they don't. We are not supplied with all of the information we need because the verses are not quoted correctly. And I do not believe that the examples that they provide as "spanking verses" are misquoted by mistake. Take for example the last verse in the examples that they have given. The verse is quoted by the Sears as such, "The rod of correction imparts wisdom, but a child left to himself disgraces his mother (Prov. 29:15)." The suggestion by the Sears that we substitute a word like "teaching" where the word "rod" appears, might work in this case if the verse were correctly quoted. But it is not.

The original verse in the King James Version of the Holy Bible is as follows, "The rod and reproof give wisdom: but a child left to himself bringeth his mother to shame." Now, if we substitute the word "rod" with the word "teaching," the verse would sound something like this. "Teaching and teaching give wisdom . . ." In the Sears version of Proverbs 29:15, the part of the verse that refers to "reproof"—the portion of the verse that refers to teaching, a lecture, a lesson given— has been left out. If the word "rod" in this verse meant "teaching," there would be no reason for the word "reproof" used in the same context. As discussed previously, it is clear from the wording in this verse that the word "rod" means the physical discipline of the child. Simply put, it means a spanking. The word "reproof" holds the meaning that the Sears attempted to convey in their explanation, which is "teaching." Unfortunately, most people reading the Sears book, unfamiliar with the deliberate meaning contained in God's word, will believe what the Sears have proclaimed.

The Sears go on to say,

> While Christians and Jews believe that the Scripture is the inspired word of God, it is also a historical text that has been interpreted in many ways over the centuries, sometimes incorrectly in order to support the beliefs of the times. These 'rod' verses have been burdened with the interpretations about corporal punishment that support human ideas. Other parts of the Bible, especially the New Testament, suggest that respect, authority, and tenderness should be the prevailing attitudes toward children among people of faith.[18]

The Sears claim that the Bible "has been interpreted in many ways over the centuries, sometimes incorrectly in order to support the beliefs of the times." It would appear that the Sears, in an effort to criticize the Christian, have indicted themselves. Those who study the Bible know that it is one complete document consisting of sixty-six books, each book substantiating the other. The elements of the Bible are intimately and closely wound together with harmoniousness between each of the books and the Bible as a whole. There are clear lines of historical evidence supporting the accuracy of the Bible. The amazingly detailed typology of the book, woven like a magnificent mosaic in God's great redemption plan from Genesis to Revelation, argues strongly for the authenticity of the Bible. Using the Sears' method of interpretation, let us rephrase their statement in this manner, "The Sears have interpreted the Bible incorrectly in order to support the beliefs of the times." There, that fits. It certainly "rings true" in this instance. The Sears continue with their "misinterpretation" of Scripture.

> Christ preached gentleness, love, and understanding, and seemed to be against any harsh use of the rod, as stated by Paul in 1 Corinthians 4:21, "Shall I come to you with the rod, or in love and with a gentle spirit?" Paul went on to teach fathers about the importance of not provoking anger in their children (which is what spanking usually does). "Fathers, do not exasperate your children" (Eph. 6:4), and "Fathers, do not embitter your children, or they will be discouraged" (Col. 3:21). In our opinion, nowhere in the Bible does it say you must spank your child to be a godly parent.[19]

Here again, the Sears use Scripture to try to convince the reader that the Bible is condemning spanking, yet they have again contradicted themselves. They refer to this passage to make their point that Paul was advocating peace (a gentle spirit) rather than violence (the rod). They have interpreted the "rod" in this passage as an instrument of physical discipline. That's fine. That is what the word means. But it also means the same thing in all of the other verses that the Sears have listed in their book, including Proverbs 22:15, "Foolishness is bound in the heart of a child; but the rod of correction shall drive it far from him." It means the same thing in Proverbs 13:24, "He that spareth his rod hateth his son: but he that loveth him chasteneth him betimes," and Proverbs 23:13–14, "Withhold not correction from the child: for if thou beatest him with the rod, he shall not die. Thou shalt beat him with the rod, and shall deliver his soul from hell." It also means the same thing in Proverbs 29:15, "The rod and reproof give wisdom: but a child left to himself bringeth his mother to shame." A simple comparison of the Hebrew and Greek text would confirm this fact.

A section in *The Discipline Book* deals with punishment. One of the major objectives of the NSA is to eliminate punishment from our culture. This humanistic attitude is beginning to take root in every aspect of our culture, from child rearing (no spanking) to the criminal justice system (no death penalty) to the medical profession (no punishment for one with a psychological disorder). It is a movement based on the philosophy that man is not responsible for his own actions, therefore he should not be punished for his wrongdoing. The Sears section of their book titled The Problems With Punishment details this philosophy. I will give credit to the Sears where credit is due. The Sears do indicate that they believe punishment is part of a balanced discipline package. They state,

> Our goal is to create an obedient attitude within the child and a structured environment around the child so that punishment is less necessary. Yet when it is needed—and it will be—the attachment approach to discipline will help you use punishment wisely, so that it helps the child obey without becoming angry or fearful.[20]

There is one part of the Sears "punishment" plan that is made very clear. They state, "By now you should realize that our position on spanking is clear: don't." In chapter 13, the Sears state,

> The main ways to shape a child's behavior are through the use of praise, selective ignoring, and time-outs; through teaching an understanding of consequences; through the use of motivators, reminders, and negotiation; and through the withdrawal of privileges.[21]

The Sears attempt to convince their readers that punishing a child is harmful in the Problems With Punishment section.

> Punishment has had an up-and-down history. In "old-fashioned" discipline, punishment was in. In fact, discipline was punishment.

In "new-fashioned" discipline, punishment is out. It is politically incorrect to even mention the p-word in behavior books. You have only to read today's newspapers to conclude that both of these extremes are unhealthy.

The child who is punished too much (or too severely) behaves more out of fear of punishment or the punisher than for the satisfaction of behaving right. For the child, fear and anger become part of his personality. A distance develops between the punisher and the child, and the parent-child relationship becomes a power struggle. Sometimes the child whose behavior is punishment-controlled seems "so good." (He knows better than to get out of line. I'll ground him.) This child doesn't know better, he only knows that punishment will occur if he misbehaves. Underneath this facade of goodness simmers an angry child ready to explode into uncontrolled behavior once the threat of punishment is lifted. If punishment overtakes the whole atmosphere on the home, fear overcomes trust and the child is at risk of becoming angry, aggressive, withdrawn, and unhappy. He is also deprived of the opportunity to be a kid, make mistakes, and realize the natural consequences of his actions.[22]

When reading this portion of the book, I realized that the Sears were describing much of what I had been taught in law enforcement about the abused child. Their statement begins by saying, "The child who is punished too much." This is an example of what I have been attempting to point out about the information being disseminated by the NSA. The Sears are describing a child who is being truly abused, either with unwarranted physical punishment or unwarranted verbal insults. Yet they have tied the emotional responses of this child to a spanked child by stating that they believe spanking is an inappropriate form of discipline. Spanking is wrong; therefore, it is "too much" punishment.

The Christian should have no trouble seeing that the information and advice being given by the Sears is in direct conflict with the manner in which God would have us rear our children. The Sears have a limited knowledge of biblical truths. With that limited knowledge of God's ways, their knowledge of man's nature and his purpose on earth is also limited. Psalms 58:3 says, "The wicked are estranged from the womb: they go astray as soon as they be born, speaking lies." God tells us that we are born with a sinful nature. We don't have to learn to be "bad." We already are! The Sears have concluded that their own experiences and wisdom authorize them to declare that God is wrong. Like those described in Romans 1:22, "Professing themselves to be wise, they became fools."

Another pediatrician contributing to the brainwashing of America is Marianne Neifert, who has been titled by the media as "Dr. Mom." In the February 1998 issue of *Parenting* magazine, Dr. Mom attempts to counsel parents on how to discipline their children who misbehave. She lists twelve "discipline strategies" that she feels will be effective in changing a child's negative behavior. I found that some of her twelve "discipline" strategies are not discipline at all. In fact, some are the complete opposite.

"Discipline strategy" number two was titled Look Away. Far from being any kind of discipline, Dr. Mom states, "By ignoring small infractions, you can avoid giving kids the negative attention they're sometimes seeking when they misbehave."[23] What Dr. Neifert is forgetting is that the child needs "negative attention" to associate with "negative behavior." This is one of the basic concepts of discipline. Imagine getting no "negative attention" from a police officer for "negative behavior" such as exceeding the speed limit. One of the reasons our roads are halfway safe to drive on is because of our fear of the "negative attention" we will get if we violate the law. Without that fear, our streets would become killing grounds where the meek would dare to venture.

"Discipline strategy" number eight written by Neifert is comical. Dr. Mom encourages parents to Insist on Paybacks. She suggests, "Children should also compensate people when they have inconvenienced them in some way. If an older child repeatedly refuses to go to bed when he's supposed to, thus depriving you and your spouse of time to yourselves, you can require him to pay back the 'bedtime owed.' You may want to let him decide which nights he'll go to bed earlier."[24] Okay, Dr. Mom, if the kid refuses to go to bed tonight, what makes you think he will agree to go to bed tomorrow night at an *earlier time*? What if he *refuses* to go to bed tomorrow night. What if you *let him decide* which night he wants to go to bed earlier, and then he *changes his mind*? My guess is that if you follow this strategy during the period this child is growing up, he will owe you several thousand hours in "bedtime owed" by the time he reaches the age of emancipation. But then you don't have to worry about collecting on the debt. By that time you probably won't be able to wait to kick him out.

"Discipline strategy" number eleven is titled Join Forces. This strategy encourages a spirit of cooperation between you and your rebellious child. This strategy begins by stating, "By presuming your child is cooperative, the two of you can work together to resolve problems."[25] At this point while reading this article, I began to wonder how many children Dr. Mom has reared. I very seldom found my own children to be cooperative. In the majority of cases I found that it took a directive, although unpopular, and the threat of punishment in order to obtain a positive end result. "Will you please do this?" very seldom worked if the child was not attracted to the activity. "Do it or else" was the solution.

"Discipline Strategy" number twelve is the epitome of what is wrong with parents today. It is titled, Call a Time-Out. Dr. Mom suggests that "This form of brief social isolation—known as a time-out—quickly helps a frustrated or angry child cope with his feelings and regain self control."[26] She continues, "Treat the time-out not as a punishment, but as a compassionate means of helping your child control his impulses."

Dr. Mom, Marianne Neifert, also makes it very clear that she feels spanking is destructive. She states, "Spanking has an adverse effect on children, resulting in aggression, low self-esteem, and depression later in life."[27] She goes on to say, "Spanking isn't a useful model for a child because it promotes the use of violence to settle disagreements."[28] She adds, "Raising your hand risks emotional harm to a child, who's likely to perceive being struck as degrading, frightening, and enraging."[29] Neifert is right about one thing. Getting spanked by your parent is frightening. That is part of the negative consequence that is associated with negative behavior. That is part of the necessary programming of the child's mind that follows them throughout his/her lifetime. That is the major problem with the out-of-control youth of today. Dr. Mom finishes her article with the statement, "Your aim is to get your child to develop self-discipline, and that goal is best achieved when you use methods that foster self-esteem."[30] My answer to that is "Bunk!" Dr. Mom is another one of the modern-day prophets of permissiveness who has caused the confusion in parenting prevalent in today's society.

13

THE THREE RS

"And ye shall teach them your children, speaking of them when thou sittest in thine house, and when thou walkest by the way, and when thou liest down, and when thou risest up" (Deuteronomy 11:19).

Once your children reach school age years, the school system in your community spends almost as much time with your child as you do. Parents who arrive home from work at six o'clock P.M. get to spend about four hours with their children. School personnel have to put up with them for almost double that.

The working relationship between my police department and our local school system is one that is envied by other communities. We have always been able to maintain a spirit of cooperation and have been able to work together to solve most crime related, school related problems. Our K-9 unit has been invited to sniff lockers in the surrounding schools, accompanied by school administrators. In 1997, when a high school student walked to a nearby pizza store and brutally shot the manager to death and then fled back to the school, it was police officers and school administrators who walked the halls side by side to locate the cold-blooded killer. When two young local teenagers attacked and robbed a youngster selling candy door to door and put him in the hospital, it was the middle school principal who conducted interviews with his students and called me the next day to supply me with the names of the two suspects. Few cities can boast of the type of support I receive from our school administrators.

That doesn't mean, however, that we are exempt from problems. There is a vast difference in ideals amongst educators and law

enforcement officers. Educators tend to be more tolerant of misconduct than police officers. Fortunately, there are still conservative
educators who provide some sort of balance to the educational
system. One of the problems that I encounter on a daily basis is the
hesitancy on the part of teachers to pursue criminal charges against
students who commit criminal acts on school property during school
hours. It appears that most teachers have a forgiving and tolerant
nature. This attitude is quickly recognized by the student population
and does nothing to deter future crime on campus. The problem is
more frustrating when the offense is a vicious attack by a student on
a teacher, and the teacher files a report to "document" the offense but
refuses to charge the juvenile in court.

Unlike parents, who have authority over their children by natural
law, educators have no natural authority over someone else's child. In
the 1800s, parents were not required by law to send their children to
school. Some parents opted to work their children in the fields rather
than educate them. When a parent decided to send their child to a
teacher for an education, it was assumed that the teacher was "in loco
parentis," a term which means "in the place of the parent." Since it was
the parent's choice to send the child to school, the teacher was
empowered with all of the authority that the parent had at home.

By the end of World War I, public education became for the most
part, compulsory. By the end of World War II, all states required that
children obtain a certain standard of education provided by the
government. In loco parentis remained for the educator, even though
parents were forced to send their child to school against their will.
Then in 1967, a court decision shaped the future of the educators'
authority over the student. In *re Gerald Gault, a Juvenile (1967) 387
U.S. 1.*, a teenager, in constant trouble with the law, was involved.
After numerous offenses and convictions, he was sentenced to the
juvenile detention facility for an extended period of time. The
Supreme Court ruled for the first time that juveniles have constitutional rights, overturning the sentence passed down by the juvenile
court. Although constitutional rights were now established for
minors, the court did not go so far as to say that children were entitled
to the same rights as adults. When the matter was reheard by the
court in 1986, it was emphasized that there had to be a balance
between the rights of the child and the safety of the majority. The
court also decided that the natural rights of the parent were still
intact. Parents could still force their children to follow their rules.

Most educators felt that they still possessed the authority of the parent when controlling their students.

A case was presented to the Supreme Court in 1969 that severely curtailed the authority of the school system over their students. Students at a Des Moines, Iowa, high school wore black armbands as a protest against the war in Vietnam. School officials banned the black armbands and forbade students from wearing them. Some students refused to comply with the rules imposed by the school and were disciplined. The parents of the students sued the school administrators, and the case eventually wound up in the Supreme Court. The court had already ruled that one of the responsibilities of a public school system was to "encourage the patriotism of its citizens and train its younger citizens to become more willing and efficient defenders of the United States in times of public danger." The school was confident that the court would rule in their favor in *Tinker v. Des Moines (1969) 89 S Ct 733.*

Guess again. The court ruled that "in loco parentis" only applies if the school has the expressed authorization of the parents to impose certain restrictions on their students. The court also ruled that the school could take action with a student if the circumstances overwhelmingly implied that the parents would give their consent under the given conditions. Even though the court ruled that society should not interfere with parents' rights to raise a child the way they wish, it did recognize that the needs and safety of the majority outweighed the recognition of parental sovereignty. Written regulations became the second source of authority that the school administrators used for maintaining order in the classroom. A written rule, if reasonable, could be used to dictate policy, and a student could be disciplined for a violation of the policy even if the parents disagreed.

It took five years for a 1980 incident that took place in a Piscataway, New Jersey, school to end up in the Supreme Court. *New Jersey v. T.L.O (1985) 105 S Ct 733* involved two girls who were observed by a teacher smoking in the restroom. The girls were escorted by force to the office where they were interrogated by the vice principal. One of the girls confessed and arrangements were made for her suspension. The other student, known as "TLO," a fourteen-year-old freshman, who had a record as a problem student, stated that she was innocent. Like many of the criminal element, TLO claimed that she was being "picked on." She refused to consent to a search of her purse and responded to the school official with an obscene gesture with her hand.

Somewhat motivated by anger, the assistant principal conducted a search of the student's purse and discovered not only cigarettes, but rolling papers, hashish, a pot pipe, and written records of TLO's drug deals. TLO admitted to the assistant principal that she had been dealing drugs. The local police officer working at the school at the time arrested TLO and transported her to the police station, where she was interrogated with her guardian present. TLO confessed to the police officer of selling drugs in the school. Subsequently, she was charged in juvenile court, and a public defender was assigned to her case. Her defense attorney filed a motion to suppress the evidence based on the claim that the search of TLO's purse was unreasonable.

The New Jersey Supreme Court ruled in TLO's favor, stating that her civil rights were violated by the search of her purse by a government official without her consent and without probable cause. The court also ruled that the school was not allowed to take any disciplinary action against TLO for the obscene gesture she made to the school official. To add insult to injury, the court ruled in TLO's favor regarding her confession, stating that her right against self-incrimination was violated when she was questioned without being first advised of her Miranda rights. I'm sure at this time, public educators all around the country were watching closely, wondering how much authority over their students they would retain by the time the courts were through. I can also imagine the frustration felt by the officials of the Piscataway school system when TLO filed a lawsuit against them. Supported by the American Civil Liberties Union, TLO was looking forward to getting rich at the expense of the public school system.

The school system appealed their position to the Supreme Court of the United States. Amongst the many issues addressed by the Supreme Court in this case was the issue of the authority of public school systems. Up to this point, the schools had claimed in loco parentis and written regulations when utilizing their authority over students. This time, the court established a third type of authority for public schools. Since each state's constitution grants the right to education, it is assumed that an education cannot take place if the atmosphere is not conducive to learning. The court ruled,

> Every student in every state has the right to an opportunity to be educated at public expense on a basis equal to the right of every other student. The government and its agents have implied power to meet the educational needs of each child. Since

education requires a safe, orderly, and secure atmosphere, the power to discipline is inherent in the power to educate.

The term "implied authority" was born.

The majority of the justices decided to refer to a prior U.S. Court of Appeals decision that addressed the "balancing test theory." This decision stated that the governmental official is obligated to weigh the rights of the citizen against the authority of the government. If the government side is paramount, the school official can proceed with its action. If the student's rights appear to be more important under the circumstances, then the school must curtail its investigative or disciplinary action. This decision caused a great deal of confusion due to its subjectivity. Educators naturally felt that their case was always stronger than the student's, and students, entering into an era of selfish individuality, usually protested that their rights were being violated.

In the meantime, the decision in *Tinker v. Des Moines* was causing far-reaching problems in the classroom. Remember, Tinker decided that students could "express themselves" by wearing black armbands even though the action was banned by the school. This newfound freedom of expression, handed to a generation of immature and unbridled classroom clowns, was resulting in a classroom environment that was less than orderly. When the TLO decision stated that a student could swear at a school official and be protected from any type of discipline because it was protected "free speech," it necessitated more "written regulation" that prohibited that specific type of behavior. If there was a specific written rule that prohibited swearing due to its threat of disrupting the learning environment, school officials were relatively safe in enforcing that rule.

Four rules finally emerged from the TLO case. The most important was the decision that children in school can be searched based on "reasonable suspicion." Because school officials were not held to the same standard as law enforcement, that requires "probable cause," they were now able to search a student even when it was unlikely that something improper would be found, as long as the "balancing test" was fulfilled. The second rule emerging from TLO was that a school official who is conducting a search in conjunction with a school-related investigation does not need to obtain a search warrant. School officials could search a student's locker over the objection of the student and the parents. The third rule stated that school officials were not required to advise students of their Miranda rights when being questioned. A student who is being questioned by school officials may invoke their Fifth Amendment right against self-incrimination and may not be punished for doing so, but confessions obtained from students by school officials are admissible in court. Rule number four stated that the school is not legally obligated to notify parents of action that involves their child unless the aid of the parent would be useful in protecting the child. On the other hand, the school must honor the student's request for parental involvement.

Whew! When it appeared that things were really getting out of hand, the Supreme Court restored a bit of common sense back into the authority area of the public school system. Schools are not bound to the same restrictions as law enforcement when it comes to searches and confessions. Both police officers and school administrators are well aware of that fact, and most communities tailor their actions against student offenders accordingly. I am well aware that if a student is suspected of possessing marijuana in his school locker, school officials can search the locker without a warrant as long as they have reasonable suspicion. School officials are also aware of the limitations that I have in searching a student's property as a police officer conducting a police investigation. Most school administrators structure their policies around this understanding. The school investigates first, then calls the police department. If a school principal calls the police to look into an illegal act, the school then becomes an extension of the police investigation. School officials cannot open a locker when ordered to do so by a police officer because the police officer is ordering the action. The school must take that action on its own in order for that action to be within the confines of the law.

Now keep in mind that the restrictions we have been reviewing here are ones placed on public school officials. In a private school, administrators and teachers are not bound to the rules set down by the Supreme Court. In loco parentis remains intact in private schools simply because attendance is a matter of choice. A child cannot be forced to go to a private school by the state, therefore the school is not subject to the same constitutional issues as the public schools. Also, when parents enroll their child in a private school, they must accept the policies of the school in order for the child to attend. The written policies are basically contracts which restrict the rights of the students. Follow the rules or else.

There are two reasons why real troublemakers are not found in private schools. One, if the child misbehaves, he/she is disciplined.

Most discipline is fair and has the blessing of the parent. I know of one mother who was advised by the private school her daughter was attending that students were paddled for specific violations of the rules, including obvious defiance of a teacher's authority. The school official advised the mother that if the need to paddle her daughter arose, the mother would first be contacted, apprised of the circumstances surrounding the discipline, and asked for her approval to spank. The mother was advised that if she did not agree with this procedure, she could take her daughter elsewhere for her education. The mother agreed. The daughter never did need to be paddled, but the fear of the consequence was always present, and the daughter conducted herself accordingly. Another reason you find few troublemakers in a private school is the "boot factor." Private schools are not obligated by law to educate children if they do not wish to do so. Kids either follow the rules, or they get the boot out the door. The direction of travel after the boot usually leads back to the public schools.

If the school system called the police department for every criminal offense that occurred on school property during school hours, the police department would be overloaded. I am thankful when school officials take matters into their own hands and refrain from calling me to solve a problem. Although most states have laws that make it illegal for someone who is aware of a crime to fail to report it, there is a term called "selective enforcement" which is used by most school systems. If every fight in the hallway or threat in the classroom were reported, the environmentalists would scream bloody murder over the trees cut down to make the paper to type the reports. Most educators report only the offenses that common sense dictates should be forwarded to the police department.

Parents can very easily request the help of the public school system in an attempt to change their child's behavior. Today's school administrators are extremely pleased to find a parent that supports their authority and any disciplinary action taken for violations of school rules. Today's teachers and school principals put up with irate parents on a daily basis who are upset because their poor little baby was treated unfairly. Much like the resistance experienced by police agencies, educators are constantly badgered by enabling parents who think their child can do nothing wrong.

In the old days, if you misbehaved in school, you got several whacks on the bucket with a paddle by the principal or disciplinarian. If you dared go home and complain to mom and dad, your parents called the school, found out you were a bad kid, and then gave you another spanking. The few parents who made the mistake of storming to the school to complain about the disciplinary action taken against their child were usually told to get lost and that if they didn't start to control their kid, he would get paddlings from the school until he did behave. Unfortunately, with the litigation in today's society, the fear of being sued has changed all that.

I have dealt with the public school system for many years, not only as a parent but also as a law enforcement officer. I can say unequivocally that in today's school system, teachers and administrators bend over backward to accommodate the troublemaker. Thirty-seven states allow corporal punishment in the public schools, but very few take advantage of that authority. The question is always present as to whether the corporal punishment used would be considered "excessive force." The possibility of being liable is too high. One Supreme Court case, *Mathis v. Berrient Co. Schools (1989, GA) 378 SE2d 505 cert den as Garcia v. Miera*, resulted when a student received a severe paddling that left bruises on the child's buttocks. The case was dismissed by the court, who ruled that the only reason medical treatment was required was for the purpose of substantiating the claim by the parents. The school, protected by state law, had not violated the portion of the law that required "serious physical harm" to be considered a violation. On the other hand, the Virginia Supreme Court denied the public school system immunity when a female student collapsed during administration of a paddling and had to be rushed to the emergency room where she was treated for shock. The court ruled that the force used by the paddler was excessive per se simply because medical treatment was necessary. In this case, the "serious physical harm" portion of the law was satisfied due to the need of a hospital stay. One can understand why the public school system is hesitant to use corporal punishment.

Unfortunately, that restriction has resulted in chaos in the classroom. I once made a visit to the high school to discuss a case with the assistant principal. As I walked into the outer office, I observed a female student sitting in the chair in front of the administrator's desk. The assistant principal was writing out a suspension form, apparently for the girl sitting in front of her. The student was not happy and kept spewing obscenities in the direction of the assistant principal. Suddenly the girl reached over and picked up the stapler from the desk, looked at it, and threw it on the floor. The administrator looked up and said, "that's another charge," and started writing again. The young lady stood up and picked up the adding machine. Smiling, she dropped it on the floor. The administrator looked up and said, "that's another charge." The girl walked to a counter where the computer was sitting. I pictured in my mind the two-thousand-dollar Apple smashing on the floor of the office. Unable to keep quiet any longer, I walked into the office and ordered the girl to sit down. She looked at me with uncertainty in her eyes. The look on my face convinced her that I would force her to sit down if she refused. "Sit down, now!" I barked. The girl frowned and sat in her chair. I then advised the girl that if she touched anything else in the office she was going directly to jail. She crossed her arm and pouted while the administrator finished writing out the "multiple charges." She handed the paper to the girl and instructed her to leave the building.

After the student stormed out of the office, I asked the assistant principal why she would allow the student to destroy her office. She explained that according to school policy, physical force could only be used against a student if the personal safety of a school employee or another student is endangered. Policy prohibited physical force against students even if they were destroying school property. This was a case where I would have arrested the girl very early on for either criminal mischief or disorderly conduct. Yet the school policy prevented laying hands on a student unless someone is in danger of being injured. The students, aware of the policy, take advantage of the entire staff.

Although some individual school policies prohibit touching students, what is termed "forced physical guidance," or the laying of hands on a student for directive purposes is specifically allowable in all fifty states and is addressed in the regulations of the U.S. Department of Education. Teachers *are* allowed to touch students, and they are protected by the law in much the same manner as the parent. I am amused by some of the school system's reports I see when an altercation takes place between a teacher and student. When one of the school staff needs to use physical force to move a student in one of our elementary schools, they use the term "supportive touch." Yes, I remember many of my fellow classmates back in the sixties receiving the "supportive touch."

It is possible for parents and schools to work together to benefit the students. If parents wish the school system to pay special attention to their child, a meeting with the school principal should be scheduled. Most administrators are pleased to work with a cooperative parent. By making it clear that you support any decision made by the teachers or administrators when it comes to disciplining your child, they will tend to relax and concentrate more on what is best for the students rather than whether or not they will be sued. On occasion parents will encounter an educator who is hesitant to spend additional time to accommodate your personal problem. If the parent hears the argument from the principal, "I can't do this for every kid," the parent should answer, "I'm not asking you to do this for every kid. Just mine!"

Parents should maintain a regular line of communication between themselves and the school. Get to know your child's teachers, counselors, and administrators. Listen to what they have to say about your child's behavior. Make it clear that you support their efforts. Remember, with the extreme exception of a psycho-teacher found once in a great while, you can depend on the word of most classroom educators. When a teacher tells you that your child is misbehaving, he/she is more than likely misbehaving. There have been times when I have arrested juveniles for an offense I witnessed with my own two eyes, completed the booking procedure, and released them to their parent, only to have Enabler Eddie call me and tell me that his kid had done nothing wrong, that I had fabricated the entire story. I'm amazed that a mature person would think that I had nothing better to do than arrest someone for doing absolutely nothing, then make up a story and get some youngster in trouble for something he didn't do.

Teachers encounter the same problem. The teacher reports that a student committed an offense and he gets suspended. The parents storm up to the school claiming that the teacher made the whole thing up. Come on now! Teachers don't get a bonus at the end of the year for filling a quota of suspended students. When a teacher claims students have acted improperly, they have. Parents tend to become protective when their child is accused of wrongdoing by an outsider. It's part of the natural protective instincts that each parent possesses. Children then realize, however, that they can manipulate the parent to work against the teacher. It takes effort on the part of the parent not to be an enabler. Parents should listen to the school staff and analyze the information being forwarded to them. They will find that the report is usually true, and by supporting the teacher, they will make the child realize that his negative behavior in the classroom will not be tolerated.

Because of the strong working relationship I have with our school system, I have had the opportunity to speak to many of our school administrators in length about their feelings and ideas to improve the public school system. A good friend of mine, Dan Barth, who headed the discipline office of the local high school for several years, became discouraged because of the lack of discipline in the school. Dan has always contended that in the public school system today, kids have "no fear" of consequences. This attitude has permeated the public school system all across our country and has contributed to the decline of education in America.

"What we have," Dan contends, "are good kids who care, and bad kids who don't care." Dan believes that the largest obstacle to overcome in the public school system is the constant disruptions in the classroom that affect the quality of the education young people are receiving. Dan believes that removing the bad kids from the learning environment would do wonders for the quality of education that the good kids would get. "The bad kids don't want to be there," Dan states, "so get rid of them." Removing the disrupter is easier to accomplish in Dan's school system. Both the middle school and high school have separate buildings for the education of behavioral problem students. Although they are labeled "academies," they could be named more appropriately "maximum security learning facilities."

Dan cited an example of the educational system's inability to offer consequences for negative behavior by a student. After numerous truancy violations, a young man was apprehended outside of the school, again, when he should have been in class. After being escorted to Dan's office, the young man sat across the desk smiling at him. "Well, James," Dan said, "I've been instructed to suspend you for three days." The young man broke into a grin. "Thanks," he said. "That's what I wanted in the first place!" Dan handed the boy his paperwork and watched him leave the building. "As punishment for not staying in school, we make him leave school," Dan states. "Go figure."

I asked Dan what he felt could be done to improve the present problems that educators are experiencing. Dan's response echoes the sentiments of many educators and law enforcement officials. He has two suggestions. First, get rid of the kids who don't want to be in school. Those kids should be placed in another area where their actions will not disrupt the classroom where the well-behaved children are learning. His second solution is to "make the parents responsible for the actions of their children." There is a growing trend in this county to make parents accountable for the actions of their children. The recent conviction of a mother and father in Michigan for their inability to control their teenage son is a landmark case in this country.

The boy had been arrested on numerous occasions, and had the reputation of "running the household." After burglarizing a church, the police conducted a search of the boy's residence. Finding weapons and drugs in plain view in the boy's bedroom, the parents were charged with the inability to control the boy's behavior.

In a small way, the city I work for has taken steps in that direction. When we implemented our daytime curfew ordinance, not only was the parent held responsible for a child cutting school, the law required that when a child was suspended or expelled from school, the child was required to be under the supervision of the parent or another responsible adult assigned by the parent. Technically, a child suspended or expelled from school is supposed to be supervised by an adult while at home during the hours he would normally be in school. This law makes it difficult for the family whose mom and dad work full time. Parental responsibility seems to be an issue that is gaining more acceptance in our society. For years we have held dog owners accountable for the actions of their pets, including everything from biting people to leaving unwanted deposits in the neighbor's yard. If a person can be cited for "dog at large" because they cannot control their pet, a parent certainly can be held accountable for the actions of his/her children, who understand much more the limitations set on their behavior by the person in charge.

What if the parent wants the school system to use stricter discipline with their child? Dan states that on one occasion a mother called his office and requested that he use corporal punishment on her son. The mother wanted the vice principal to spank her kid! When Dan went to the top administrators, he was told that although state law permitted paddling in the schools, the system policy prohibited such action. Can school policy be changed? Certainly it can, if enough people insist on the change.

A close friend of my oldest son (you know, the kind that eats dinner with your family more often than his own family) went on to also follow in his father's footsteps. While my son went on to become a police officer, his friend Bob Bushok went on to become a school teacher like his father Bill, who was an educator for thirty-four years. Being a strict conservative, Bob found out in a very short period of time what it is like to be a public school teacher. Some of his stories are hilarious; some are sad. Bob feels as many of us do about special educational programs, such as "employment-education" programs. Every public school system has them. These are programs designed to accommodate kids who don't want to sit in the classroom. The school system that Bob teaches in calls it the Occupational Work Adjustment program, or "OWA." Bob calls it more appropriately "Out Walking Around." Bob tells a story about having trouble with one of his middle school students completing his assignments and getting homework turned in on time. Bob called the boy's mother and attempted to explain the problem and ask for the assistance of the parent in addressing the problem. Mom responded by saying, "I'm tired of coming home and having to do your job!" Can you imagine a parent who dumps completely onto the school system the responsibility of educating her child? All teachers will tell you that the major factor in the success of a child is the parent. Period.

Bob does admit that there are weaknesses in the system. He claims that almost all teachers are afraid to take any disciplinary action against a student because of the fear of liability. I have heard from many educators that approximately one third of the students in the public school system make trouble throughout the school year. That means that two thirds of the students, the ones who come to learn, are being disrupted on a regular basis by those who like to cause trouble. Teachers are reluctant to use any type of enforcement action because they are afraid of getting sued. Recently the school system was attempting to pass a levy that would add a substantial amount to the area's property tax. One of the teachers who was having a difficult time with a student took the disciplinary action she felt necessary against the student. The administrators, feeling that the action would look bad just before voting day, reversed the decision of the teacher. The teacher, considered by many to be a good educator, quit. Sometimes the politics of education can be tough.

We've been discussing how many of those in positions of authority have little or no idea what actually constitutes child abuse. We've discovered that social workers and even police officers sometimes do not realize that parents have the authority to use corporal punishment within reason when disciplining their child. Another horror story came to my attention when I was writing this chapter. A teacher in one of the local public schools told me that one of the students claimed to the principal that she had been struck by her father. The principal insisted that the department of children's services be contacted. When I asked the teacher why social services had to be contacted, the teacher responded by saying, "Because her father had hit her." The law demands that the school administrators notify the department of social services when they have information that a child is being abused. The simple claim that a father struck the daughter does not constitute abuse. So why did the principal call the social worker? The teacher replied, "I don't know." Isn't it time we learn?

Bob Bushok agrees that making parents accountable for their child's actions is the best method to change a child's behavior. Bob suggests that if the student receives a three-day in-school suspension, the parent should be required to supervise the child in the suspension room. If the parent is employed, he/she would be required to take off work. Face it folks, as juveniles become more out of control, the government is placing more of the liability on the parent. Recently, Ohio passed a House Bill which demands that the parent of a student who has been suspended from school attend parenting classes. If the parent refuses, the offense becomes a fourth degree misdemeanor, an offense that the parent can be jailed for. For years parents have been responsible for the actions of their children under civil law. Now, there is a movement in this country to make parents responsible under criminal law. There could come a day when parents are forced to address the problem of their out-of-control children or suffer criminal consequences. It could happen because it's a method that works.

One of the best analogies I have ever heard that demonstrates how spanking should be viewed came from an educator. His viewpoint on corporal punishment compared to an inoculation against disease. We all agree that children differ in many ways, including genetic structure, personality, and will. Some children need stronger discipline than others. Some children respond to alternative forms of discipline better than others. The major problem is determining what child will act in what manner when they reach the early teenage years. Parents who decide not to spank their child may learn too late that spanking was needed to instill the fear factor into the child. I've talked to parents who have insisted that they never spanked their child, and the child turned out to be good. Is that possible? I would argue that those exceptions are rare but will concede that it is possible.

When our children are very young, we inoculate them against disease. When I was a small child, my mother took me to the doctor to be immunized against polio. Was my mother sure that I was going to contract that disease when I got older? Of course not. Was there a possibility that I would contract polio as I grew older. Yes, there was that possibility. Did the inoculation harm me? No, but it was insurance that I would not contract polio if I came in contact with the disease.

Spanking accomplishes one thing. It ensures that children have instilled in their nature the necessary fear that results in respect for authority. Will children always grow into "in-your-face" teenagers if they are not spanked when they are young? No, not always. Is there a chance that children will develop attitudes of "no fear" if they are not spanked when they are young? Yes, there is a good chance of that. The only problem is knowing in advance which children will reach adolescence with an attitude of defiance. We can't tell. What we need is an insurance policy. Spanking, when used properly, is never harmful to a child and is the insurance policy that guarantees that the child develops the respect for authority that is essential to survive in our society. It's an insurance policy that guarantees there will never be an attitude of "no fear."

14

A Matter of Perception

"To know wisdom and instruction; to perceive the words of understanding" (Proverbs 1:2).

It's been said that "We are not what we think we are. We are not even what other people think we are. We are what we think other people think we are." Now if that sounds confusing, it is. People perceive reality in different ways. The way your child perceives you results in how your child acts toward you. If your child perceives that you have no authority to force him to behave in a certain way, he will not comply with your demands. Unless you display an air of authority and possess the means with which to enforce the consequence, no one will listen to you.

An excellent example of this theory was made clear to me in 1988 when President Reagan was campaigning throughout the country for Vice President George Bush. One of his stops was in the Cleveland area, and the decision was made by the administration to hold one of the campaign speeches at a Cleveland area college in our jurisdiction. A great deal of preparation took place prior to the president's arrival. Members of our department were briefed by the secret service days before the event. We were all given our instructions in writing and assigned stations throughout the city, including the escort from the airport and the officers guarding the entrances to the building where the president would speak. Hoping to be assigned a position near the stage where the speech would take place, you can imagine my disappointment when I was assigned to the area outside the rear stage door of the building. During the briefing, we were instructed as to what was expected of us during the president's stay and what we were to do under certain circumstances.

My partner was a secret service agent, whose southern drawl and dry sense of humor made the detail interesting. As we were being briefed, officers who were stationed at the doors of the building were instructed as to the procedure if someone attempted to pass through our post. If someone were to attempt to walk or drive past our position, we were to verbalize the command "Stop, do not come any closer." If the intruder into your zone were to continue toward the building, we were to draw our weapon and verbalize the command "Stop, or I'll shoot." Fortunately, we were advised that it would not be necessary for us to pull the trigger. There would be a sniper on the roof who would quickly pick off any unlucky moron who wouldn't listen. "Wow," I thought. "These guys don't mess around."

The problem was, I didn't think these secret service agents knew anything about the public in these parts. With the erosion of police power, and the perception by the public that the cops couldn't do anything to you, I began to imagine the pile of bodies near the back door of the auditorium when nobody listened to my commands. Didn't these federal agents know that people around here didn't listen to anything we said? When we try to pull them over on the road, they take off and we have to chase them. When we order them to halt, they run off and we have to run after them on foot. Nobody listens to the cops anymore. What makes these secret service agents think these people are going to stop when we tell them?

We were fortunate that the weather was clear and sunny on the day of the president's visit. The secret service agent and myself positioned ourselves in the area just outside the rear stage door. We could hear the buzz of activity as the president's motorcade pulled up in front of the auditorium. Soon we could hear the public address system reverberating the president's voice throughout the campus as he began his speech. We settled back and watched the large groups of people scurrying about the area.

Then it happened. A middle-aged man ventured past the cordoned off area in an effort to take a shortcut to the front of the building. "Sir," I hollered. He looked in my direction as he shuffled across the lawn. I summoned all the authority that I could and shouted, "Stop! Do not come any closer!"

This guy froze in his tracks as though I had fired a warning shot across his bow. "You are in a restricted area, get on the other side of that rope!" This poor guy bolted for the safety of the sidewalk as though he were being chased by a bunch of Doberman pinschers. I watched in amazement as the man complied immediately with my order. My secret service agent partner chuckled. I shook my head as I said, "I can't believe it! Why did he listen so well?" The agent, who was used to this type of reaction on this kind of detail had the answer. "We're talking about protecting the president here, not some security guard protecting some merchandise at K-Mart! They know you mean business!"

At least fifty people attempted to cut through our restricted area that afternoon. Not once did I have to draw my weapon. Not once did we have to repeat our command. Not once did we have to shoot anyone. I was flabbergasted that all of these people perceived our authority as final, and the consequence for disobeying, fatal. True, I did possess much more authority to use deadly force than I would have had under other circumstances. The public also realized it, and their perception of my ability to enforce the rules caused them to comply with my orders.

Our children are no different. Their perception of their parents' authority and their perception of their parents' ability to enforce the rules and impose the consequences determines how they react. Sometimes force is never needed; just the threat of force and the parents' authority to use it is enough.

Before the implementation of our city's new daytime curfew law that enabled our officers to arrest students who were playing hookie, there was little or no enforcement clout. We depended on the school's truancy officer to file any charges in juvenile court. Because of the volume of serious juvenile crime in our county, most of the minor offenses were simply ignored by the court. When I drafted our community's daytime curfew ordinance and presented it to city council, its major objective was to make the parents responsible for their child cutting school. The law said that if a child was arrested for truancy, on the first offense the parents were responsible for $100 in fines and $80 in court costs. On the second and each subsequent offense, the fine went to $250 and $80 in court costs. The legislation passed, and for the first time, our city had some bite in its truancy law.

Two days after the law went into effect, one of our most frequent school skippers got pinched. Observed walking down a side street, he was stopped and detained while the officer checked with the attendance officer. Sure enough, he was supposed to be in class at that moment. He was placed under arrest and booked, and his father was notified. When dad came to pick up his son, he expressed his displeasure when he found out that he was being cited also. The vein in the front of his forehead swelled as he called us every name in the book and proclaimed his inability to control his son's actions. He was much kinder to the judge the following week when sentence was imposed, and he paid his fines.

Not more than four days later, Tommy Truant got busted again. This time he made a valiant attempt to evade the arresting officer, running through backyards until he was corralled several blocks from the school. When dad came to pick up his offspring and discovered that he was receiving another citation, his facial vein threatened to pop. "What do you mean, two hundred and fifty dollars?" he yelled. "My kid is the one breaking the law, not me!" He grabbed junior by the nape of his neck as he dragged him out of the lobby of the police station, growling about the endless ways he could impose pain upon the youngster.

We heard nothing from the habitual truant or his father for quite a while. About a month later, while visiting the high school on another matter, I was approached by the vice principal. He humorously conveyed some information to me about the youngster who had missed so much school prior to his two arrests. The vice principal explained how each teacher thought it was a real treat that the youngster had been in every class during the last month and wondered what had taken place to produce such spectacular results.

I talked to the father later that week. What I discovered was that the father had never touched his son. Although he had considered knocking some sense into the young man's head, he indicated that after his second court appearance, he had simply stated in a quiet, non-violent tone, "Son, don't you *ever* cut school again!"

The way your child perceives your authority determines how he reacts to your demands.

What changed junior's behavior? Why did the young man feel it was in his best interest to go to class every day? The young man *perceived* his father's authority and his ability to carry out the consequences. The court had stated loud and clear that his father was responsible for the offense he had committed. Therefore, his father must be authorized to enforce the rules. His father had never cared before whether he went to school or not. But the lightening of the wallet gave dad some incentive to encourage his son to attend classes. When dad figured out that he would lose $330 every time his son got caught cutting class, he suddenly became concerned about the boy's education. That's really what this law was designed for—to get parents directly involved in their child's school attendance.

I have held numerous meetings in my office and in homes with families whose teenage son or daughter thinks their parent has no authority or ability to enforce the rules. The very first thing that I make clear is the parent's authorization under the law to use corporal punishment in the discipline of the child. I don't necessarily believe that spanking a fifteen year old is the most productive type of discipline to use, but I want that teenager to think that the possibility is there. And I want that teen to know that flagrant defiance of the reasonable rules imposed by his/her parents will not be tolerated under any circumstances. Mom and dad do not need the police to solve their discipline problems. I want them to know that the police are supporting everything that the parents do within the law to bring their child under control.

There are many examples of how the perception of a person's ability to follow through with a threat or promise determines what action is taken. Many years ago, a student in a classroom could make a comment about buying a gun and killing other students, and the comment was not taken seriously. In today's climate, and with the number of recent school shootings by students, a comment made in the classroom about killing other students is perceived as a likely possibility, and the student is arrested and charged with aggravated menacing. The difference is the perception that the student is capable of doing what he claims he will do.

When I was first assigned to the detective bureau, I had the opportunity to meet with a single mom and her fifteen-year-old son. The boy had been in trouble for some time and had been charged with numerous crimes such as aggravated burglary, assault, and unruly child. When he sat down in my office with his mother, I explained the rules of our meeting as I do with every juvenile who enters our police department. No swearing, no disrespecting your parents, and no getting up and leaving. Our conversation began easily enough, but eventually got to that point when the young man didn't feel like listening anymore. He voiced his opinion of me and stood up to leave the room.

When you enter our police department, you cannot get out without the assistance of a police officer. The doors lock from both sides and must be opened with a key. The city jail is housed in our building, and if a prisoner were to somehow get out of his cell, he could not exit the building. In the same area as my office is the patrol squad room and armory. There are times when guns are left out in the open. When Danny Defiant got up out of his chair and began walking out of my office, my reaction was to prevent him from walking down the hallway toward the squad room. When I told the boy to sit back down in his chair, he waved at me with one of his fingers. I stood up from my chair and grabbed Danny by the shirt.

I'm sure anyone just walking into my office would think that Danny and I were doing the Blue Danube Waltz in the middle of the floor. Danny was trying to pull away, and I was trying to get him back in his chair. Mom sat in her chair grinning, probably enjoying the fact that someone else was having difficulty with her son. As Danny tried to get away, he wriggled out of my grasp and fell backward, right into the glass window in the door of my office. The shattering glass brought everyone in the general vicinity running in our direction. The lieutenant in charge of patrol was the first one there. Mom pointed her finger at her son lying on the floor bleeding from the arm and said, "He should have listened to Detective Surgenor! He doesn't listen to me; he's going to find out he has to listen to somebody!" The paramedics were summoned, and the boy was transported to the hospital to treat his wounds. Mom shook my hand and left asking, "Am I allowed to do that at home?"

The next day I got a call from the high school principal. "What in the world did you do to Danny Defiant yesterday?" he asked. When I tried to explain the circumstances surrounding Danny's injuries, the principal interrupted. "I understand he got mouthy with you, and you picked him up out of his chair and threw him through a plate glass window!" The silence on my end of the telephone conversation was not because of a loss for words on my part. It was due to the visions of lawsuits running through my head. The principal, waiting for an indication from me as to whether I had tossed one of his less favorite students through a window onto the pavement below, asked, "Well, did you?"

It took some convincing for the principal to believe the actual facts. The entire school was talking about the new juvenile officer who was short-tempered and unbelievably strong, able to pick up young men and heave them through windows with no effort at all. And to top it off, he got away with it! The young man's mother had sided with the officer and there would be no lawsuit. Poor Danny Defiant, lying near death in the hospital room, weak from a loss of blood and wishing he had never tried to confront this new breed of police officer. I believe the principal was disappointed when he heard how the incident actually occurred.

It was about two weeks later when I had my next parent/child conference. As the young man walked into my office with his mother, he warily eyed the door, looking up and down at its construction and the area around it. As he sat down in the chair, his eyes met mine. He casually motioned toward the door and asked, "Is that the window?" My answer was honest. "No," I replied. "That's the replacement." Mom quickly piped up and pointed her finger at her son. "I would suggest that you listen to the detective, or he might throw *you* through it!"

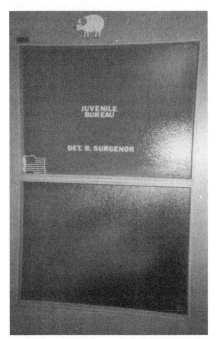

The infamous "Danny Defiant" window, viewed by many a wayward juvenile as they enter the author's office.

Since that time, I have never had a juvenile attempt to leave my office during a conversation. I have had many ask me if that was the infamous "Danny Defiant window." The word had spread that there was a chance that the consequences for not following the rules in Detective Surgenor's office were severe. None of those juveniles had any idea that to take that kind of action would lead to my dismissal from the police department and the filing of criminal charges. But the perception of my ability to perform that act keeps them all from getting out of line in my office.

Most of the time, we never know if our actions have the results we desire. Very seldom do we realize that the action we took deterred negative behavior. Unfortunately, there are times when parents don't make the "common sense" decision and regret it for the rest of their life. A mother in the Cleveland area did not like her son driving with one of his friends. The friend had reckless driving habits, and the mother had personally observed the boy peeling tires and driving at fast speeds. When her son asked her if he could go with other friends to an amusement park thirty miles away, the mother's instincts told her to say no when she found out that the driver was Reckless Randy. Her son pleaded with her, and because she did not want her son angry with her, she consented. Two hours later, the police were at her door, advising her that her son was killed in a head-on crash when the driver of the car he was in lost control at high speed and swerved into oncoming traffic. Mom should have done what she knew was best.

There are times when we are rewarded with information that lets us know how our enforcement of the rules has affected another person's perception. While on patrol one early Sunday morning, I was traveling down one of our main streets when I observed the railroad gates going down at the train crossing. The lights were flashing and the bells were ringing. The gates actually block the roadway, so in order to proceed past the crossing, the motorist must pass around the gate on the wrong side of the street and continue on. As I approached the crossing, I observed a red corvette approaching the crossing from the opposite direction. The vehicle stopped at the crossing and waited. I observed the front tires turn to the left, and with horror, I watched the vehicle begin to accelerate around the gates. The train was nearing the crossing, and the engineer blew his horn frantically as the car spun its tires over the tracks. The rear of the car just cleared the crossing as the train sped past. "Alright," I said to myself. "This one is getting a ticket!"

I performed a u-turn behind the corvette as it passed me. The driver was an attractive girl in her early-to-mid twenties. Sitting next to her was a male about the same age. As I pulled in behind the car and activated my overheads, the male threw up his hands in disgust. When I walked up to the car, the first words I heard were out of the young man's mouth. "It's my fault, officer. I told her to do it." Although I really dislike the "would you jump off a cliff" analogy, in this case, I used it. The man, obviously upset with the inconvenience of being detained on a beautiful Sunday morning, began arguing with me and suggesting that I should be looking for real criminals somewhere else. The young lady quietly handed me her driver's license with tears in her eyes. It appeared that she was shaken a great deal by her close call with the large diesel locomotive. I went back to the cruiser and wrote the girl a citation, motivated not only by the girl's reckless act but also by the boyfriend's big mouth. When I handed the girl her ticket, she quietly thanked me with tears in her eyes and slowly drove on her way.

I felt bad for the rest of the day. I realized that sometimes issuing a traffic ticket wasn't the best way to handle a traffic violation. If violators realized their mistakes and were truly repentant, I usually sent them on their way with a warning and a note of concern for their safety. One of the reasons I had written the girl the ticket was because of her boyfriend's big mouth, certainly not something she had any control over. It took several days for me to forget her teary eyes and the stiff fine she was going to be required to pay in court.

It was almost one year later, while patrolling the city in the cruiser, that I received a radio call from dispatch to return to the station. There was a female in the lobby who wished to speak to me. When I walked into the lobby, I recognized the girl's face but could not remember where I had seen her. She began by asking me if I knew who she was. She went on to ask me if I remembered a red corvette and her loud-mouth boyfriend. I immediately recalled the incident and wondered why this young lady had come back a year later to complain about her ticket. It was at that point that the girl's bottom lip began to tremble. She looked much more familiar as tears began to well up in her eyes.

"I just wanted to thank you for giving me that ticket last year," she said. She smiled when she saw the amazed look on my face. Very seldom did anyone thank me for a traffic ticket, much less one year after the fact. The girl continued, "I just wanted you to know that I was sitting at the railroad crossing on Sterns Road yesterday . . . " Before she said another word, I knew what she was going to tell me. I had heard on the news that several teenagers had been killed at that crossing the previous day. The teenagers had been waiting at the crossing for a slow eastbound train, and when the train cleared the crossing, the teens had crossed the tracks in violation of the warning lights, only to be struck by a westbound train that had been hidden from view by the other train. All of the kids in the car were killed immediately.

The girl in the lobby wept as she described what happened. "I was the first car at the crossing," she explained. "When the slow train cleared the crossing, I turned my wheels to go over the tracks. It was then that I thought to myself, 'I wonder if there's a cop sitting on the other side of this crossing. That's all I need is another two-hundred-dollar fine!' So I stopped." The girl described the carload of teenagers behind her, blowing the horn and encouraging her to either go across the tracks or get out of their way. She explained how she motioned them to go around.

Her description of the look of horror on the young girl's face in the backseat of that car as she saw the oncoming train was vivid. She tried to explain to me her feelings as she watched the train slam into the side of the car and drag it hundreds of yards down the track. The tears ran down her face as she told me how she will never forget the screams that came from the car as it disappeared in front of the diesel locomotive. The girl then looked at me and said, "If you hadn't given me that ticket, that would have been me!" She went on to explain how the consequence of her violation a year ago kept her from breaking the law again. Her perception of the police officer's ability to punish her for her irresponsible action deterred her from recommitting the offense. This time, it saved her life.

Parents may never know that the implementation of strict rules and the enforcement of severe consequences may save their child's life. Most parents will never realize that their child's life was spared because he/she was afraid to violate the rules. Most parents will never realize that their child's addiction to heroin was averted because of fear of dad's enforcement action. Most parents will never realize that their child's perception of the parent's ability to impose swift and sure punishment for defiance of authority kept him/her out of trouble with the teacher, the police, and the judge. On the other hand, too many parents realize too late that their permissiveness resulted in a child who had no respect for authority, would not follow the rules, and developed an attitude of "no fear."

15

CHANGING BEHAVIOR

"For I know him, that he will command his children and his household after him, and they shall keep the way of the Lord, to do justice and judgment" *(Genesis 18:19).*

One of the biggest problems I encounter is the fact that most kids who have not been disciplined as they were growing up, begin committing crimes at the age of twelve or thirteen. Depending on the size of the child, we now face a much larger and stronger individual than the two year old who had temper tantrums to get his own way. Although some begin their life of crime at an earlier age, the majority of our repeat offenders start as they reach their early teen years.

If the parents have done little to instill the fear factor in the child up to that point, mom and dad have a rough road ahead. By the time the child reaches fifteen years of age, the parents are looking at a possible physical confrontation with the teen if an attempt is made to tighten the screws. Do you remember what I said about the saying, "As the twig is bent, so grows the tree?" A small sapling that has its trunk bent is much easier to straighten while it is still small. If you wait till the tree is full grown, major surgery is needed. Instilling the fear factor into an older teenager requires maximum effort on the part of the parent. However, it's not impossible. I have seen out-of-control teenagers go into the Marine Corps only to emerge years later as respectful, responsible human beings. What it takes is rules, structure, discipline, and consequences. And those all dished out with consistency.

What can parents do with a teenager who is suddenly defying their authority and disobeying every rule? The most important thing for the

175

*There is always
something that works to
change the child's
behavior, even if it means
having them locked up.*

parent to remember is that the parent is the one in charge, not the child. The law says so. The police officer says so. The judge says so. Parents need to remember that society expects them to take control of their child. It is their responsibility to do so. Parents are liable for everything their child does. Therefore, the law gives them a great deal of latitude in dealing with the child. The child is obligated by law to comply with the reasonable control of the parents. Period.

A rule such as a time for curfew is considered "reasonable control" by the courts. If parents demand that their teenager be in the house by ten o'clock on a school night, the child is obligated to obey their parents. What if the child decides to leave the house against the parents' wishes? Then physical force should be used by the parent to restrain the child and keep him/her in the house. In every state, parents are allowed to use physical force against their child in order to keep them from violating the rules of the home. A child is never allowed to use physical force against a parent.

Kids Don't Hit Parents

Children who use force against their mother or father or other family member are guilty of domestic violence. Most communities have mandatory arrest policies for those charged with this offense. If a child pushes, pokes, or punches a parent, he/she should be arrested immediately. Parents who overlook their child using force against them can expect much more serious problems by the time that child reaches the age of eighteen. A young man in my city began his violent history at the age of thirteen when he shoved his mother for attempting to keep him in the house. The mother called our department but refused to pursue the domestic violence charge against him, claiming that he was "really a good boy." Good boys don't use physical force against mom. Less than six months later, the boy punched his mother during an argument. Mom refused to call the police because she feared her son would be taken to the detention facility. The boy assaulted his parents two more times over the next several months before a neighbor called our department and reported a fist fight going on inside the house. This time the fighter went to the detention home, over the objections of mom and dad. In no uncertain terms, the boy was told that if he ever touched his parents again, he would be spending a lot of time behind bars. The fear of a lengthy stay in the kiddie jail has kept him from hitting his parents again.

There is no excuse for a teenager assaulting a parent and should not be tolerated. Most police departments and officers in charge of the juvenile unit are receptive to meeting with parents who are fearful of their children. Most departments will explain their arrest policies and will work with the parents to design a plan of attack in case the parent is assaulted. I have not yet met a police officer who does not take pleasure in slapping the cuffs on a young punk who has given his mother a bloody nose.

The Intake Managers for the Cuyahoga County Juvenile Court. From left to right: Gary Gavin, drug offense specialist; Greg Weimer, chief intake manager; Jim Young, domestic violence specialist.

Do Without

One of the toughest things for a parent to do is tolerate a loud, inconsiderate child who takes everything that the parent does for granted and complains about how unfortunate they are. I have suggested to parents that in order to make the child understand a bit more of reality, try taking away some of the benefits the child receives on a daily basis. It's amazing how even a parent forgets that the comforts we all enjoy are easily removed. I had a couple, sitting in my office, who looked puzzled when I suggested that they remove certain luxuries so their teenage daughter would start to realize what her parents actually provided for her. Her mother insisted, "She doesn't care about her television being taken away," she said. "She doesn't seem to care about anything!"

There is always *something* that a child enjoys during daily living that would make things uncomfortable if eliminated. The couple's eyes lit up when I asked them if their daughter knew how to turn the hot water heater on or off. I suggested that before leaving for work early in the morning, they shut the water valve coming from the hot water tank. When the little darling gets up to go to school, she suddenly realizes that her shower is freezing cold. Unable to shower or wash her hair, she goes to school dirty and uncomfortable. When she arrives home from school, she is advised by her parents that she *will* do the dishes tonight as instructed or there will be no hot water the next morning. Better yet, every time she gets in the shower without doing her chores, turn the hot water off after she gets lathered up. It's a very effective consequence for not accepting her responsibilities.

Bob Reitman gives an example of a family he was dealing with. They thought they had taken everything away from their fifteen-year-old son as consequences for his violations of the rules and defiance of their authority. It seemed that he continued to disobey at will, not coming home when he was supposed to, walking out of the house against the parents' wishes, and refusing to do his designated chores. About to give up, mom walked into his room one evening and observed junior fast asleep with his arm around Fido, the boy's German shepherd. Bingo! The next day when junior came home from school, Fido was nowhere to be found. After an extensive search, junior asked mom and dad if they knew where Fido was. Their answer was clear. When you start following the rules, Fido can come back home. Until then, he is being kept in a kennel in an undisclosed location. Because of the boy's strong attachment to Fido, he discovered that it was in his best interest to follow the rules. After a short period of reformed behavior, Fido was returned home, with the understanding that he could very easily be returned to the kennel if junior were to slip back into his old ways. The parents had found the one consequence that junior dreaded, being separated from his dog.

It's Recorded

I have suggested to many parents that they arm themselves with an electronic device to record the actions of their out-of-control child. It can be a mini-tape recorder or a video camera. As long as it can record the shenanigans of the in-your-face youth, parents feel a confidence that they will be believed when presenting their case to the police, judge, or social worker. When the child accuses the parent of excessive force or abuse, the parent is able to produce the recording of the child spewing obscenities and threatening the parent with harm.

A mother called me one day to ask that I meet with her and her sixteen-year-old son. The mother, who was single, stated that she was having a terrible time controlling the boy, who was defying every rule and threatening her. On one occasion he had grabbed her wrists and forced her onto her knees, advising her that he would kill her if she didn't leave him alone. I agreed to meet with mom and her son.

When they arrived at the police department, I was impressed with the intelligence of the boy. He was extremely bright and acted in the most courteous manner. He shook my hand firmly and called me sir. As they sat in my office and the mother explained her concerns, the boy looked at the floor with a forlorn look on his face. When his mother accused him of wrongdoing, he slowly shook his head no and looked away. He said nothing during the meeting and when asked to contribute to the conversation replied, "No sir, I really can't defend myself." He then refused to elaborate on his statement. As the mother and son left my office, the boy turned toward me, shook my hand, and whispered, "She's crazy, you know!"

The next day I called the high school and talked with the principal. We discussed the young man who was in my office the previous day, accused by his mother of being Damion of *Omen II*. The principal filled me in on the young man. He was extremely intelligent, currently carrying a 4.6 grade point average. He got along with all of his teachers and had never been a discipline problem. He was most likely going to be the class valedictorian and was planning to attend Harvard University when he graduated.

I was starting to have real doubts about the mother's credibility and the validity of her claims. The boy had never been in trouble with the law and seemed to possess all of the qualities of a well-trained child. I decided to call the mother and get more information. The mother immediately indicated that she knew I didn't believe that her son was dangerous. I suggested to the mother that she purchase a small microcassette recorder and carry it with her at all times. When her son became violent, she should push the record button. She should then call me at her earliest convenience and forward the tape to me.

It was less than a week later that I got a call from the mother. She indicated that she wanted to bring a tape in for me to hear. She was in my office shortly thereafter and set the little recorder on my desk. When she pushed the play button, I was shocked when I heard the boy using profane language toward his mother, calling her stupid and ignorant, and threatening to kill her if she reported his antics to the police department. When the mother had attempted to turn off the computer at midnight, the boy grabbed her arms and twisted them, forcing her onto the floor. The resulting conversation was convincing evidence that the mother was living in constant fear of her son. The mother was relieved that I finally believed her. The recorder had done the trick. Furthermore, the mother indicated that while the recorder was running, she felt less afraid than she had in the past, knowing that the entire incident was being taped.

I can attest to the fact that knowing your argument is being recorded gives a sense of "peace" and reduces the level of anxiety. Before I installed a video camera in my police cruiser in 1987, I found myself getting extremely upset when a traffic violator would argue his/her case with me. I personally observed the traffic light turn red and observed the violator drive through the intersection a few seconds later. How dare the motorist call me a liar! How dare he tell me to buy myself a new pair of glasses! How dare he call me that name! You're the moron, mister, not me! How would you like to go to jail? What's that you said? I told you once to quit running your mouth, now you can get out of the car! Why? Because you're under arrest for disorderly conduct, that's why!

After the video camera was installed on the dashboard of my cruiser along with a wireless microphone worn in my pocket to pick up all of the interesting conversation, arguments with motorists took on a whole new angle. The first time I recorded a confrontation with a traffic violator, I actually found it humorous. I suppose the smile on my face didn't make matters easier for him because he kept getting louder and more vulgar. I patiently listened to his verbal assault, glancing at the little microphone on my lapel, hoping it was picking up every word. His reference to me as one of the less intelligent members of the animal kingdom caused me to chuckle. He looked at me with eyes slit. "You really think this is funny, don't you?" he said. I answered calmly, "No sir, I think you are making a complete fool of yourself. Are you finished?"

Watching a replay of the tape at roll call the next day brought thunderous laughter from the other officers. "Man," one of them said, "I would have pulled him right out of that car! How in the world did you keep your cool?" It was then that I realized that while that confrontation was taking place, I was documenting every word for others to hear. The judge would actually see and hear what the traffic stop was like. When Victor Violator showed up in court acting like the epitome of politeness, his story would be blown out of the water when the judge saw the tape. While the argument was taking place, I felt none of the anger that I had experienced in the past under similar circumstances. The fact that I was documenting the whole thing gave me the "peace" I needed to control my own temper.

When parents are recording the out-of-control behavior of their child, they find that their anger, which is usually impossible to control, is lessened. They find themselves remarkably in control of their emotions. If the parent does need to use force, like restraining the youngster when he is ready to leave the house at midnight, the parent has documentation as to why that action needed to be taken. The parent can verbalize clues that can be useful later, such as, "It's midnight and you have school tomorrow. I am forbidding you to leave this house." If the child defies the parent, the recorder picks it all up to be used against the child in future court proceedings.

Black and White

Have you ever had the opportunity as a parent to give your child an order knowing full well that he is going to do exactly as you told him, not what you meant. If there was one thing that frustrated me with my own children was the necessity to explain, down to the smallest details, what I expected them to do. For instance, if I were to ask one of them to vacuum the living room before our company arrived, they just might vacuum the carpet like you requested. Then the doorbell rings, you rush to answer the door and trip over the hoover, which is sitting in the middle of the floor. You spot the fireplace tools balancing precariously on the coffee table, and you notice that the newspaper basket and all of the throw rugs are still piled on the couch, where they were placed in order to vacuum the carpet under it. As your guests wait patiently at the door repeatedly ringing your doorbell, you shove the hoover in the closet, put the throw rugs back down in front of the fireplace along with the fireplace tools, and toss the basket behind the Lazy-Boy. Shame on you that you were not more specific in your instruction. You forgot to tell the boy to vacuum *plus* put things back.

I would suggest that in order to make life less confusing, put it in writing. If chores are a part of your child's activities, list them and post them where they can be reviewed. If your teenager is to be home by midnight on weekends and ten o'clock P.M. on weekdays, then type it out and post it. Make it black and white. For a task that needs to be completed in a certain amount of time, set a time limit. For those kids who are too slow to get out of their own way, that's the only way of ensuring the job gets done. To instruct the child to simply "vacuum the living room" can result in the living room getting vacuumed, maybe by bedtime. It is much more effective to have posted on the refrigerator "Vacuum the entire living room carpet, replace all items removed from the carpet, and complete by 4:30 P.M." It helps to put the consequence for failing to perform this task in writing also. "Failure to complete this chore in the allotted time will result in dish washing duty after dinner." If the child doesn't want to do the dinner dishes, vacuuming the living room in the proper manner appears more attractive. If the parent is consistent with the enforcement, it works.

Being consistent in enforcing the rules is extremely important. Bob Reitman uses "the airplane reservation" story when he speaks to parents about enforcing rules that require promptness. When your child is to be home at midnight and he walks in the door at 12:10 A.M. with his hands dirty from changing a flat tire, do you change the consequence? Reitman believes that teenagers should learn lessons that will apply to them in real life. He got the crowd laughing as he pretended to make a cellular telephone call. "Hello. Is this American Airlines? Hey, I am scheduled on a flight to Mexico at noon, but I have a flat tire and I'll be a little late. Can you hold the plane?" Point well made.

I Can't Do It Alone

One of the most frustrating situations encountered by law enforcement officers is the victim who refuses to take action against the offender. Before Ohio instituted the "preferred arrest" policy for domestic violence offenses, officers would respond to a family free-for-all and find the wife with two black eyes and bleeding from the nose. Unable to make an arrest without the cooperation of the victim, many officers were sent on their way because of the reluctance of the wife to pursue charges.

Whether it was from fear of retaliation or the uncertainty of a future without hubby, beaten and abused wives were dying all over this country because they refused to charge their husbands with domestic violence and have them arrested. Any person in law enforcement will tell you that this type of behavior doesn't stop by itself. It escalates to the point where the assault doesn't stop with a punch to the head. The assaults become more frequent and more serious as time goes on. I recall one couple who engaged in the weekend ritual of "beat the little woman." The husband got drunk every weekend and pummeled his wife with his fists. We would get the call from neighbors and respond to the residence. One evening, as I talked to the bleeding wife, she explained why she would not sign the charge against her husband. "I can't do it alone," she said.

The preferred arrest policy changed all that. When Ohio decided that wives were unable to "do it alone," a law was passed that enabled police officers to arrest the primary aggressor of a domestic violence offense without the cooperation of the victim. When the officers showed up at a family fight, usually called in by a neighbor, whoever appeared to have started the assault or was the primary aggressor in the altercation was taken to jail. There is no bond available, so Bobby Boxer can't return home to retaliate against the spouse. The victim, usually the wife, could now say, "I'm really sorry, honey, if I had my choice you wouldn't have gone to jail, but I had nothing to do with it." Women soon found out that the *fear* of going to jail changed their husband's behavior. Wives soon discovered that the way to stop their husband from using them as a punching bag was to offer a negative consequence. Husbands soon found out that the second time they got arrested, the offense was classified as a felony.

Parents occasionally need help to bring their children under control. Some parents, especially single moms, can't always "do it alone." Those parents need someone else to be the "bad guy." That bad guy should be one who already has some authority over the child. It can be a relative, like grandpa or Uncle Joe. It can be a member of the educational system, like the school principal or a teacher. It can be someone from a local church, like a minister or priest. It can be a member of the police department, like the juvenile detective or a patrolman in your area who is familiar with your case. No matter what the size of your community, parents have many resources at their fingertips. Although my workload is tremendous, I have never turned down a parent who has requested special attention to a child.

Some parents need someone else to play the tough role. It is important for children to understand that if they get out of line, they won't necessarily only get in trouble with mom or dad. If the juvenile officer has stated unequivocally that he will file the charge of unruly in juvenile court if the child runs away one more time whether or not mom agrees, that can act as a deterrent. Most children know how far they can push the parent, and by the time children are twelve or thirteen, they know whether or not mom will follow through on her promise. If the child is certain that mom will not follow through, the certainty of what the juvenile officer will do may deter the action considered by the child.

James Robertson, the intake manager of the southwest branch of juvenile court, processes each of Detective Surgenor's juvenile charges.

Hester and Venita, two of the secretaries for juvenile court who direct all of the calls for the southwest branch.

It's Alright, Honey!

Another frustrating part of my job is dealing with the enabler. These are parents who constantly cover up for their children's mistakes. They fix the damage caused by the child and offer no consequences when the child does something wrong. I learned shortly after being assigned to the juvenile crime unit that this type of behavior by the parent can be extremely destructive to the child.

I once dealt with a single mother whose young teenage boy (we'll call him Matthew Miller) was starting to get into trouble. His first criminal offense at thirteen years old was shoplifting. Because he had no prior criminal record, he was recommended for our city's diversion program. This program gave first-time offenders the opportunity to perform community service instead of going to juvenile court. If the offender successfully completed the community service, the charge was dropped. The program works for some and not for others. The deciding factor is usually how the parent approaches the offense and how they handle the situation in the home. I found out quickly that this mother was an enabler. Instead of teaching her children that there are negative consequences to negative behavior, she attempted to "fix" everything.

I next had contact with this mother when her sixteen-year-old daughter stole her checkbook, wrote checks to herself totaling almost five hundred dollars, and forged her mother's name to them in order to get them cashed. When the mother called me to make a report, she requested that I not file charges against her daughter in juvenile court. I then asked the mother why she was even bothering to file a criminal offense report if she did not intend on pursuing the offense. Mama Miller explained that the bank had agreed to reimburse her for the missing money from her account, even though it was stolen by her own daughter, as long as the mother filed a report with the police department to make it official. I double checked with the bank to make sure that the mother wasn't trying to pull a fast one on me, and sure enough, the bank was willing to replace the "stolen" money. What was mom going to do with the daughter who was so considerate of her mother that she ripped her off while her back was turned? Mama Miller's answer to that question was, "What can I do?"

Less than one month later, I received a tip that her son (the shoplifter/diversion youngster) had stolen an item from a local music store and was keeping it hooked up to his amplifier in his bedroom.

Based on that information, I considered getting a search warrant for the Miller home. Instead, I decided to call Mama Miller and advise her of the information I had received. Mom seemed shocked that her Matthew would actually steal anything from the local music store since he spent a lot of time and money at the place because of his involvement with his rock band. I supplied mom with a description of the stolen item along with the serial number. She assured me that she would look for the item and get back to me.

She called me two days later to advise me that she had searched the entire house, including her sticky fingered son's bedroom, and had come up empty. I thanked her for her cooperation and decided that the information I had received was possibly incorrect. Silly me! That was the first and last time I trusted a parent to nail his/her kid to the wall. About one week later, the stolen item was hand delivered to me at the police station. It seems that Matthew Miller started feeling the heat and decided to unload the hot item before he got caught with it. He got the word out in school that he had the item for sale. A young man who knew the music store owner decided to try to retrieve it. When Matthew sold it to him, he stated, "My mom said I had to get this thing out of the house before the police found it." Not only did Matthew get charged with the theft of the item, mom got charged with obstructing official business for lying to the police about the stolen item being in her house.

For those parents who feel that they are doing their child a favor by helping them elude the consequences of the law, guess again. Parents who cover up for their child's violations of the law are doing their child a great disservice. Although parents feel that they are protecting their child from danger, they are teaching them that they can violate the law and then depend on mom or dad to "undo" the wrong. I am pleased to hear stories about parents who drag their kid back to a store after realizing that the child took something without paying. I have had parents who have called our department and requested that an officer respond to their home because they found something illegal in the child's possession. Whether it be marijuana or something the child shoplifted, the child will soon realize that his parents will not only impose their own consequence but will also be subject to the law of the land and any consequence that the court deems necessary. Remember, the *fear* of the consequence deters further action. If you don't want your child to violate the law, make sure he is subject to the legal consequences.

Step Syndrome

One issue that needs to be discussed in this chapter is something I call the "Step Syndrome." With the divorce rate hovering around fifty percent in this country and many children suddenly being thrust into a second marriage where they receive a new "non-bio-parent," the problem is becoming more prevalent. Although I did not understand this problem years ago, I suddenly realized when I remarried and inherited two stepsons that the relationship between stepparents and stepchildren is a difficult one. When I was dating the woman who is now my wife, the relationship between myself and her sons was uncomplicated and simple. I had no authority over them, and they lived under their mother's roof. She was their ultimate authority.

Suddenly, a man whom they have known for a very small percentage of their lives becomes another boss that they have to deal with. The average child has enough trouble dealing with the restrictions placed on them by their biological parents, let alone a person who has no biological connection to them at all. Many children have problems with grandpa and grandma telling them what to do, and they were the people who bossed mom or dad around for years. There's no way that mom's new husband is going to tell them what to do.

What most kids don't realize is that the new stepparent has married into a complete package of new liabilities. Even though the new dad or mom did not have anything to do with the decision to bring the child into this world, they have now decided to assume the responsibilities that the natural parent should have.

Do you think that the child will understand this and accept it unconditionally? Not on your life! There is something unnatural about a nonbiological parent barking orders. It seems that no matter how hard one tries, one will never get children to respond to the authority of a stepparent as willingly as they respond to their biological parents. Children may not even understand why they are reacting the way they are, they just know that they don't want to be ordered around by a stranger.

Does that mean that the stepparents don't make any decisions at all about their new child's behavior? That is not what I'm suggesting. A stepparent must try to understand the complications involved in a new marriage that include children. Most adults feel that children should be submissive. The new father understands that he is now liable for the child's actions. The new parent understands that he could lose everything he owns because his stepchild messes up. Don't expect the child to understand that.

After I married Nancy, I soon realized that the relationship between myself and her two sons changed. Although I tried very hard not to be the heavy, if mom was working late and the chores weren't done, it was up to me to encourage them to get them done. I started noticing the glares and the slight resistance to my authority. The boys felt deep down inside that I shouldn't be allowed to tell them what to do. Who was I anyway?

Then the oldest boy got his driver's license. He was placed on our insurance policy, and for the first few months of his driving experience he was given strict restrictions on his driving freedom. He was to advise us where he was going and was to go nowhere else without permission. There was to be nobody else in the car with him when he was driving. He was restricted to using the car for transportation to and from work and school events. That was it.

The day after he was allowed to use the car to drive to a school swim meet, I got in the car and started driving down the street. Hearing a noise I wasn't used to hearing, I discovered the driver's side rear window was rolled down about one half inch. Being the detective that I am, I made several deductions. The boy didn't roll down the rear window from the front seat. Someone else did. Since the right front passenger seat would be the first seat chosen by a single rider, that meant that at least two other people were in the car with the boy the prior night. He had violated the rule of no passengers in the car while he was using it.

What he didn't realize was that the liability coverage that we had on the insurance policy was limited. If he were to cause an accident that severely injured or killed the occupants of the vehicle he was driving, there was a chance that his mother and I would end up paying for damages over and above those covered by our insurance policy. Since his mother and I were now married and "what's hers was mine and what's mine was hers," the boy's failure to follow instruction could result in us losing everything we owned, much of which I had worked for all of my life. I was willing to take on the responsibility of Nancy's son until he was eighteen years old. But I also needed some authority to enforce the rules. I could very easily lose my home because of the actions of the boy. I therefore need to have the authority to control his behavior.

It is extremely important for the stepchild to understand this liability and authority connection. Remember, responsibility without authority is futility. But the parent must remember that authority without responsibility is tyranny. The stepparent must also understand that the child will always have difficulty accepting the new parent's authority and may never understand it completely. When making important discipline decisions, it is wise for the biological parent to state the demands and impose the consequences. The parents should never let the stepparent's authority be defied, but every effort should be made to reduce the chance that the stepparent appears to be the sole enforcer in important discipline decisions.

Doing It Alone

More difficult than the stepparent syndrome is the single-parent syndrome. According to the U.S. Bureau of the Census, there has been a 200 percent growth in single-parent households since 1970. That number rose from four million homes to eight million homes. An alarming statistic is one released by the F.B.I. Uniform Crime Reports that says an estimated 70 percent of juvenile offenders come from single-parent families. The overwhelming majority of single-parent households are headed by the mother. Single mothers are usually forced to go to work outside the home. According to the U.S. Bureau of Labor Statistics, the number of married moms leaving home for work each morning rose 65 percent from 10.2 million in 1970 to 16.8 million in 1990. The number for single or divorced moms is much higher.

Feminists can say what they wish, but they will never be able to convince me that there are not major differences between men and women—physically, psychologically, and emotionally. I have dealt for years with single-parent families. Most of the kids who I see getting into trouble come from single-parent homes headed by mothers. Those kids tend to be less respectful of authority and harder to control. On the other hand, the single-mom kids tend to be more forgiving and compassionate. They tend to end up with a liberal outlook on life. Why is this? It seems to be because women tend to be more forgiving and less strict about following the rules. Yes, there are exceptions to the rule, but most moms are weak when it comes to being tough. Unfortunately, feminists have tried to make women think that they are capable of anything that a man is capable of, including being as tough. Then when mom finds it more difficult to play the tough role, she feels inadequate, when the way she is reacting is normal.

I see much less of those kids who are raised in single-parent households where the father is the head. On occasion I will be handed a case that involves a dad trying to rear his children on his own. I have noticed a marked difference in the attitude of those children being raised by dad. Most are much more respectful of authority. I believe this is the "fear" factor caused by a parent who is capable of being a stronger disciplinarian than his female counterpart. On the other hand, those children reared in homes with no mothers are less loving and compassionate. Although there are exceptions, most fathers use corporal punishment when disciplining their children. Most single mothers do not.

Just recently there was a news story on television that demonstrated one of the major differences between men and women. The story included a videotape of a shooting in a city's council chambers. The tape showed six members of council standing in the room talking. Three were men and three were women. An angry citizen, obviously upset with city council, walked into the room while the videotape was rolling, and pulled a gun. As he cranked off a round at the council president, the reaction of the three women was to scream and run away from the gunman. The three men immediately rushed the gunman and wrestled him to the ground, taking the gun from his hand. Were the three men specially trained to deal with a crazed gunman? No. It is part of a man's nature to be aggressive. It is also part of a woman's nature to be more nurturing than a man. In today's society, that balance is missing in many of our youth because one of the parents is not in the home to contribute that influence.

I feel compassion for a single mother who, for one reason or another, is left to rear her children on her own. She doesn't have the luxury of telling her children, "Wait till your father gets home." She must play the role of nurturer and the role of disciplinarian. I have encouraged single mothers to employ the assistance of male members of her family to assist her in the rearing of her children. Whether it be a brother, her father, or a cousin, the influence of a male in the child's life is extremely important. If mom can call "Uncle Fred" when junior starts to defy the rules, she gets the support of a male member of the family who can step in and play the role of the tough guy—something that is needed to maintain the fear factor in the children. Before Nancy married me, she depended a great deal on her three brothers to provide that male influence in her two sons' lives. Although she used corporal punishment when rearing her boys on her own, the uncles provided an additional factor to keep their nephews from stepping over the line. The fear of consequences helped shape them into the respectful boys they are today.

Evicted

When a child reaches the age of emancipation, in most states eighteen years of age, the parent is no longer liable for the actions of that child. The parent can no longer be sued for any damages caused by the child and cannot be held accountable for any of the child's decisions. The parent is also no longer obligated to provide a "duty of care, protection, or support." Former juveniles, now adults, can be ordered to leave the home. They do not have the right to take any property with them; they can be forced to leave only with the clothes on their back. In most states, if the young adult refuses to leave, the police can be called and the subject arrested. To trespass or remain on the land or property of the owner without the owner's consent is considered criminal trespass.

I have very seldom encountered parents who are willing to take such drastic action against their own child. Unless the circumstances are extremely volatile and the parent is extremely angry, most parents find it difficult to push the young bird over the edge of the nest to "fly or die." But this is an option that most parents must be aware of. If the child is aware of the parents' authority to have him tossed out and the child believes that the parents are able to take that action, his behavior may change in order to prevent that eviction from occurring.

Trust Your Instincts

I could share thousands of situations where parents felt that they should follow a certain direction or take a certain type of action but did not because of something they had heard or read. Something that Bob Reitman pounds into every parent that he deals with is, "Does it make sense?" When I meet with families to discuss the law enforcement aspect of their problem, I also encourage them to do "what makes sense." When we look at society today there are so many things that are "nonsensical nit-wittery," we wonder where half the population's brains are. Parents come equipped with instincts that tell them what to do with their children. How in the world has mankind survived all of these years without "parenting classes"? I once attended a parenting class in our city out of curiosity. What I listened to was some of the most nonsense that I had ever heard.

If it makes sense, do it! There are times when common sense must prevail. If you are sitting in the counselor's office and he suggests something that makes no sense, tell him it makes no sense. Too often parents follow the advice of an "expert" knowing deep down inside that they are doing the wrong thing. Parents need to make the determination every time a decision is made about their child, "Does it make sense?"

There was a recent newspaper article in the Cleveland area that addressed the causes of school violence. All of us are concerned about recent school shootings and much of the violence that is occurring in the school environment. The reporter interviewed numerous "experts," from psychologists to ministers to police chiefs. From the very lengthy article, I found one bit of common sense. A local police chief stated,

> In the early seventies, when I was teaching, we were permitted to use corporal punishment. Remember when we were in school? I feared the reaction of my parents more than I did the school. Back then, you lived in fear that the teacher would call your parents. Then you'd really be in trouble. Since corporal punishment—and apparently, parental backbone—have gone the way of the dodo bird, what is a community to do?[1]

The police chief poses a good question. What does the community do when time-tested methods of rearing children go the way of the "dodo bird?" I have an answer. We, as a community, suffer the consequences. I am opposed to the theory that "it takes a village" to rear a child. There is one major flaw in that theory. What if the village is full of idiots? Then the village idiot is rearing your child! If parents depend on "experts" to tell them what to do with their children, their parental authority is going to disappear. I have only had one "discipline" conference in our local school system involving one of my own children. My young teenage daughter went to the school counselor to convey her concerns about not being allowed to do what her friends were allowed to do. She discovered that she could bring a family matter out into the open to be considered by an "expert." The school counselor called and requested a meeting to discuss this "crisis." I went along reluctantly and sat while the child and the counselor talked about her "feelings" and the restrictions placed on her by her father. When the counselor asked me if I was willing to compromise my position, I replied with an emphatic no. The counselor frowned and stated, "It appears what we have here are two very stubborn people, both of whom are not willing to give in." I'm sure my answer angered the counselor. "Yes," I said. "Fortunately, I'm the father and she's the daughter. I win!" I then took my daughter's hand and walked out of the "village idiot's" office.

Parents must realize that they are the best chance for their children. There is no one else in this world who knows more about those children than the parents who are rearing them. Our instincts often do not always reveal why we are feeling the way we are; we just know. I had a couple in my office with their son who looked like something out of the movie *Night of the Living Dead*. Wearing black baggy pants and a black heavy metal t-shirt, his white skin and black lipstick made him look like a zombie. His earrings and lip rings made him look like a sequin doll. I asked dad what he thought about his son's attire. Dad indicated that he didn't like it at all. I asked dad and mom why they allowed their son to dress that way. Donnie Death piped up, "Because they can't give me a reason why I shouldn't dress like this!"

Alright, it was time to wake up the brains. I probed the minds of mom and dad and put the zombie on the spot. "Why do you look the way you do?" I asked him. "Because I like it," he answered. Further prodding resulted in the boy admitting that he liked to dress this way because his friends also looked like death warmed over. I avoided the "If your friends jumped off a cliff" analogy, since it seldom made an impression on this type of individual. Instead, I educated mom and dad about their instinctive feelings. I explained that most people convey their attitude about society and life in general by the way they look. Dad smiled and nodded when I mentioned the long hair of the sixties. Remember how young men grew their hair down to the middle of their back. Do you remember why? It was to show everyone that we were not conforming to the rules and restrictions of our society. So here is your son, dressing like this, and your instincts are screaming at you telling you that normal people won't accept him looking like he is. He's dressing the way he is to transmit his defiance of the rules. The gothic look means something. The skinhead and neo-Nazi look means something. The skater look means something.

As for the ear/nose/lip/eyelid rings, they mean something also. Since the pharaohs of Egypt, cultures where the men wore earrings were defiant of any other authority. How about the pirates of the high seas? They recognized no other authority over them. The same with gypsies. Gypsy men wore earrings to convey an attitude to the rest of society. Those cultures failed to recognize any other authority above their own. When modern-day rebellious youth began to stick pins in their left ears, parents' instincts told them that it wasn't right. Yet after years of conditioning, more and more men are wearing earrings as a fashion statement. Think about it, do you see any policemen wearing earrings? Do you see mature male government officials wearing earrings? Most men you see wearing earrings are nonconformists who see a need to tell everyone "I'm a rebel." Parents who want to allow their child to display his defiance can ignore the baggy pants hanging off the child's rear end. Parents who are fed up with their children publicly announcing their displeasure with our society can confiscate the offensive clothing and throw it in the trash. If parents wish to keep their child from embarrassing them, they have the right to insist that the child dress in a normal fashion. Go ahead, ask me what normal is. It's what the parents' common sense tells them it is.

Peer Fear

When I look back at the advice I gave my children as they were growing up, there is one subject that I found later in life was easier to preach than practice. Although I remember the fear of rejection when I was young and I recall my desire to be accepted by others my age, I considered myself a strong individual as an adult who was able to voice my convictions without fear of ridicule and to stand up for what I believed. I tried very hard to instill in my children the ability to resist peer pressure and to do what they wanted to do instead of what others wanted them to do.

When I joined the police department, I knew very little about the police community. I perceived police officers as bigger than life. I had always thought of policemen as strong robot-like creatures who had little emotion and a great deal of wisdom. When I was shipped off to the police academy, I wondered if I would ever fit into the police family. I wondered if I would ever measure up.

When I graduated from the academy and showed up in the squad room for my first shift of crime fighting, I recognized the looks of uncertainty amongst the veterans on the department. I tried hard to keep the new leather gun belt from squeaking too loud as I sat down for my first roll call. When the shift sergeant assigned me to another officer I knew only as "Rooster," I saw the look of disgust on his face and heard him say, "Oh no!" I learned very early to keep my mouth shut and take lots of notes. I was trying very hard to fit in and be accepted by my fellow officers.

I enjoyed second shift most. I enjoyed sleeping in and not having to be at work until three o'clock P.M. Most people were out during the evening hours, and at eleven o'clock P.M., it was nice to drive home, fix some supper, watch some late-night television, tuck the three kids in bed, and relax. I enjoyed my home and looked forward to getting there after an exciting day in the police cruiser.

One evening after a busy day of arrests and traffic tickets, I sat back at debriefing and loosened my gun belt. I was looking forward to my dinner at home and relaxing in the recliner while I watched a late night movie. Then one of the other officers on my shift popped the question. "Hey Bob, do you want to come on down to the Eastland Inn with us and have a few?"

Do you think that perhaps I succumbed to peer pressure? Do you think that perhaps I went along with the rest of the shift when I would have rather gone home? Do you think that perhaps I did something that I didn't want to do in order to be accepted by others? Of course I did! My desire to be accepted by the other police officers on the department was more important to me than I had realized. When placed in the situation where acceptance by others is paramount, most people will succumb to the pressure and even abandon what they believe is right in order to gain that acceptance.

Face it, parents, your children are even weaker than you are. They have a fear of rejection and an intense need to be accepted by their peers. Your children will violate their own moral code in order to be accepted by their friends. How do you keep your child from committing crimes in order to be accepted by friends? Keep your child from associating with the criminal element. How do you keep your child from shoplifting in order to be accepted by their friends. Keep your child from associating with the shoplifting crowd. How do you keep your child from taking drugs in order to be accepted by friends. Keep your child from associating with the drug crowd. But, how do you find out what type of friends your child is associating with?

There are two main sources of information for the parent. First, the officer in the local police department who is in charge of the juvenile unit is a wealth of information. Most police officers are familiar with the kind of kids you don't want your son or daughter to be hanging around with. Most juvenile officers will offer that information to the concerned parent who is trying to keep their child out of trouble. The second source is the teacher and administrator in your local school system. Ask any teacher which kids are bad news, and you'll get a list of undesirables. Teachers have no problem advising parents of their children's acquaintances and whether or not they are hanging with the wrong crowd.

When a parent does discover that their child is associating with a known drug user, or someone who has a reputation for shoplifting, or is sexually active, or just has an in-your-face attitude, then it is the responsibility of the parent to dissolve the relationship. Keeping your child away from those who can influence your child's behavior in a negative way is extremely important. Remember, adults succumb to peer pressure. Keep your child out of the situation where they have to resist every temptation to do wrong by limiting the chances that those temptations will arise. Keep your child away from bad kids.

Parents have the authority to keep another juvenile from associating with their child. Remember, the child who disobeys his or her parents is an unruly child. If the parent orders the child to stay away from Sammy Shoplifter, then the child must comply with the wishes of the parent. I encourage parents who are meeting with resistance from their child to take control and make the restriction official. I suggest that the parent mail a certified letter to the parent or guardian of the undesirable associate and advise them that you will no longer tolerate Sammy Shoplifter being near your son or daughter. Advise the parents of the young criminal that if he continues to associate with your child, he is contributing to your child's unruliness, which the law addresses specifically. If he doesn't lay off, you will charge him with contributing to the unruliness of a child, namely yours. I have found this method extremely effective when attempting to control the types of influences in your child's life.

Live the Life

Are you living the kind of life that you want your child to live? An area of conversation that is inevitable with families in my office is the "practice what you preach" accusation. Face it, parents. The way you live says more to your children than anything you can say. I have a sign hanging in my office. The sign reads, "You are acting so loudly, I can't hear what you are saying." I have it hanging right where parents can see it. It simply means that there is nothing you can do to impress your children more than the way you live.

When I was a child, I vividly remember my father being given too much change by a cashier in a store. My father carefully recounted the change, separated the extra, and handed it back to the clerk. "You gave me too much money back," he said. I remember the look of amazement on the clerk's face as she thanked him. She went on to say that she was responsible for any shortage in the cash drawer at the end of her shift. My dad had actually saved her some money. I remember being proud to be with my father on that occasion. Then again, there were times when I didn't appreciate my parents' quest for total honesty. I recall a friend who I was trying to avoid kept calling my house to talk to me. My mother answered the telephone. As I frantically motioned to her that I was not home, she answered, "Yes, he's here. Hold on a minute." After my conversation was over, I asked my mom why she told my friend I was home. "I'm not going to lie about anything," was her reply. I never doubted that my parents were ever telling me anything but the truth.

I carried that philosophy over into my own life. I tried very hard to teach my children the values that I held important. We all make mistakes as parents, and sometimes I found myself doing something in front of my kids that I later regretted. They were simple things, like exceeding the speed limit while off duty, knowing I would probably not be ticketed. I remember my son asking, "Are you allowed to go fast because you are a policeman, dad?" I then realized that my children were watching everything I did. I didn't bother to tell them that I had been trained to drive fast and had even been to a high speed pursuit racing school. That didn't exempt me from the law.

When I wasn't making irresponsible mistakes, I was making an effort to teach them two major ideals. The first and most important was respect for authority. The way I instilled that into their souls was to offer quick and severe consequences for a defiant act. The second ideal that I attempted to teach my children was honesty. There were also stinging consequences for a dishonest act, but the way I lived in front of them reinforced their thinking. I believe that these are the two most important qualities that a human being can possess. An honest person who respects authority will go further in this world than a lying thief. Ask any employer.

There is a difference between the way parents lived years ago as a child or young adult and the way they are living at the present time. Many times I have had teenagers argue that their parents cannot criticize them for a certain behavior because the parents acted the same way when they were young. Phooey! Does that mean that a reformed drug addict can't recommend to his son that he shouldn't take drugs? He's been there and done that. He knows better than anyone else what the consequences of addiction are. He's in a better position to counsel his son than a father who has never tried drugs.

But the parent who is taking drugs today finds it extremely difficult to advise his children not to take drugs. For those parents who smoke cigarettes, don't expect to make a big impact on your child when you find that pack of Winstons in his book bag. And for those parents who drink on a regular basis and spend the majority of their time in an intoxicated state, don't expect to get much respect from your child when you find the bottle of Mad Dog 20-20 in a dresser drawer.

Do you cheat on your income tax? Do you manufacture deductions that don't exist? Do you return the extra change to the cashier? Do you deliberately violate traffic laws when your children are in the car? Do you lie to your children? Do you lie for your children? Do you tell the person on the telephone that your child is not home when he's standing right near you? Do you call in sick to work when you are not really sick? Do you treat your spouse with respect? Do you treat your parents with respect? If so, I'm sorry, but you are acting so loudly that I cannot hear what you are saying!

Epilogue

There are those who, after digesting the information contained in these pages, will change their approach to child rearing. I doubt this book will change the minds of those parents who have felt all along that spanking harms a child. For them, it will take an out-of-control teenager to make them reevaluate their method of discipline. I do believe that there are millions of parents who believe that corporal punishment is a valuable disciplinary tool but hesitate to spank their child because an "expert" has told them that it is harmful or that they will be arrested for child abuse. There are thousands of Christians who hesitate to follow God's plan of child discipline due to the doubt placed in their minds by the nonspanking advocate. It is those parents who will recognize the "common sense" contained herein and realize that the wisdom of Solomon and the word of God far outweighs the theory of modern-day psychology.

Today's generation of teenagers and adolescents have an attitude that has not been common in our past. Kids today have "no fear" of consequences for negative behavior. Any person who has been alive for any length of time has recognized that difference in attitude during the recent generation. Kids today are taunting adults in the shopping malls—something that was rare years ago. Kids today are swearing at their school teachers—something that teachers will tell you was unheard of thirty years ago. Kids today are assaulting their parents— something that was never tolerated fifty years ago. Yet today, the frequency of such behavior is increasing at an alarming rate.

We've read how today's "experts" claim that spanking a child causes them to grow up angry and aggressive. Psychologists are "teaching" us that if a parent spanks a child, that child will eventually turn on the parent in violent ways. For those of you who were spanked by your parents, have you ever beat up your mother? In my city, children committing domestic violence offenses against their parents has increased by 700 percent over the past ten years. Is that because more parents are spanking their children now than in the past? No. The opposite is true. In my city, of the juveniles arrested for assaulting their parents, less than 2 percent were spanked as youngsters. Yet psychologists continue to try to convince parents that spanking produces violent children.

Today's "experts" are claiming that spanking children is counterproductive and causes the child to indulge in criminal activity as they grow older. Yet, as parents spank their children less, the juvenile crime rate continues to rise. The F.B.I.'s Uniform Crime Reports show that murders committed by children increased from 1,175 in 1983 to 2,982 in 1994, an increase of over 153 percent. During that same time period, adults committing murders went from 14,260 to 14,675, an increase of only 10 percent. Can the increase in murders committed by children be attributed to more kids being spanked? Not on your life! Domestic violence offenses committed nationwide by juveniles between 1983 and 1997 has increased by 348 percent. Are more kids hitting their parents because more parents are spanking their kids? No. The opposite is true.

We have been offered alternative forms of discipline by the "experts." Remember the doctor who suggested that we "change the mood" when the willful child gets out of hand. Common sense should tell us that a spanking is in order when an eight-year-old defiant child screams at his mother and attempts to assault her. The expert suggests that the parent balance a toy on her head. Common sense?

What would have happened to us when we were children if we were told to go to bed, now, and we had refused? The "expert" suggests that when a child refuses to go to bed, when he flagrantly defies mom or dad's authority and states that he is *not* going to do what he is told, the parent should make him promise he will go to bed earlier on another night of his choice. Common sense?

Then there are those "experts" who suggest that when a child misbehaves, the parent should ignore it and look away. Remember when you were small and you did something you knew was wrong and you realized that dad was looking right at you? The only reason dad would look away was to look for the location of the belt. If parents fall for this "expert" advice, then common sense has truly gone the way of the dodo bird. It is the responsibility of parents to instill in their child the connection between negative behavior and negative consequences. To "look away" is to abandon that parental responsibility.

"Experts" contend that the self-esteem of the child is paramount. We are being told that we should never make our children feel "bad." So when the child spray paints vulgar graffiti on the wall, we should not admonish him for vandalizing the property; instead, we should commend him for spelling the obscenities correctly. From outcome-based education to restrictions on the way we discipline our children, our culture has placed more emphasis on individual feelings and self-esteem than on society as a whole. We have sacrificed courtesy and respect for a feeling of self-worth, whether or not it is deserved.

We've learned that although nonspanking advocates profess to be knowledgeable in biblical facts, *they are not.* The nonspanking "experts" claim that Christians are confused when interpreting scriptures that pertain to corporal punishment. However, those who claim that spanking is harmful to the child are referred to by God as "natural," who "receiveth not [rejects] the things of the Spirit of God [the Scriptures]: for they [the Scriptures] are foolishness unto him: neither can he know them, because they are spiritually discerned" (1 Corinthians 2:14). The Bible clearly advocates corporal punishment in the upbringing of our children. Those that try to discredit the Bible are trying to discredit God.

But then we've also learned that there is an overwhelming number of professionals who endorse spanking as a necessary part of child discipline. From Focus on the Family's Dr. James Dobson to Boston College's William Kilpatrick, from Dr. Diana Baumrind of the Institute of Human Development at the University of California to Dr. Henry Harbin and Dr. Denis Madden of the University of Maryland's Medical School, we find "common sense" experts who dispute the claims of those who suggest that spanking is harmful. These professionals have studied the results of the permissive parenting era and, not surprisingly, they have discovered what law enforcement and the courts have known for years. The lack of corporal punishment has resulted in a generation of kids with "no fear."

We've learned that it is never too late to change a child's behavior. An adult who is trained to react a certain way to certain stimuli does so without thinking. A police officer trained to shoot in a certain manner will do exactly as he was trained when under fire. Children who are conditioned as they grow up to react certain ways to certain circumstances will do so when they mature. God's word tells us in Proverbs

22:6, "Train up a child in the way he should go: and when he is old, he will not depart from it."

We've learned that when the child abuse laws were written, legislators were careful not to remove all of the parents' authority to use corporal punishment in the discipline of their child. In most states, the law protects the parent who wishes to do so. Parents who have a knowledge of the law can defend themselves when accused of abuse by investigators. When the social worker says, "You can't do that," the parent can say, "The law says I can. What law are you referring to?"

We've learned that public school administrators and teachers encounter many of the same problems and frustrations as those of the parent. Most school administrators are pleased and relieved to know that you support their efforts to bring your child under control. Many times they will work with the parent to coordinate a plan of attack, as long as the parent accepts responsibility in attempting to control the child.

We've learned that there is always something that works. Children take everything in life for granted. My wife once said to her brother on the telephone, "You know, my kid has to be the most selfish, ungrateful person in the world." Her brother answered, "No he's not, my kid is!" Sometimes, it pays to hit them with a dose of reality. It's hard to take a shower in ice cold water and that consequence just might make them change their behavior. Maybe it's the child's dog that goes away until the child starts following the rules. Since the parent owns everything and the child owns nothing, the parent has every right to remove property from the home. Sometimes being left with nothing shocks the youngster into reality.

We've learned that sometimes it's necessary to ask for the help of others, as long as it isn't the village idiot. Relatives, with the biological connection, can lend a great deal of support if you let them. The staff at the child's school will offer their help if you just ask. And you won't have to ask the juvenile officer of your local police department twice to give you a hand. There is always the support of other Christians—those who also trust God to direct their way. All of these are no more than a telephone call away. But most importantly, we can turn to God's word. He has supplied us with "a lamp unto my feet and a light unto my path" (Psalms 119:105). We should strive to "receive the word with all readiness of mind, and search the scriptures daily, whether those things are so" (Acts 17:11). In the pages of God's word we will find guidance regarding our daily living, including the rearing of our children.

But the child's best hope is you, the parent. No matter what some of the experts say, a child knows when a parent is disciplining out of love. A child knows whether his parent is conveying love or hatred. A child knows that the reason he is being spanked is because mom and dad love him dearly and cannot allow him to act in such a negative manner. To allow your young child to defy your authority without swift and stinging consequences is inviting much larger problems years down the road. No matter what some of the experts say, attempting to rear your child "without fear" is laying the groundwork for a teenager who isn't afraid to flagrantly disobey your rules. To seek other forms of discipline rather than spanking when your four year old tells you "no," is guaranteeing that he will defy your authority when he's seventeen. King Solomon wrote, "He that spareth his rod, hateth his son" (Proverbs 13:24). For parents who love their children with all their hearts, it's time to trust the wisdom of Solomon and the infinite wisdom of God rather than the rhetoric of the village idiot.

Appendix

Although each state's child abuse laws are addressed here, it is impossible to include all statutes involved in the area of child abuse and parental authority. When the law refers to another section, limitations on space might prevent that section from being included in this text. It will, however, give you an idea of where to search for the law in your local library or legal website. Some laws pertaining to sexual abuse are not included, since there is no question that sexual acts involving or against children are abusive.

Alabama
26-14-1. Definitions.

For the purposes of this chapter, the following terms shall have the meanings respectively ascribed to them by this section:

(1) Abuse. Harm or threatened harm to a child's health or welfare. Harm or threatened harm to a child's health or welfare can occur through nonaccidental physical or mental injury, sexual abuse or attempted sexual abuse or sexual exploitation or attempted sexual exploitation.

(2) Neglect. Negligent treatment or maltreatment of a child, including the failure to provide adequate food, medical treatment, supervision, clothing or shelter.

(3) Child. A person under the age of 18 years.
26-14-7.2. Child denied medical treatment due to parents' religious beliefs.

When an investigation of child abuse or neglect by the Department of Human Resources determines that a parent or legal guardian legitimately practicing his or her religious beliefs has not provided specific medical treatment for a child, the parent or legal guardian shall not be considered a negligent parent or guardian for that reason alone. This exception shall not preclude a court from ordering that medical services be provided to the child when the child's health requires it.

Alaska
Sec. 11.51.100.

Endangering the welfare of a child in the first degree.

(a) A person commits the crime of endangering the welfare of a child in the first degree if, being a parent, guardian, or other person legally charged with the care of a child under 16 years of age, the person

(1) intentionally deserts the child in a place under circumstances creating a substantial risk of physical injury to the child;

(2) leaves the child with another person who is not the parent, guardian, or lawful custodian of the child knowing that the person

(A) is registered or required to register as a sex offender under AS 12.63 or a law or ordinance in another jurisdiction with similar requirements;

(B) has been charged by complaint, information, or indictment with a violation of AS 11.41.410 - 11.41.455 or a law or ordinance on another jurisdiction with similar elements; or

(C) has been charged by complaint, information, or indictment with an attempt, solicitation, or conspiracy to commit a crime described in (B) of this paragraph; or

(3) leaves the child with another person knowing that the person has previously physically mistreated or had sexual contact with any child, and the other person causes physical injury or engages in sexual contact with the child.

(b) In this section, "physically mis-treated" means

(1) having committed an act punishable under AS 11.41.100 - 11.41.250; or

(2) having applied force to a child that, under the circumstances in which it was applied, or

considering the age or physical condition of the child, constitutes a gross deviation from the standard of conduct that a reasonable person would observe in the situation because of the substantial and unjustifiable risk of

(A) death;

(B) serious or protracted disfigurement;

(C) protracted impairment of health;

(D) loss or impairment of the function of a body member or organ;

(E) substantial skin bruising, burning, or other skin injury;

(F) internal bleeding or subdural hematoma;

(G) bone fracture; or

(H) prolonged or extreme pain, swelling, or injury to soft tissue

(c) Endangering the welfare of a child in the first degree under (a)(1) or (2) of this section is a class C felony

(d) Endangering the welfare of a child in the first degree under (a)(3) of this section is a

(1) class B felony if the child dies;

(2) class C felony if the child suffers sexual contact, sexual penetration, or serious physical injury; or

(3) class A misdemeanor if the child suffers physical injury.

Arizona
8-201. Definitions.

In this title, unless the context otherwise requires:

1. "Abandoned" means the failure of the parent to provide reasonable support and to maintain regular contact with the child, including the providing of normal supervision. Abandoned includes a judicial finding that a parent has made only minimal efforts to support and communicate with the child. Failure to maintain a normal parental relationship with the child without just cause for a period of six months shall constitute prima facia evidence of abandonment.

2. "Abuse" means the infliction or allowing of physical injury, impairment of bodily function or disfigurement or the infliction of or allowing another person to cause serious emotional damage as evidenced by severe anxiety, depression, withdrawal or untoward aggressive behavior and which emotional damage is diagnosed by a medical doctor or psychologist pursuant to section 8-821 and which is caused by the acts or omissions of an individual having care, custody and control of a child.

6. "Child," "youth" or "juvenile" means any individual who is under the age of eighteen years.

20. "Neglect" or "neglected" means the inability or unwillingness of a parent, guardian or custodian of a child to provide that child with supervision, food, clothing, shelter or medical care if that inability or unwillingness causes substantial risk of harm to the child's health or welfare, except if the inability of a parent or guardian to provide services to meet the needs of a child with a disability or chronic illness is solely the result of the unavailability of reasonable services.

Arkansas
12-12-503. Definitions.

As used in this subchapter, unless the context otherwise requires:

(1) "Child" or "juvenile" means an individual who:

(A) Is under the age of eighteen (18) years;

(B) Is under the age of twenty-one (21) years; whether married or single, who was adjudicated delinquent under the Arkansas Juvenile Code § 9-27-301 et seq., for an act committed prior to the age of eighteen (18) years, and for whom the court retains jurisdiction; or

(C) Was adjudicated delinquent-neglected under the Arkansas Juvenile Code, § 9-27-301 et seq., before reaching the age of eighteen (18) years, and who, while engaged in a course of instruction or treatments, requests the court to retain jurisdiction until the course has been completed;

(3) "Child maltreatment" means abuse, sexual abuse, neglect, sexual exploitation, or abandonment;

(4)(A) "Abuse" means any of the following acts or omissions by a parent, guardian, custodian, foster parent, or any person who is entrusted with the juvenile's care by a parent, guardian, custodian, or foster parent, including, but not limited to, an agent or employee of a public or private residential home, child care facility, public or private school, or any person legally responsible for the juvenile's welfare:

(i) Extreme and repeated cruelty to a juvenile; or

(ii) Physical, psychological, or sexual abuse of any juvenile which includes, but is not limited to, intentionally, knowingly, or negligently and without justifiable cause:

(a) Engaging in conduct creating a substantial possibility of death, permanent or temporary disfigurement, illness, impairment of any bodily organ, or an observable and substantial impairment in the intellectual or psychological capacity of the juvenile to function within his normal range of performance and behavior with due regard to his culture;

(b) Any nonaccidental physical injury or mental injury; or

(c) Any injury which is at variance with the history given.

(B)(i) "Abuse" shall not include physical discipline of a child when it is reasonable and moderate and is inflicted by a parent or guardian for purposes of restraining or correcting the child.

(ii) The following actions are not reasonable or moderate when used to correct or restrain a child:

(a) Throwing, kicking, burning, biting, or cutting a child;

(b) Striking a child with a closed fist;

(c) Shaking a child under age three (3);

(d) Striking or other actions which result in any nonaccidental injury to a child under the age of eighteen (18) months;

(e) Interfering with a child's breathing;

(f) Threatening a child with a deadly weapon;

(g) Striking a child on the face; or

(h) Doing any other act that is likely to cause, and which does cause, bodily harm greater than transient pain or minor temporary marks.

(iii) The age, size, and condition of the child, and the location of the injury and the frequency or recurrence of injuries shall be considered when determining whether the bodily harm is reasonable or moderate.

(iv) This list is illustrative of unreasonable action and is not intended to be exclusive;

(6) "Neglect" means those acts or omissions of a parent, guardian, custodian, foster parent, or any person who is entrusted with the juvenile's care by a parent, custodian, guardian, or foster parent, including, but not limited to, an agent or employee of a public or private residential home, child care facility, public or private school, or any person legally responsible under state law for the juvenile's welfare, which constitute:

(A) Failure or refusal to prevent the abuse of the juvenile when such person knows or has reasonable cause to know the juvenile is or has been abused;

(B) Failure or refusal to provide the necessary food, clothing, shelter, and education required by law, or medical treatment necessary for the juvenile's well-being, except when the failure or refusal is caused primarily by the financial inability of the person legally responsible and no services for relief have been offered or rejected;

(C) Failure to take reasonable action to protect the juvenile from abandonment, abuse, sexual abuse, sexual exploitation, neglect, or parental unfitness where the existence of such condition was known or should have been known.

(D) Failure or irremediable inability to provide for the essential and necessary physical, mental, or emotional needs of the juvenile;

(E) Failure to provide for the juvenile's care and maintenance, proper or necessary support, or medical, surgical, or other necessary care; or

(F) Failure, although able, to assume responsibility for the care and custody of the juvenile or participate in a plan to assume such responsibility;

(10) "Severe maltreatment" means sexual abuse, sexual exploitation, acts or omissions which may or do result in death, abuse involving the use of a deadly weapon as defined by the Arkansas Criminal Code, § 5-1-101 et seq., bone fracture, internal injuries, burns, immersions, suffocation, abandonment, medical diagnosis of failure to thrive, or causing a substantial and observable change in the behavior or demeanor of the child;

(15) "Serious bodily injury" means bodily injury which involves substantial risk of death, extreme physical pain, protracted and obvious disfigurement, or protracted loss or impairment of the function of a bodily member, organ, or mental faculty.

California

Section 11165. Child.

As used in this section, "child" means a person under the age of 18 years.

Section 11165.2. Neglect; severe neglect; general neglect.

As used in this article, "neglect" means the negligent treatment or the maltreatment of a child by a person responsible for the child's welfare under circumstances indicating harm or threatened harm to the child's health or welfare. The term includes both acts and omissions on the part of the responsible person.

(a) "Severe neglect" means the negligent failure of a person having the care of custody of a child to protect the child from severe malnutrition or medically diagnosed nonorganic failure to thrive. "Severe neglect" also means those situations of neglect where any person having the care of custody of a child willfully causes or permits the person or health of the child to be placed in a situation such that his or her person or health is endangered, as proscribed by section 11165.3, including the intentional failure to provide adequate food, clothing, shelter, or medical care.

(b) "General neglect" means the negligent failure of a person having the care or custody of a child to provide adequate food, clothing, shelter, medical care, or supervision where no physical injury to the child has occurred.

Section 11165.3. Willful cruelty or unjustifiable punishment of a child.

As used in this article, "willful cruelty or unjustifiable punishment of a child" means a situation where any person willfully causes or permits any child to suffer, or inflicts thereon, unjustifiable physical pain or mental suffering, or having the care or custody of any child, willfully causes or permits the person or health of the child to be placed in a situation such that his or her person or health is endangered.

Section 11165.4. Unlawful corporal punishment or injury.

As used in this article, "unlawful corporal punishment or injury" means a situation where any person willfully inflicts upon any child any cruel or inhuman corporal punishment or injury resulting in a traumatic condition. It does not include an amount of force that is reasonable and necessary for a person employed by or engaged in a public school to quell a disturbance threatening physical injury to person or damage to property, for purposes of self-defense, or to obtain possession of weapons or other dangerous objects within the control of the pupil, as authorized by section 49001 of the Education Code. It does not include an amount of force that is reasonable and necessary for a peace officer to quell a disturbance threatening physical injury to person or damage to property to prevent physical injury to person or damage to property for purposes of self-defense, to obtain possession of weapons or other dangerous objects within the control of the child, or to apprehend an escapee.

Section 11165.6. Child abuse.

As used in this article, "child abuse" means a physical injury which is inflicted by other than accidental means on a child by another person. "Child abuse" also means the sexual abuse of a child or any act or omission proscribed by section 273a (willful cruelty or unjustifiable punishment of a child) or 273d (unlawful corporal punishment or injury). "Child abuse" also means the neglect of a child or abuse in out-of-home care, as defined in this article. "Child abuse" does not mean a mutual affray between minors. "Child abuse" does not include an injury caused by reasonable and necessary force used by a peace officer to quell   a disturbance threatening physical injury to person or damage to property to prevent physical injury to person or damage to property for purposes of self-defense, to obtain possession of weapons or other dangerous objects within the control of the child, or to apprehend an escapee.

Section 300. Minors subject to jurisdiction;

Any minor who comes within any of the following descriptions is within the jurisdiction of the juvenile court which may adjudge that person to be a dependent child of the court.

(a) The minor has suffered, or there is a substantial risk that the minor will suffer, serious physical harm inflicted nonaccidentally upon the minor by the minor's parent or guardian. For the purposes of this subdivision, a court may find there is substantial risk of serious future injury based on the manner in which a less serious injury was inflicted, a history of repeated inflictions of injuries on the minor or the minor's siblings, or a combination of these and other actions by the parent or

guardian which indicate the child is at risk of serious physical harm. For purposes of this subdivision, "serious physical harm" does not include reasonable and age appropriate spanking to the buttocks where there is no evidence of serious physical injury.

§ 273a. Willful harm or injury to child; endangering persons or health; punishment;

(a) Any person who, under circumstances or conditions likely to produce great bodily harm or death, willfully causes or permits any child to suffer, or inflicts thereon unjustifiable physical pain or mental suffering, or having the care or custody of any child, willfully causes or permits the person or health of that child to be injured, or willfully causes or permits that child to be placed in a situation where his or her person or health is endangered, shall be punished by imprisonment in a county jail not exceeding one year, or in a state prison for two, four, or six years.

(b) Any person who, under circumstances or conditions other than those likely to produce great bodily harm or death, willfully causes or permits any child to suffer, or inflicts thereon unjustifiable physical pain or mental suffering, or having the care or custody of any child, willfully causes or permits the person or health of that child to be injured, or willfully causes or permits that child to be placed in a situation where his or her person or health is endangered, is guilty of a misdemeanor.

Colorado

18-6-401. Child abuse.

(1) A person commits child abuse if such person causes an injury to a child's life or health, or permits a child to be unreasonably placed in a situation which poses a threat of injury to the child's life or health, or engages in a continued pattern of conduct which results in malnourishment, lack of proper medical care, cruel punishment, mistreatment, or an accumulation of injuries which ultimately results in the death of a child or serious bodily injury to a child.

(2) In this section, "child" means a person under the age of sixteen years.

(3) The statutory privilege between patient and physician and between husband and wife shall not be available for excluding or refusing testimony in any prosecution for a violation of this section.

(4) No person, other than the perpetrator, complicitor, coconspirator, or accessory, who reports an instance of child abuse to law enforcement officials shall be subjected to criminal or civil liability for any consequence of making such report unless he knows at the time of making it that it is untrue.

(5) Deferred prosecution is authorized for a first offense under this section unless the provisions

of subsection (7.5) of this section or section 18-6-401.2 apply.

(6) A parent, guardian, or legal custodian who chooses and legitimately practices treatment by spiritual means through prayer in accordance with section 19-3-103, C.R.S., shall not be considered to have injured or endangered the child and to be criminally liable under the laws of this state solely because he fails to provide medical treatment for the child, unless such person inhibits or interferes with the provision of medical treatment for the child in accordance with a court order, or unless there is an additional reason, other than health care, to consider the said child to be injured or endangered.

(7) (a) Where death or injury results, the following shall apply:

(I) When a person acts knowingly or recklessly and the child abuse results in death to the child, it is a class 2 felony except as provided in paragraph (c) of this subsection (7).

(II) When a person acts with criminal negligence and the child abuse results in death to the child, it is a class 3 felony.

(III) When a person acts knowingly or recklessly and the child abuse results in serious bodily injury to the child, it is a class 3 felony.

(IV) When a person acts with criminal negligence and the child abuse results in serious bodily injury to the child, it is a class 4 felony.

(V) When a person acts knowingly or recklessly and the child abuse results in any injury other than serious bodily injury, it is a class misdemeanor.

(VI) When a person acts with criminal negligence and the child abuse results in any injury other than serious bodily injury to the child, it is a class 2 misdemeanor.

(b) Where no death or injury results, the following shall apply:

(I) An act of child abuse when a person acts knowingly or recklessly is a class 2 misdemeanor.

(II) An act of child abuse when a person acts with criminal negligence is a class 3 misdemeanor.

(c) When a person knowingly causes the death of a child who has not yet attained twelve years of age and the person committing the offense is one in a position of trust with respect to the child, such person commits the crime of murder in the first degree as described in section 18-3-102 (1) (f).

(7.5) If a defendant is convicted of the class 2 or class 3 felony of child abuse under subparagraph (I) or (III) of paragraph (a) of subsection (7) of this section, the court shall sentence the defendant in accordance with section 18-1-105 (9) (d).

19-1-103. Definitions. As used in this title or in the specified portion of this title, unless the context otherwise requires:

(1) (a) "Abuse" or "child abuse or neglect," as used in part 3 of article 3 of this title, means an act or omission in one of the following categories that threatens the health or welfare of a child:

(I) Any case in which a child exhibits evidence of skin bruising, bleeding, malnutrition, failure to thrive, burns, fracture of any bone, subdural hematoma, soft tissue swelling, or death and either: Such condition or death is not justifiably explained; the history given concerning such condition is at variance with the degree or type of such condition or death; or the circumstances indicate that such condition may not be the product of an accidental occurrence;

(II) Any case in which a child is subjected to sexual assault or molestation, sexual exploitation, or prostitution;

(III) Any case in which a child is in need of services because the child's parents, legal guardian, or custodian fails to take the same actions to provide adequate food, clothing, shelter, medical care, or supervision that a prudent parent would take. The requirements of this subparagraph (III) shall be subject to the provisions of section 19-3-103.

(IV) Any case in which a child is subjected to emotional abuse. As used in this subparagraph (IV), "emotional abuse" means an identifiable and substantial impairment of the child's intellectual or psychological functioning or development or a substantial risk of impairment of the child's intellectual or psychological functioning or development.

(V) Any act or omission described in section 19-3-102 (1) (a), (1) (b), or (1) (c).

(b) In all cases, those investigating reports of child abuse shall take into account accepted child-rearing practices of the culture in which the child participates. Nothing in this subsection (1) shall refer to acts that could be construed to be a reasonable exercise of parental discipline or to acts reasonably necessary to subdue a child being taken into custody pursuant to section 19-2-502 that are performed by a peace officer, level I, as defined in section 18-1-901 (3) (l), acting in the good faith performance of the officer's duties.

(19) "Child abuse," as used in article 3.5 of this title, means any act that reasonably may be construed to fall under the definition of abuse or child abuse or neglect in subsection (1) of this section.

(78) "Neglect," as used in part 3 of article 3 of this title, means acts that can reasonably be construed to fall under the definition of child abuse or neglect as defined in subsection (1) of this section.

Connecticut
§ 46b-120. Definition.

The terms used in this chapter shall, in its interpretation and in the interpretation of other statutes, be defined as follows:

(1) "Child" means any person under sixteen years of age;

(2) "youth" means any person sixteen to eighteen years of age;

(3) "abused" means that a child or youth

(A) has had physical injury or injuries inflicted upon him other than by accidental means, or

(B) has injuries which are at variance with the history given of them, or

(C) is in a condition which is the result of maltreatment such as, but not limited to, malnutrition, sexual molestation or exploitation, deprivation of necessities, emotional maltreatment or cruel punishment;

(9) a child or youth may be found "uncared for" who is homeless or whose home cannot provide the specialized care which his physical, emotional or mental condition requires. For the purposes of this section the treatment of any child by an accredited Christian Science practitioner in lieu of treatment by a licensed practitioner of the healing arts, shall not of itself constitute neglect or maltreatment;

§ 53-20. Cruelty to persons

Any person who tortures, torments, cruelly or unlawfully punishes or wilfully or negligently deprives any person of necessary food, clothing, shelter or proper physical care; and any person who, having the control and custody of any child under the age of sixteen years, in any capacity whatsoever, maltreats, tortures, overworks, cruelly or unlawfully punishes or wilfully or negligently deprives such child of necessary food, clothing, or shelter shall be fined not more than five hundred dollars or imprisoned not more than one year or both.

§ 53-21. Injury or risk of injury to, or impairing morals of, children

Any person who

(1) wilfully or unlawfully causes or permits any child under the age of sixteen years to be placed in such a situation that the life or limb of such child is endangered, the health of such child is likely to be injured or the morals of such child are likely to be impaired, or does any act likely to impair the health or morals of any child, or

(2) has contact with the intimate parts, as defined in section 53a-65, of a child under the age of sixteen years or subjects a child under sixteen years of age to contact with the intimate parts of such person, in a sexual and indecent manner likely to impair the health or morals of such child, or

(3) permanently transfer the legal or physical custody of a child under the age of sixteen years to another person for money or other valuable consideration or acquires or receives the legal or physical custody of a child under the age of sixteen years from another person upon payment of money or other valuable consideration to such other person or

a third person, except in connection with an adoption proceeding that complies with the provisions of chapter 803 shall be guilty of a class C felony.

Delaware

§ 1102. Endangering the welfare of a child; class A misdemeanor.

(a) A person is guilty of endangering the welfare of a child when:

(1) Being a parent, guardian or other person legally charged with the care or custody of a child less than 18 years old the person:

a. Knowingly acts in a manner likely to be injurious to the physical, mental or moral welfare of the child; or

b. Intentionally does or fails to do any act, with the result that the child becomes a neglected child;

(b) Endangering the welfare of a child shall be punished as follows:

(1) When the death of a child occurs while the child's welfare was endangered as defined in subsection (a) of this section, endangering the welfare of a child is a class E felony;

(2) When serious physical injury to a child occurs while the child's welfare was endangered as defined in subsection (a) of this section, endangering the welfare of a child is a class G felony;

(3) In all other cases, endangering the welfare of a child is a class A misdemeanor.

(c) For the purpose of imposing the penalties prescribed in paragraph (b)(1) or (b)(2) of this section, it is not necessary to prove the person's state of mind or liability for causation with regard to the resulting death or serious physical injury of the child, notwithstanding the provisions of §§ 251, 252, 261, 262, 263 or 264 of this title, or any other statutes to the contrary.

§ 1103. Definitions relating to children.

(a) "Abuse" means causing any physical injury to a child through unjustified force as defined in § 468(1)(c) of this title, torture, negligent treatment, sexual abuse, exploitation, maltreatment, mistreatment or any means other than accident.

(c) "Neglect" means threatening or impairing the physical, mental or emotional health and well-being of a child through inadequate care or protection, nontreatment or abandonment by the child's custodian or other person in whose temporary custodial care the child is left, when such custodian or other person has the ability and financial means to provide adequate care or protection, but does not or will not do so. A child subjected to the conditions defined in this subsection is considered a "neglected child." Nothing in this subsection shall be construed to mean that a child is neglected for the sole reason that the child's custodian, or other person in whose custodial care the child is left, provided treatment by spiritual means alone through prayer in lieu of medical treatment, provided that such custodian is a member or adherent of an organized church or religious group, the tenets of which prescribe prayer as the principal treatment for illness, and the treatment provided conformed to such tenets.

(e) "Child" shall mean any individual 18 years of age or less.

Florida

827.03 Abuse, aggravated abuse, and neglect of a child; penalties.

(1) "Child abuse" means:

(a) Intentional infliction of physical or mental injury upon a child;

(b) An intentional act that could reasonably be expected to result in physical or mental injury to a child; or

(c) Active encouragement of any person to commit an act that results or could reasonably be expected to result in physical or mental injury to a child.

A person who knowingly or willfully abuses a child without causing great bodily harm, permanent disability, or permanent disfigurement to the child commits a felony of the third degree.

(2) "Aggravated child abuse" occurs when a person:

(a) commits aggravated battery on a child;

(b) Willfully tortures, maliciously punishes, or willfully and unlawfully cages a child; or

(c) Knowingly or willfully abuses a child and in doing so causes great bodily harm, permanent disability, or permanent disfigurement to the child.

A person who commits aggravated child abuse commits a felony of the second degree.

Georgia

16-5-70 Cruelty to children.

(a) A parent, guardian, or other person supervising the welfare of or having immediate charge or custody of a child under the age of 18 commits the offense of cruelty to children in the first degree when such person willfully deprives the child of necessary sustenance to the extent that the child's health or well-being is jeopardized.

(b) Any person commits the offense of cruelty to children in the first degree when such person maliciously causes a child under the age of 18 cruel or excessive physical or mental pain. Any person commits the offense of cruelty to children in the second degree when such person intentionally allows a minor to witness the commission of a forcible felony.

(c) A person convicted of the offense of cruelty to children in the first degree as provided in this

Code section shall be punished by imprisonment for not less than five nor more than 20 years.

19-7-5

(a) The purpose of this Code section is to provide for the protection of children whose health and welfare are adversely affected and further threatened by the conduct of those responsible for their care and protection. It is intended that the mandatory reporting of such cases will cause the protective services of the state to be brought to bear on the situation in an effort to prevent further abuses, to protect and enhance the welfare of these children, and to preserve family life wherever possible. This Code section shall be liberally construed so as to carry out the purposes thereof.

(b) As used in this Code section, the term:

(3) "Child abuse" means:

(A) Physical injury or death inflicted upon a child by a parent or caretaker thereof by other than accidental means; provided, however, physical forms of discipline may be used as long as there is no physical injury to the child;

Hawaii

§350-1 Definitions. For the purposes of this chapter, unless the context specifically indicates otherwise:

"Child abuse or neglect" means the acts or omissions of any person who, or legal entity which, is in any manner or degree related to the child, is residing with the child, or is otherwise responsible for the child's care, that have resulted in the physical or psychological health or welfare of the child, who is under the age of eighteen, to be harmed, or to be subject to any reasonably foreseeable, substantial risk of being harmed. The acts or omissions are indicated for the purposes of reports by circumstances that include but are not limited to:

(1) When the child exhibits evidence of:

(A) Substantial or multiple skin bruising or any other internal bleeding;

(B) Any injury to skin causing substantial bleeding;

(C) Malnutrition;

(D) Failure to thrive;

(E) Burn or burns;

(F) Poisoning;

(G) Fracture of any bone;

(H) Subdural hematoma;

(I) Soft tissue swelling;

(J) Extreme pain;

(K) Extreme mental distress;

(L) Gross degradation;

(M) Death; and such injury is not justifiably explained, or when the history given concerning such condition or death is at variance with the degree or type of such condition or death, or circumstances indicate that such condition or death may not be the product of an accidental occurrence; or

(2) When the child has been the victim of sexual contact or conduct, including, but not limited to, sexual assault as defined in the Penal Code, molestation, sexual fondling, incest, or prostitution; obscene or pornographic photographing, filming, or depiction; or other similar forms of sexual exploitation; or

(3) When there exists injury to the psychological capacity of a child as is evidenced by an observable and substantial impairment in the child's ability to function; or

(4) When the child is not provided in a timely manner with adequate food, clothing, shelter, psychological care, physical care, medical care, or supervision; or

(5) When the child is provided with dangerous, harmful, or detrimental drugs as defined by section 712-1240; provided that this paragraph shall not apply when such drugs are provided to the child pursuant to the direction or prescription of a practitioner, as defined in section 712-1240.

Idaho

16-1602. DEFINITIONS. For purposes of this chapter:

(a) "Abused" means any case in which a child has been the victim of:

(1) Conduct or omission resulting in skin bruising, bleeding, malnutrition, burns, fracture of any bone, subdural hematoma, soft tissue swelling, failure to thrive or death, and such condition or death is not justifiably explained, or where the history given concerning such condition or death is at variance with the degree or type of such condition or death, or the circumstances indicate that such condition or death may not be the product of an accidental occurrence; or

(2) Sexual conduct, including rape, molestation, incest, prostitution, obscene or pornographic photographing, filming or depiction for commercial purposes, or other similar forms of sexual exploitation harming or threatening the child's health or welfare or mental injury to the child.

(b) "Abandoned" means the failure of the parent to maintain a normal parental relationship with his child, including but not limited to reasonable support or regular personal contact. Failure to maintain this relationship without just cause for a period of one (1) year shall constitute prima facie evidence of abandonment.

(e) "Child" means an individual who is under the age of eighteen (18) years.

(j) "Custodian" means a person, other than a parent or legal guardian, to whom legal or joint legal custody of the child has been given by court order or who is acting in loco parentis.

(s) "Mental injury" means a substantial impairment in the intellectual or psychological ability of a child to function within a normal range of performance and/or behavior, for short or long terms.

(t) "Neglected" means a child:

(1) Who is without proper parental care and control, or subsistence, education, medical or other care or control necessary for his well-being because of the conduct or omission of his parents, guardian or other custodian or their neglect or refusal to provide them; provided, however, no child whose parent or guardian chooses for such child treatment by prayers through spiritual means alone in lieu of medical treatment, shall be deemed for that reason alone to be neglected or lack parental care necessary for his health and well-being, but further provided this subsection shall not prevent the court from acting pursuant to section 16-1616, Idaho Code; or

(2) Whose parents, guardian or other custodian are unable to discharge their responsibilities to and for the child because of incarceration, hospitalization, or other physical or mental incapacity; or

(3) Who has been placed for care or adoption in violation of law.

18-1501. INJURY TO CHILDREN.

(1) Any person who, under circumstances or conditions likely to produce great bodily harm or death, willfully causes or permits any child to suffer, or inflicts thereon unjustifiable physical pain or mental suffering, or having the care or custody of any child, willfully causes or permits the person or health of such child to be injured, or willfully causes or permits such child to be placed in such situation that its person or health is endangered, is punishable by imprisonment in the county jail not exceeding one (1) year, or in the state prison for not less than one (1) year nor more than ten (10) years.

(2) Any person who, under circumstances or conditions other than those likely to produce great bodily harm or death, willfully causes or permits any child to suffer, or inflicts thereon unjustifiable physical pain or mental suffering, or having the care or custody of any child, willfully causes or permits the person or health of such child to be injured, or willfully causes or permits such child to be placed in such situation that its person or health may be endangered, is guilty of a misdemeanor.

(3) A person over the age of eighteen (18) commits the crime of injury to a child if the person transports a minor in a motor vehicle while under the influence of alcohol, intoxicating liquor, a controlled substance, or any combination thereof, in violation of section 18-8004, Idaho Code. Any person convicted of violating this subsection is guilty of a misdemeanor. If a child suffers bodily injury or death due to a violation of this subsection, the violation will constitute a felony punishable by imprisonment

for not more than ten (10) years, unless a more severe penalty is otherwise prescribed by law.

(4) The practice of a parent or guardian who chooses for his child treatment by prayer or spiritual means alone shall not for that reason alone be construed to have violated the duty of care to such child.

Illinois

Chapter 325. Children Act 5. Abused and Neglected Child Reporting Act.

5/3. Definitions

§ 3. As used in this Act unless the context otherwise requires:

"Child" means any person under the age of 18 years, unless legally emancipated by reason of marriage or entry into a branch of the United States armed services.

"Abused child" means a child whose parent or immediate family member, or any person responsible for the child's welfare, or any individual residing in the same home as the child, or a paramour of the child's parent:

(a) inflicts, causes to be inflicted, or allows to be inflicted upon such child physical injury, by other than accidental means, which causes death, disfigurement, impairment of physical or emotional health, or loss or impairment of any bodily function;

(b) creates a substantial risk of physical injury to such child by other than accidental means which would be likely to cause death, disfigurement, impairment of physical or emotional health, or loss or impairment of any bodily function;

(c) commits or allows to be committed any sex offense against such child, as such sex offenses are defined in the Criminal Code of 1961, as amended, [FNI] and extending those definitions of sex offenses to include children under 18 years of age;

(d) commits or allows to be committed an act or acts of torture upon such child; or

(e) inflicts excessive corporal punishment.

"Neglected child" means any child who is not receiving the proper or necessary nourishment or medically indicated treatment including food or care not provided solely on the basis of the present or anticipated mental or physical impairment as determined by a physician acting alone or in consultation with other physicians or otherwise is not receiving the proper or necessary support or medical or other medical care recognized under State law as necessary for a child's well-being, or other care necessary for his or her well-being, including adequate food, clothing and shelter; or who is abandoned by his or her parents or other person responsible for the child's welfare without a proper plan of care.

A child shall not be considered neglected for the sole reason that the child's parent or other person

responsible for his or her welfare has left the child in the care of an adult relative for any period of time. A child shall not be considered neglected or abused for the sole reason that such child's parent or other person responsible for his or her welfare depends upon spiritual means through prayer alone for the treatment or cure of disease or remedial care as provided under Section 4 of this Act. A child shall not be considered neglected or abused solely because the child is not attending school in accordance with the requirements of Article 26 of The School Code, as amended. [FN3]

Indiana

35-46-1-4 Neglect of a dependent; child selling.

Sec. 4. (a) A person having care of a dependent, whether assumed voluntarily or because of a legal obligation, who knowingly or intentionally:

(1) places the dependent in a situation that may endanger his life or health;

(2) abandons or cruelly confines the dependent;

(3) deprives the dependent of necessary support; or

(4) deprives the dependent of education as required by law;

commits neglect of a dependent, a Class D felony. However, except for a violation of subdivision (4), the offense is a Class B felony if it results in serious bodily injury. It is a defense that the accused person, in the legitimate practice of his religious belief, provided treatment by spiritual means through prayer, in lieu of medical care, to his dependent.

Iowa

232.68 Definitions.

As used in sections 232.67 through 232.77 and 235A.12 through 235A.23, unless the context otherwise requires:

1. "Child" means any person under the age of eighteen years.

2. "Child abuse" or "abuse" means:

a. Any nonaccidental physical injury, or injury which is at variance with the history given of it, suffered by a child as the result of the acts or omissions of a person responsible for the care of the child.

b. Any mental injury to a child's intellectual or psychological capacity as evidenced by an observable and substantial impairment in the child's ability to function within the child's normal range of performance and behavior as the result of the acts or omissions of a person responsible for the care of the child, if the impairment is diagnosed and confirmed by a licensed physician or qualified mental health professional as defined in section 622.10.

d. The failure on the part of a person responsible for the care of the child to provide for the adequate food, shelter, clothing or other care necessary for the child's health and welfare when financially able to do so or when offered financial or other reasonable means to do so. A parent or guardian legitimately practicing religious beliefs who does not provide specific medical treatment for a child for that reason alone shall not be considered abusing the child, however this provision shall not preclude a court from ordering that medical service be provided to the child where the child's health requires it.

726.6 Child endangerment

1. A person who is the parent, guardian, or person having custody or control over a child or a minor under the age of eighteen with a mental or physical disability, commits child endangerment when the person does any of the following:

a. Knowingly acts in a manner that creates a substantial risk to a child or minor's physical, mental or emotional health or safety.

b. By an intentional act or series of intentional acts, uses unreasonable force, torture or cruelty that results in physical injury, or that is intended to cause serious physical injury.

c. By an intentional act or series of intentional acts, evidences unreasonable force, torture or cruelty which causes substantial mental or emotional harm to a child or minor.

2. A person who commits child endangerment resulting in serious injury to a child or minor is guilty of a class "C" felony.

3. A person who commits child endangerment not resulting in serious injury to a child or minor is guilty of an aggravated misdemeanor.

Kansas

21-3609. Abuse of a child. Abuse of a child is intentionally torturing, cruelly beating, shaking which results in great bodily harm, or inflicting cruel and inhumane corporal punishment upon any child under the age of 18 years.

Abuse of a child is severity level 5, person felony 38-1502. Definitions. As used in this code, unless the content otherwise indicates:

(a) "Child in need of care" means a person less than 18 years of age who:

(1) Is without adequate parental care, control or subsistence and the condition is not due solely to the lack of financial means of the child's parents or other custodian;

(2) is without the care or control necessary for the child's physical, mental or emotional health;

(3) has been physically, mentally or emotionally abused or neglected or sexually abused;

(b) "Physical, mental or emotional abuse or neglect" means the infliction of physical, mental or emotional injury or the causing of a deterioration of a child and may include, but shall not be limited to, failing to maintain reasonable care and treatment, negligent treatment or maltreatment or exploiting a child to the extent that the child's health or emotional well-being is endangered. A parent legitimately practicing religious beliefs who does not provide specific medical treatment for a child because of religious beliefs shall not for that reason be considered a negligent parent; however, this exception shall not preclude a court from entering an order pursuant to subsection (a)(2) of K.S.A. 38-1513 and amendments thereto.

Kentucky

508.090 Definitions for KRS 508.100 to 508.120.

The following definitions apply in KRS 508.100 to 508.120 unless the context otherwise requires:

(1) "Abuse" means the infliction of physical pain, injury, or mental injury, or the deprivation of services by a person which are necessary to maintain the health and welfare of a person, or a situation in which an adult, living alone, is unable to provide or obtain for himself the services which are necessary to maintain his health or welfare.

508.100 Criminal Abuse in the First Degree

(1) A person is guilty of criminal abuse in the first degree when he intentionally abuses another person or permits another person of whom he has actual custody to be abused and thereby;

(a) Causes serious physical injury; or

(b) Places him in a situation that may cause him serious physical injury; or

(c) Causes torture, cruel confinement or cruel punishment;

to a person twelve (12) years of age or less, or who is physically helpless or mentally helpless.

(2) Criminal abuse in the first degree is a Class C felony.

508.110 Criminal Abuse in the Second Degree

(1) A person is guilty of criminal abuse in the first degree when he wantonly abuses another person or permits another person of whom he has actual custody to be abused and thereby;

(a) Causes serious physical injury; or

(b) Places him in a situation that may cause him serious physical injury; or

(c) Causes torture, cruel confinement or cruel punishment;

to a person twelve (12) years of age or less, or who is physically helpless or mentally helpless.

(2) Criminal abuse in the first degree is a Class D felony.

508.100 Criminal Abuse in the Third Degree

(1) A person is guilty of criminal abuse in the first degree when he recklessly abuses another person or permits another person of whom he has actual custody to be abused and thereby;

(a) Causes serious physical injury; or

(b) Places him in a situation that may cause him serious physical injury; or

(c) Causes torture, cruel confinement or cruel punishment;

to a person twelve (12) years of age or less, or who is physically helpless or mentally helpless.

(2) Criminal abuse in the third degree is a Class A misdemeanor.

Louisiana

§ 403. Abuse of children; missing or abused children; reports; immunity; central registry; investigations; definitions; waiver of privilege; penalties; limitations

A. Purpose. The purpose of this Section is to protect children whose physical or mental health and welfare are substantially at risk of harm by abuse, neglect, or sexual abuse, and may be further threatened by the conduct of those responsible for their care and protection or by any other person, by providing for either mandatory or permissive reporting by certain persons having reasonable cause to believe that any child is so endangered. It is the intention to provide professional screening of these reports which will minimize unnecessary interference with family privacy act and yet, will authorize the protective an preventative intervention needed to safeguard and enhance the health and well-being of the children. This Section shall be administered and interpreted to provide the greatest possible protection as promptly as possible for such children.

B. Definitions. For the purpose of this Section, the following terms shall mean;

"(1) For the purpose of reporting, 'abuse' is the infliction, by a caretaker or any other person, of physical or mental injury or the causing of the deterioration of a child, including, but not limited to, such means as sexual abuse, sexual exploitation, or the exploitation or overwork of a child to such an extent that his health, moral or emotional well-being is endangered."

"(3) 'Child' is any individual under the age of eighteen years."

"(5) For the purpose of reporting, 'neglect' is the failure by a caretaker to provide for a child the proper or necessary support or medical, surgical, or any other care necessary for his well-being. Whenever, in lieu of medical care, a child is being provided treatment in accordance with the tenets of a well-recognized religious method of healing which has a reasonable proven record of success, the child shall not for that reason alone be considered to be neglected or abused."

Maine

Title 22, MRSA Chapter 1071.

§4002. Definitions

As used in this chapter, unless the context indicates otherwise, the following terms have the following meanings.

(1) Abuse or neglect. "Abuse or neglect" means a threat to a child's health or welfare by physical, mental or emotional injury or impairment, sexual abuse or exploitation, deprivation or essential needs or lack of protection from these, by a person responsible for the child.

(1-A) Abandonment. "Abandonment" means any conduct on the part of the parent showing an intent to forgo parental duties or relinquish parental claims. The intent may be evidenced by:

(A) Failure, for a period of at least 6 months, to communicate meaningfully with the child;

(B) Failure, for a period of at least 6 months, to maintain regular visitation with the child;

(C) Failure to participate in any plan or program designed to reunite the parent with the child;

(D) Deserting the child without affording means of identifying the child and his parent or custodian;

(E) Failure to respond to notice of child protective proceedings; or

(F) Any other conduct indicating an intent to forgo parental duties or relinquish parental claims.

(1-B) Aggravating Factor. "Aggravating factor" means any of the following circumstances with regard to the parent.

(A) The parent has subjected the child to aggravated circumstances including, but not limited to, the following:

(1) Rape, gross sexual misconduct, gross sexual assault, sexual abuse, incest, aggravated assault, kidnapping, promotion of prostitution, abandonment, torture, chronic abuse or any other treatment that is heinous or abhorrent to society; or

(2) Refusal for 6 months to comply with treatment required in a reunification plan.

(6) Jeopardy to health or welfare or jeopardy. "Jeopardy to health or welfare" or "jeopardy" means serious abuse or neglect as evidenced by:

(A) Serious harm or threat of serious harm;

(B) Deprivation of adequate food, clothing, shelter, supervision or care, including health care when that deprivation causes a threat of serious harm;

(C) Abandonment of the child or absence of any person responsible for the child, which creates a threat of serious harm; or

(D) The end of voluntary placement, when the imminent return of the child to his custodian causes a threat of serious harm.

(10) Serious harm. "Serious harm" means:

(A) Serious injury;

(B) Serious mental or emotional injury or impairment, which now or in the future is likely to be evidenced by serious mental, behavioral or personality disorder, including severe anxiety, depression or withdrawal, untoward aggressive behavior, seriously delayed development or similar serious dysfunctional behavior; or

(C) Sexual abuse or exploitation.

(11) Serious injury. "Serious injury" means serious physical injury or impairment.

§4009. Penalty for violations

A person who knowingly violates a provision of this chapter commits a civil violation for which a forfeiture of not more than 500% may be adjudged.

§4010. Spiritual Treatment.

(1) Treatment not considered abuse or neglect. Under subchapters I to VII, a child shall not be considered to be abused or neglected, in jeopardy of health or welfare or in danger of serious harm solely because treatment is by spiritual means by an accredited practitioner of a recognized religious organization.

Maryland

5-701. Definitions.

(b) Abuse.—"Abuse" means:

(i) the physical or mental injury of a child by a parent or other person who has permanent or temporary care or custody of responsibility for supervision of a child, or by any household member, under circumstances that indicate that the child's health or welfare is harmed or at substantial risk of being harmed; or

(ii) sexual abuse of a child, whether physical injuries are sustained or not.

(2) "Abuse" does not include, for that reason alone, providing a child with nonmedical religious remedial care and treatment recognized by State law.

(d) Child.—"Child" means any individual under the age of 18 years.

(p) Neglect.—"Neglect" means the leaving of a child unattended or other failure to give proper care and attention to a child by a parent or other person who has permanent or temporary care or custody or responsibility for supervision of the child under circumstances that indicate;

(1) that the child's health or welfare is harmed or placed at substantial risk of harm; or

(2) mental injury to the child or a substantial risk of mental injury.

Massachusetts

119 § 51A Physical or emotional injury.

(3) Injury

The term "serious physical or emotional injury" in the context of this section includes all but the most negligible or de minimis injuries to children and the standard thus established applies to those instances in which certain enumerated professionals are required to make reports to the department of public welfare. Serious physical or emotional injury applies only to those instances in which certain enumerated professionals are required, as a matter of law, to make reports to the department of public welfare but the reporting of injury and access to services is in no manner restricted to serious injury.

119 § 51B Physically or emotionally injured children;

A report required under section fifty-one A and this section of, after an investigation and evaluation undertaken pursuant to clause (1), the department has reasonable cause to believe that any of the following conditions has resulted from abuse or neglect; provided, however, that the department may immediately report cases of serious physical injury to the appropriate office of the district attorney:

(a) a child has died;

(c) a child has suffered brain damage, loss or substantial impairment of a bodily function or organ, or substantial disfigurement;

(e) a child has suffered serious physical abuse or injury that includes, but is not limited to:

(i) a fracture of any bone, severe burn, impairment of any organ, or any other serious injury;

(ii) an injury requiring the child to be placed on life-support systems;

(iii) any other disclosure of physical abuse involving physical evidence which may be destroyed;

(iv) any current disclosure by the child of sexual assault; or

(v) the presence of physical evidence of sexual assault.

Michigan

722.622. Definitions.

Sec. 2. As used in this act:

(b) "Child" means a person under 18 years of age.

(c) "Child abuse" means harm or threatened harm to a child's health or welfare by a parent, legal guardian, or any other person responsible for the child's health or welfare, or by a teacher or teacher's aide, that occurs through nonaccidental physical or mental injury; sexual abuse; sexual exploitation; or maltreatment.

(d) "Child neglect" means harm or threatened harm to a child's health or welfare by a parent, legal guardian, or any other person responsible for the child's health or welfare that occurs through either of the following:

(i) Negligent treatment, including the failure to provide adequate food, clothing, shelter, or medical care.

(ii) Placing a child at an unreasonable risk to the child's health or welfare by failure of the parent, legal guardian, or any other person responsible for the child's health or welfare to intervene to eliminate that risk when that person is able to do so and has, or should have, knowledge of the risk.

750.136b. Child abuse; degrees, punishment, definitions; reasonable discipline and force

Sec. 136b.

(1) As used in this section:

(a) "Child" means a person who is less than 18 years of age and is not emancipated by operation of law as provided in section 4(1) of Act No. 293 of the Public Acts of 1968, being section 722.4 of the Michigan Compiled Laws.

(b) "Omission" means a willful failure to provide the food, clothing, or shelter necessary for a child's welfare or the willful abandonment of a child.

(c) "Person" means a child's parent or guardian or any other person who cares for, has custody of, or has authority over a child regardless of the length of time that a child is cared for, in the custody of, or subject to the authority of that person.

(d) "Physical harm" means any injury to a child's physical condition.

(e) "Serious physical harm" means an injury of a child's physical condition or welfare that is not necessarily permanent but constitutes substantial bodily disfigurement, or seriously impairs the function of a body organ or limb.

(f) "Serious mental harm" means an injury to a child's mental condition or welfare that is not necessarily permanent but results in visibly demonstrated manifestations of a substantial disorder of thought or mood which significantly impairs judgment, behavior, capacity to recognize reality, or ability to cope with the ordinary demands of life.

(2) A person is guilty of child abuse in the first degree if the person knowingly or intentionally causes serious physical or serious mental harm to a child. Child abuse in the first degree is a felony punishable by imprisonment for not more than 15 years.

(3) A person is guilty of child abuse in the second degree if the person's omission causes serious physical harm or serious mental harm to a child or if the person's reckless act causes serious physical harm to a child. Child abuse in the second degree is a felony punishable by imprisonment for not more than 4 years.

(4) A person is guilty of child abuse in the third degree if the person knowingly or intentionally causes physical harm to a child. Child abuse in the third degree is a misdemeanor punishable for not more than 2 years.

(5) A person is guilty of child abuse in the fourth degree if the person's omission or reckless act causes physical harm to a child. Child abuse in the fourth degree is a misdemeanor punishable for not more than 1 year.

(6) This section shall not be construed to prohibit a parent or guardian, or other person permitted by law or authorized by the parent or guardian, from taking steps to reasonably discipline a child, including the use of reasonable force.

Minnesota

260.015 Definitions.

Subd. 24. Domestic child abuse. "Domestic child abuse" means:

(1) any physical injury to a minor family or household member inflicted by an adult family or household member other than by accidental means; or

(2) subjection of a minor family or household member by an adult family or household member to an act which constitutes a violation of sections 609.321 to 609.324, 609.342, 609.343, 609.344, 609.345, or 617.246.

Subd. 28. Child abuse. "Child abuse" means an act that involves a minor victim and that constitutes a violation of section 609.221, 609.222, 609.223, 609.224, 609.2242, 609.322, 609.323, 609.324, 609.342, 609.343, 609.344, 609.345, 609.377, 609.378, or 617.246.

609.377 Malicious Punishment of a Child.

A parent, legal guardian, or caretaker who, by an intentional act or a series of intentional acts with respect to a child, evidences unreasonable force or cruel discipline that is excessive under the circumstances is guilty of malicious punishment of a child and may be sentenced to imprisonment for not more than one year or to payment of a fine of not more than $3,000, or both. If the punishment results in substantial bodily harm, that person may be sentenced to imprisonment for not more than five years or to payment of a fine not more than $10,000, or both. If the punishment results in great bodily harm, that person may be sentenced to imprisonment for not more than ten years or to payment of a fine of not more than $20,000, or both. If the punishment is to a child under the age of four and causes bodily harm to the head, eyes, neck, or otherwise causes multiple bruises to the body, the person may be sentenced to imprisonment for not more than five years or a fine of $10,000, or both.

609.378 Neglect or Endangerment of a Child.

Subd. 1. Persons guilty of neglect or endangerment.

(1) A parent, legal guardian, or caretaker who willfully deprives a child of necessary food,

clothing, shelter, health care, or supervision appropriate to the child's age, when the parent, guardian, or caretaker is reasonably able to make the necessary provisions and the deprivation harms or is likely to substantially harm the child's physical, mental, or emotional health is guilty of neglect of a child and may be sentenced to imprisonment for not more than one year or to payment of a fine of not more than $3,000, or both. If the deprivation results in substantial harm to the child's physical, mental, or emotional health, the person may be sentenced to imprisonment for not more than five years or to payment of a fine of not more than $10,000, or both. If a parent, guardian, or caretaker responsible for the child's care in good faith selects and depends on spiritual means or prayer for treatment or care of disease or remedial care of the child, this treatment or care is "health care" for the purposes of this clause.

(b) Endangerment. A parent, legal guardian, or caretaker who endangers the child's person or health by:

(1) intentionally or recklessly causing or permitting a child to be placed in a situation likely to substantially harm a child's physical, mental, or emotional health or cause the child's death.

If the endangerment results in substantial harm to the child's physical, mental, or emotional health, the person may be sentenced to imprisonment for not more than five years or to payment of a fine of not more than $3,000, or both.
626.556 Definitions. As used in this section, the following terms have the meanings given them unless the specific content indicates otherwise.

(d) "Physical abuse" means any physical or mental injury, or threatened injury, inflicted by a person responsible for the child's care on a child other than by accidental means, or any physical or mental injury that cannot reasonably be explained by the child's history of injury or injuries, or any aversive and deprivation procedures that have not been authorized under section 245.825.

Mississippi

SEC. 97-5-39. Contributing to the neglect or delinquency of a child; felonious abuse and/or battery of a child.

(1) Any parent, guardian or other person who willfully commits any act or omits the performance of any duty, which act or omission contributes to or tends to contribute to the neglect or delinquency of any child or which act or omission results in the abuse and/or battering of any child, as defined in Section 43-21-105 (m) of the Youth Court Law . . . shall be guilty of a misdemeanor, and upon conviction shall be punished by a fine not to exceed One Thousand Dollars ($1,000.00), or by imprisonment

not to exceed one (1) year in jail, or by both such fine and imprisonment.

(2) Any person who shall intentionally (a) burn any child, (b) torture any child or, (c) except in self-defense or in order to prevent bodily harm to a third party, whip strike or otherwise abuse or mutilate any child in such a manner as to cause serious bodily harm, shall be guilty of felonious abuse and/or battery of a child and, upon conviction, may be punished by imprisonment in the penitentiary for not more than twenty (20) years.
SEC. 43-21-105. Definitions

(m) "Abused child" means a child whose parent, guardian or custodian or any person responsible for his care or support, whether legally obligated to do so or not, has caused or allowed to be caused upon said child sexual abuse, sexual exploitation, emotional abuse, mental injury, nonaccidental physical injury or other maltreatment. Provided, however, that physical discipline (not to include any form of sexual abuse) performed on a child by a parent, guardian or custodian shall only be deemed to be abuse under this paragraph when a licensed physician has determined that physical injury has occurred.

Missouri

210.110. Definitions—As used in sections 210.109 to 210.165, and sections 210.180 to 210.183, the following terms mean:

(1) "Abuse," any physical injury, sexual abuse, or emotional abuse inflicted on a child other than by accidental means by those responsible for the child's care, custody, and control, except that discipline including spanking administered in a reasonable manner, shall not be considered to be abuse;

(3) "Child," any person, regardless of physical or mental condition, under eighteen years of age;

(8) "Neglect," failure to provide, by those responsible for the care, custody, and control of the child, the proper or necessary support, education as required by law, nutrition, or medical, surgical, or any other care necessary for the child's well-being;
210.165. Penalties for violations.

(1) Any person violating any provision of sections 210.110 to 210.165 is guilty of a class A misdemeanor.

Montana

45-2-101. General definitions. Unless otherwise specified in the statute, all words will be taken in the objective standard rather than in the subjective, and unless a different meaning plainly is required, the following definitions apply in this title:

(5) "Bodily injury" means physical pain, illness, or any impairment of physical condition and includes mental illness or impairment.

(22) "Felony" means an offense in which the sentence imposed upon conviction is death or imprisonment in the state prison for any term exceeding 1 year.

(26) "Harm" means loss, disadvantage, or injury or anything so regarded by the person affected, including loss, disadvantage, or injury to any person or entity in whose welfare the affected person is interested.

(41) "Misdemeanor" means an offense for which the sentence imposed upon conviction is imprisonment in the county jail for any term or a fine, or both, or for which the sentence imposed is imprisonment in the state prison for any term of 1 year or less.

(64) (a) "Serious bodily injury" means bodily injury that:

(i) creates a substantial risk of death;

(ii) causes serious permanent disfigurement or protracted loss or impairment of the function or process of any bodily member or organ; or

(iii) at the time of injury, can reasonably be expected to result in serious permanent disfigurement or protracted loss or impairment of the function or process of any bodily member or organ.

(b) The term includes serious mental illness or impairment.

45-5-622. Endangering welfare of children.

(1) A parent, guardian, or other person supervising the welfare of a child less than 18 years old commits the offense of endangering the welfare of children if the parent, guardian, or other person knowingly endangers the child's welfare by violating a duty of care, protection, or support.

(2) Except as provided in 16-6-305, a parent or guardian or any person who is 18 years of age or older, whether or not the parent, guardian, or other person is supervising the welfare of the child, commits the offense of endangering the welfare of children if the parent, guardian, or other person knowingly contributes to the delinquency of a child less than:

(a) 18 years old by:

(i) supplying or encouraging the use of an intoxicating substance by the child; or

(ii) assisting, promoting, or encouraging the child to enter a place of prostitution; or

(b) 16 years old by assisting, promoting, or encouraging the child to:

(i) abandon the child's place of residence without the consent of the child's parents or guardian; or

(ii) engage in sexual conduct.

(4) A person convicted of endangering the welfare of children shall be fined an amount not to exceed $500 or be imprisoned in the county jail for any term not to exceed 6 months, or both. A person convicted of a second offense of endangering the welfare of children shall be fined an amount not to exceed $1,000 or be imprisoned in the county jail for any term not to exceed 6 months, or both.

(5) On the issue of whether there has been a violation of the duty of care, protection, and support, the following, in addition to all other admissible evidence, is admissible: cruel treatment; abuse; infliction of unnecessary and cruel punishment; abandonment; neglect; lack of proper medical care, clothing, shelter, and food; and evidence of past bodily injury.

Nebraska
§ 28-707. Child abuse; privileges not available; penalties.

(1) A person commits child abuse if he or she knowingly, intentionally, or negligently causes or permits a minor child to be:

(a) Placed in a situation that endangers his or her life or physical or mental health;

(b) Cruelly confined or cruelly punished;

(c) Deprived of necessary food, clothing, shelter or care;

(3) Child abuse is a Class I misdemeanor if the offense is committed negligently.

(4) Child abuse is a Class IIIA felony if the offense is committed knowingly and intentionally and does not result in serious bodily injury as defined in section 28-109.

(5) Child abuse is a Class III felony if the offense is committed knowingly and intentionally and results in serious bodily injury as defined in such section.

(6) Child abuse is a Class IB felony if the offense is committed knowingly and intentionally and results in the death of such child.

Nevada
NRS 432B.020 "Abuse or neglect of a child" defined.

1. "Abuse or neglect of a child" means:

(a) Physical or mental injury of a nonaccidental nature;

(b) Sexual abuse or sexual exploitation; or

(c) Negligent treatment or maltreatment as set forth in NRS 432B.140, of a child caused or allowed by a person responsible for his welfare under circumstances which indicate that the child's health or welfare is harmed or threatened with harm.

2. A child is not abused or neglected, nor is his health or welfare harmed or threatened for the sole reason that his parent or guardian, in good faith, selects and depends upon nonmedical remedial treatment for such child, if such treatment is recognized and permitted under the laws of this state in lieu of medical treatment. This subsection does not limit the court in ensuring that a child receive a

medical examination and treatment pursuant to NRS 62.231.

3. As used in this section, "allow" means to do nothing to prevent or stop the abuse or neglect of a child in circumstances where the person knows or has reason to know that a child is abused or neglected.

NRS 432B.040 "Child" defined. "Child" means a person under the age of 18 years.

NRS 432B.070 "Mental injury" defined. "Mental injury" means an injury to the intellectual or psychological capacity or the emotional condition of a child as evidenced by an observable and substantial impairment of his ability to function within his normal range of performance or behavior.

NRS 432B.090 "Physical injury" defined. "Physical injury" includes, without limitation:

1. A sprain or dislocation;

2. Damage to cartilage;

3. A fracture of a bone or the skull;

4. An intracranial hemorrhage or injury to another internal organ;

5. A burn or scalding;

6. A cut, laceration, puncture or bite;

7. Permanent or temporary disfigurement; or

8. Permanent or temporary loss or impairment of a part or organ of the body.

NRS 432B.140 Negligent treatment or maltreatment. Negligent treatment or maltreatment of a child occurs if a child has been abandoned, is without proper care, control and supervision or lacks the subsistence, education, shelter, medical care or other care necessary for the well-being of the child because of the faults or habits of the person responsible for his welfare or his neglect or refusal to provide them when able to do so.

NRS 432B.150 Excessive corporal punishment may constitute abuse or neglect. Excessive corporal punishment may result in physical or mental injury constituting abuse or neglect of a child under the provisions of this chapter.

New Hampshire
RSA 169-C:3 Definitions.

I. "Abandoned" means the child has been left by his parent, guardian or custodian, without provision for his care, supervision or financial support although financially able to provide for such support.

II. "Abused child" means any child who has been:

(a) Sexually abused; or

(b) Intentionally physically injured; or

(c) Psychologically injured so that said child exhibits symptoms of emotional problems generally recognized to result from consistent mistreatment or neglect; or

(d) Physically injured by other than accidental means.

V. "Child" means any person who has not reached his eighteenth birthday.

XIX. "Neglected child" means a child:

(a) Who has been abandoned by his parents, guardian, or custodian; or

(b) Who is without proper parental care or control, subsistence, education as required by law, or other care or control necessary for his physical, mental, or emotional health, when it is established that his health has suffered or is very likely to suffer serious impairment; and the deprivation is not due primarily to the lack of financial means of the parents, guardian or custodian, or

(c) Whose parents, guardian or custodian are unable to discharge their responsibilities to and for the child because of incarceration, hospitalization or other physical or mental incapacity;

Provided, that no child who is, in good faith, under treatment solely by spiritual means through prayer in accordance with the tenets and practices of a recognized church or religious denomination by a duly accredited practitioner thereof shall, for that reason alone, be considered to be a neglected child under this chapter.

XXIII. "Probable cause" means facts and circumstances based upon accurate and reliable information, including hearsay, that would justify a reasonable person to believe that a child subject to a report under this chapter is abused or neglected.

RSA 169-C:39 Penalty for Violation

Anyone who knowingly violates any provision of this subdivision shall be guilty of a misdemeanor.

RSA 625:8 Limitations

I. Except as otherwise provided in this section, prosecutions are subject to the following periods of limitations:

(a) For a class A felony, 6 years;

(b) For a class B felony, 6 years;

(c) For a misdemeanor, one year;

(d) For a violation, 3 months;

(e) For an offense defined by RSA 282-A, 6 years.

RSA 631:1 First Degree Assault

I. A person is guilty of a class A felony if he:

(d) Knowingly or recklessly causes serious bodily injury to a person under 13 years of age.

RSA 631:2 Second Degree Assault

I. A person is guilty of a class B felony if he:

d) Purposely or knowingly causes bodily injury to a child under 13 years of age.

New Jersey
9:6-1. Abuse, abandonment, cruelty and neglect of child; what constitutes

Abuse of a child shall consist in any of the following acts:

(a) disposing of the custody of a child contrary to law;

(b) employing or permitting a child to be employed in any vocation or employment injurious to its health or dangerous to its life or limb, or contrary to the laws of this State;

(c) employing or permitting a child to be employed in any occupation, employment or vocation dangerous to the morals of such child;

(d) the habitual use by the parent or by a person having the custody and control of a child, in the hearing of such child, of profane indecent or obscene language;

(e) the performing of any indecent, immoral or unlawful act or deed, presence of a child, that may tend to debauch or endanger the morals of the child;

(f) permitting or allowing any other persons to perform any indecent, immoral or unlawful act in the presence of the child that may tend to debauch or endanger the morals of such child;

(g) using excessive physical restraint in the child under circumstances which do not indicate that the child's behavior is harmful to himself, others or property; or

(h) in an institution as defined in section 1 of P.L.1974, c. 119(C. 9:6-8.21), willfully isolated the child from ordinary social contact under circumstances which indicate or emotional deprivation.

Abandonment of a child shall consist in any of the following acts by anyone having custody or control of the child:

(a) willfully forsaking a child;

(b) failing to care for and keep the control and custody of a child so that the child shall be exposed to physical or moral risk without proper and sufficient protection;

(c) failing to care for and keep the control and custody of a child so that the child shall be liable to be supported and maintained at the expense of the public, or by child caring societies or private persons not legally chargeable with its or their care, custody and control.

Cruelty to a child shall consist in any of the following acts:

(a) inflicting unnecessary severe corporal punishment upon a child;

(b) inflicting upon a child unnecessary suffering or pain, either mental or physical;

(c) habitually tormenting, vexing or afflicting a child;

(d) any willful act of omission or commission whereby unnecessary pain and suffering, whether mental or physical, is caused or permitted to be inflicted on a child;

(e) or exposing a child to unnecessary hardship, fatigue or mental or physical strains that may tend to injure the health or physical or moral well-being of such child,

Neglect of a child shall consist in any of the following acts, by anyone having the custody or control of the child:

(a) willfully failing to provide proper and sufficient food, clothing, maintenance, regular school education as required by law, medical attendance or surgical treatment, and a clean and proper home, or

(b) failure to do or permit to be done any act necessary for the child's physical or moral well-being.

Neglect also means the continued inappropriate placement of a child in an institution, as defined in section 1 of P.L.1974, c. 119 (C.9:6-8.21), with the knowledge that the placement has resulted and may continue to result in harm to the child's mental or physical well-being.

Notes Of Decision: Corporal Punishment—The offense intended to be prevented by this Act is not the infliction of severe corporal punishment but unnecessarily inflicting it, and the questions to be tried when such a case is presented are whether there was a necessity for the punishment, and, if so, was it severe. Richardson v. State Board of Control of Institutions and Agencies, 98 N.J.L. 690, 121 A. 457 (1923), affirmed 99 N.J.L. 516, 123 A. 720.

9:6-8.21. Definitions

(c) "Abused or neglected child" means a child less than 18 years of age whose parent or guardian, as herein defined,

(1) inflicts or allows to be inflicted upon such child physical injury by other than accidental means which causes or creates a substantial risk of death, or serious or protracted disfigurement, or protracted impairment of physical or emotional health or protracted loss or impairment of the function of any bodily organ;

(2) creates or allows to be created a substantial or ongoing risk of physical injury to such child by other than accidental means which would be likely to cause death or serious or protracted disfigurement, or protracted loss or impairment of the function of any bodily organ;

No child who in good faith is under treatment by spiritual means alone through prayer in accordance with the tenets and practices of a recognized church or religious denomination by a duly accredited practitioner thereof shall for this reason alone be considered to be abused or neglected.

9:6-3. Cruelty and neglect of children; crime of fourth degree; remedies

Any parent, guardian or person having the care, custody or control of any child, who shall abuse, abandon, be cruel to or neglectful of such child, or any person who shall abuse, be cruel to or neglectful of any child shall be deemed to be guilty of a crime of the fourth degree.

L.1990, c. 26, § 5, provided person found guilty of child abuse, abandonment, cruelty or neglect was guilty of a crime in the fourth degree, rather than a misdemeanor subject to a fine of up to $500 or imprisonment with or without hard labor for a term not to exceed three years, or both.

New Mexico
32A-4-2. Definitions.

As used in the Abuse and Neglect Act [this article]:

B. "abused child" means a child:

(1) who has suffered physical abuse, emotional abuse or psychological abuse inflicted by the child's parent, guardian or custodian;

(2) who has suffered sexual abuse or sexual exploitation inflicted by the child's parent, guardian or custodian;

(3) whose parent, guardian or custodian has knowingly, intentionally or negligently placed the child in a situation that may endanger the child's life or health; or

(4) whose parent, guardian or custodian has knowingly or intentionally tortured, cruelly confined or cruelly punished the child;

C. "neglected child" means a child:

(1) who has been abandoned by the child's parent, guardian or custodian;

(2) who is without proper parental care and control or subsistence, education, medical or other care or control necessary for the child's well-being because of the faults or habits of the child's parent, guardian or custodian or the neglect or refusal of the parent, guardian or custodian, when able to do so, to provide them;

(5) who has been placed for care or adoption in violation of the law; provided that nothing in the Children's Code [this chapter] shall be construed to imply that a child who is being provided with treatment by spiritual means alone through prayer, in accordance with the tenets and practices of a recognized church or religious denomination, by a duly accredited practitioner thereof, is for that reason alone a neglected child within the meaning of the Children's Code;

D. "physical abuse" includes, but is not limited to, any case in which the child exhibits evidence of skin bruising, bleeding, malnutrition, failure to thrive, burns, fracture of any bone, subdural hematoma, soft tissue swelling or death and:

(1) there is not a justifiable explanation for the condition or death;

(2) the explanation given for the condition is at variance with the degree or nature of the condition;

(3) the explanation given for the death is at variance with the nature of the death; or

(4) circumstances indicate that the condition or death may not be the product of an accidental occurrence;

New York
§ 260.10 Endangering the welfare of a child.

A person is guilty of endangering the welfare of a child when:

(1) He knowingly acts in a manner likely to be injurious to the physical, mental or moral welfare of a child less than seventeen years old or directs or authorizes such child to engage in an occupation involving a substantial risk of danger to his life or health; or

(2) Being a parent, guardian or other person legally charged with the care or custody of a child less than eighteen years old, he fails or refuses to exercise reasonable diligence in the control of such child to prevent him from becoming an "abused child," a "neglected child," a "juvenile delinquent" or a "person in need of supervision," as those terms are defined in articles ten, three and seven of the family court act.

Endangering the welfare of a child is a class A misdemeanor.

§ 260.11 Endangering the welfare of a child; corroboration

A person shall not be convicted of endangering the welfare of a child, or of an attempt to commit the same, upon the testimony of a victim who is incapable of consent because of mental defect or mental incapacity as to conduct that constitutes an offense or an attempt to commit an offense referred to in section 130.16, without additional evidence sufficient pursuant to section 130.16 to sustain a conviction of an offense referred to in section 130.16, or of an attempt to commit the same.

§ 1012. Definitions

When used in this article and unless the specific context indicates otherwise;

(a) "Respondent" includes any parent or other person legally responsible for a child's care who is alleged to have abused or neglected such child;

(b) "Child" means any person or persons alleged to have been abused or neglected, whichever the case may be;

(e) "Abused child" means a child less than eighteen years of age whose parent or other person legally responsible for his care

(i) inflicts or allows to be inflicted upon such child physical injury by other than accidental means which causes or creates a substantial risk of death, or serious or protracted disfigurement, or protracted impairment of physical or emotional health or protracted loss or impairment of the function of any bodily organ, or

(ii) creates or allows to be created a substantial risk of physical injury to such child by other than accidental means which would be likely to cause death or serious or protracted disfigurement, or protracted impairment of physical or emotional health or protracted loss or impairment of the function of any bodily organ.

(f) "Neglected child" means a child less than eighteen years of age

(i) whose physical, mental or emotional condition has been impaired or is in imminent danger of becoming impaired as a result of the failure of his parent or other person legally responsible for his care to exercise a minimum degree of care

(A) in supplying the child with adequate food, clothing, shelter or education in accordance with the provisions of part one of article sixty-five of the education law, or medical, dental, optometrical or surgical care, though financially able to do so or offered financial or other reasonable means to do so; or

(B) in providing the child with proper supervision or guardianship, by unreasonably inflicting or allowing to be inflicted harm, or a substantial risk thereof, including the infliction of excessive corporal punishment; or by misusing a drug or drugs; or by misusing alcoholic beverages to the extent that he loses self-control of his actions; or by any other acts of a similarly serious nature requiring the aid of the court; provided, however, that where the respondent is voluntarily and regularly participating in a rehabilitative program, evidence that the respondent has repeatedly misused a drug or drugs or alcoholic beverages to the extent that he loses self-control of his actions shall not establish that the child is a neglected child in the absence of evidence establishing that the child's physical, mental or emotional condition has been impaired or is in imminent danger of becoming impaired as set forth in paragraph (i) of this subdivision; or

(ii) who has been abandoned, in accordance with the definition and other criteria set forth in subdivision five of section three hundred eighty-four-b of the social services law, by his parents or other person legally responsible for his care.

(h) "Impairment of emotional health" and "impairment of mental or emotional condition" includes a state of substantially diminished psychological or intellectual functioning in relation to, but not limited to, such factors as failure to thrive, control of aggressive or self-destructive impulses, ability to think and reason, or acting out misbehavior, including incorrigibility, ungovernability or habitual truancy; provided, however, that such impairment must be clearly attributable to the unwillingness or inability of the respondent to exercise a minimum degree of care toward the child.

North Carolina
§ 7A-517. Definitions.

Unless the context clearly requires otherwise, the following words have the listed meanings:

(1) Abused juveniles.—Any juvenile less than 18 years of age whose parent, guardian, custodian, or caretaker:

a. Inflicts or allows to be inflicted upon the juvenile a serious physical injury by other than accidental means; or

b. Creates or allows to be created a substantial risk of serious physical injury to the juvenile by other than accidental means; or

b1. Uses or allows to be used upon the juvenile cruel or grossly inappropriate procedures or cruel or grossly inappropriate devices to modify behavior; or

d. Creates or allows to be created serious emotional damage to the juvenile. Serious emotional damage is evidenced by a juvenile's severe anxiety, depression, withdrawal or aggressive behavior toward himself or others; or

e. Encourages, directs, or approves of delinquent acts involving moral turpitude committed by the juvenile.

(20) Juvenile.—Any person who has not reached his eighteenth birthday and is not married, emancipated, or a member of the armed services of the United States. A juvenile who is married, emancipated, or a member of the armed forces, shall be prosecuted as an adult for the commission of a criminal offense.

(21) Neglected juvenile.—A juvenile who does not receive proper care, supervision, or discipline from the juvenile's parent, guardian, custodian, or caretaker; or who has been abandoned; or who is not provided necessary medical care; or who is not provided necessary remedial care; or who lives in an environment injurious to the juvenile's welfare; or who has been placed for care or adoption in violation of law.
§ 14-318.2.

Child abuse a Class 1 misdemeanor.

(a) Any parent of a child less than 16 years of age, or any other person providing care to or supervision of such child, who inflicts physical injury, or who allows physical injury to be inflicted, or who creates or allows to be created a substantial risk of physical injury, upon or to such child by other than accidental means is guilty of the Class 1 misdemeanor of child abuse.

(b) The Class 1 misdemeanor of child abuse is an offense additional to other civil and criminal provisions and is not intended to repeal or preclude any other sanctions or remedies.
§ 14-318.4. Child abuse a felony.

(a) A parent or any other person providing care to or supervision of a child less than 16 years of age who intentionally inflicts any serious physical injury upon or to the child or who intentionally commits an assault upon the child which results in any serious physical injury to the child is guilty of a Class E felony.

(a1) Any parent of a child less than 16 years of age, or any person providing care to or supervision of the child, who commits, permits, or encourages any act of prostitution with or by the juvenile is guilty of child abuse and shall be punished as a Class E felon.

(a2) Any parent or legal guardian of a child less than 16 years of age who commits or allows the commission of any sexual act upon a juvenile is guilty of a Class E felony.

(b) The felony of child abuse is an offense additional to other civil and criminal provisions and is not intended to repeal or preclude any other sanctions or remedies.

North Dakota

14-09-22. Abuse or neglect of child—Penalty.

1. Except as provided in subsection 2, a parent, guardian, or other custodian of any child who willfully commits any of the following offenses is guilty of a class C felony:

a) Inflicts, or allows to be inflicted, upon the child, physical or mental injury.

b) Fails to provide parental care or control, subsistence, education as required by law, or other care or control necessary for the child's physical, mental, or emotional health, or morals.

c) Permits the child to be, or fails to exercise reasonable diligence in preventing the child from being, in a disreputable place or associating with vagrants or vicious or immoral persons.

d) Permits the child to engage in, or fails to exercise reasonable diligence in preventing the child from engaging in, an occupation forbidden by the laws of this state or an occupation injurious to the child's health or morals or the health or morals of others.

50-25.1-02. Definitions.

(2) "Abused child" means an individual under the age of eighteen years who is suffering from serious physical harm or traumatic abuse caused by other than accidental means by a person responsible for the child's welfare, or who is suffering from or was subjected to any act involving that individual in violation of sections 12.1-20-01 through 12.1-20-08.

(5) "Harm" means negative changes in a child's health which occur when a person responsible for the child's welfare:

a) Inflicts, or allows to be inflicted, upon the child, physical or mental injury, including injuries sustained as a result of excessive corporal punishment; or

b) Commits, allows to be committed, or conspires to commit, against the child, a sex offense as defined in chapter 12.1-20.

Ohio

[§ 2151.031] § 2151.031 Abused child defined

As used in this chapter, an "abused child" includes any child who:

(B) Is endangered as defined in section 2919.22 of the Revised Code . . .

(C) Exhibits evidence of any physical or mental injury or death, inflicted other than by accidental means, or an injury or death which is at variance with the history given of it. Except as provided in division (D) of this section, a child exhibiting evidence of corporal punishment or other physical disciplinary measure by a parent, guardian, custodian, person having custody or control, or person in loco parentis of a child is not an abused child under this division if the measure is not prohibited under section 2919.22 of the Revised Code.

(D) Because of the acts of his parents, guardian, or custodian, suffers physical or mental injury that harms or threatens to harm the child's health or welfare.

§ 2919.22 Endangering children

(B) No person shall do any of the following to a child under eighteen years of age or a mentally or physically handicapped child under twenty-one years of age:

(1) Abuse the child;

(2) Torture or cruelly abuse the child;

(3) Administer corporal punishment or other disciplinary measure, or physically retrain the child in a cruel manner for a prolonged period, which punishment, discipline, or restraint is excessive under the circumstances and creates a substantial risk of serious physical harm to the child;

(4) Repeatedly administer unwarranted disciplinary measures to the child, when there is a substantial risk that such conduct, if continued, will seriously impair or retard the child's mental health or development;

§ 2901.01 Definitions

(5) "Serious physical harm to persons" means any of the following:

(a) Any mental illness or condition of such gravity as would normally require hospitalization or prolonged psychiatric treatment;

(b) Any physical harm that carries a substantial risk of death;

(c) Any physical harm that involves some permanent incapacity, whether partial or total, or that involves some temporary, substantial incapacity;

(d) Any physical harm that involves some permanent disfigurement, or that involves some temporary, serious disfigurement;

(e) Any physical harm that involves acute pain of such duration as to result in substantial suffering, or that involves any degree of prolonged or intractable pain.

Oklahoma
§43-107.3.

C. As used in this section:

1. "Child abuse" means:

a. that a child has been physically, emotionally, or psychologically abused by a parent,

b. that a child has been:

(1) sexually abused by a parent through criminal sexual penetration, incest, or criminal sexual contact of a minor as those acts are defined by state law, or

(2) sexually exploited by a parent through allowing, permitting, or encouraging the child in obscene or pornographic photographing or filming or depicting a child for commercial purposes as those acts are defined by state law,

c. that a child has been knowingly or intentionally or negligently placed in a situation that may endanger the child's life or health, or

d. that a child has been knowingly or intentionally tortured, cruelly confined, or cruelly punished; provided, that nothing in this paragraph shall be construed to imply that a child who is or has been provided with treatment by spiritual means alone through prayer, in accordance with the tenets and practices of a recognized church or religious denomination, by a duly accredited practitioner of the church or denomination, is for that reason alone a victim of child abuse within the meaning of this paragraph;

§10-7102.

A. 1. It is the policy of this state to provide for the protection of children who have been abused or neglected and who may be further threatened by the conduct of persons responsible for the care and protection of such children.

2. It is the policy of this state that in responding to a report of child abuse or neglect, in any necessary removal of a child from the home, in placements of a child required pursuant to the Oklahoma Child Abuse Reporting and Prevention Act and in any administrative or judicial proceeding held pursuant to the provisions of the Oklahoma Child Abuse Reporting and Prevention Act, the best interests of the child shall be of paramount consideration.

B. As used in the Oklahoma Child Abuse Reporting and Prevention Act:

1. "Abuse" means harm or threatened harm to a child's health or safety by a person responsible for the child's health or safety including sexual abuse and sexual exploitation;

2. "Harm or threatened harm to a child's health or safety" includes, but is not limited to:

a. nonaccidental physical or mental injury,

b. sexual abuse,

c. sexual exploitation,

d. neglect, or

e. failure or omission to provide protection from harm or threatened harm;

3. "Neglect" means failure or omission to provide:

a. adequate food, clothing, shelter, medical care, and supervision, or

b. special care made necessary by the physical or mental condition of the child;

4. "Child" means any person under the age of eighteen (18) years except any person convicted of a crime specified in Section 7306-1.1 of this title or any person who has been certified as an adult pursuant to Section 7303-4.3 of this title and convicted of a felony;

5. "Person responsible for a child's health or safety" includes a parent; a legal guardian; custodian; a foster parent; a person eighteen (18) years of age or older with whom the child's parent cohabitates or any other adult residing in the home of the child; an agent or employee of a public or private residential home, institution, facility or day treatment program as defined in Section 175.20 of this title; or an owner, operator, or employee of a child care facility as defined by Section 402 of this title;

Oregon
SECTION 1. ORS 419B.005 Child Abuse.

(1)(a) "Abuse" means:

(A) Any assault, as defined in ORS chapter 163, of a child and any physical injury to a child which has been caused by other than accidental means, including any injury which appears to be at variance with the explanation given of the injury.

(B) Any mental injury to a child, which shall include only observable and substantial impairment of the child's mental or psychological ability to function caused by cruelty to the child, with due regard to the culture of the child.

(G) Threatened harm to a child, which means subjecting a child to a substantial risk of harm to the child's health and welfare.

(b) "Abuse" does not include reasonable discipline unless the discipline results in one of the conditions described in paragraph (a) of this subsection.

418.990 Criminal Penalties.

(1) A person who violates ORS 418.130 or 418.140 (1) commits a Class A misdemeanor.

(2) A person who violates ORS 418.250 (2), 418.255, 418.290 or 418.300 commits a violation punishable by a fine not exceeding $100.

(3) A person who violates ORS 418.215, 418.250 (1) or 418.327 (3) is a Class A misdemeanor. Each day of violation is a separate offense. [Formerly part of 419.990; subsection (2) enacted as 1961 c.341 §3;]

Pennsylvania

§ 3490.4. Definitions

The following words and terms, when used in this chapter, have the following meanings, unless the context clearly indicates otherwise:

(1) "Child"—A person 17 years of age or younger.

(2) "Child abuse"—Serious physical or mental injury which is not explained by the available medical history as being accidental, or sexual abuse or sexual exploitation, or serious physical neglect of a child under 18 years of age if the injury, abuse or neglect has been caused by the acts or omissions of the child's parents, or by a person responsible for the child's welfare, or an individual residing in the same home as the child, or a paramour of a child's parent. No child may be deemed to be physically or mentally abused for the sole reason that he is in good faith being furnished treatment by spiritual means through prayer alone in accordance with the tenets and practices of a recognized church or religious denomination by an accredited practitioner thereof or is not provided specified medical treatment on the practice of religious beliefs, or solely on the grounds of environmental factors which are beyond the control of the person responsible for the child's welfare such as inadequate housing, furnishings, income, clothing and medical care.

(3) "Serious bodily injury"—Injury which creates a substantial risk of death or which causes serious permanent disfigurement or protracted loss or impairment of the function of a body member or organ.

(4) "Serious mental injury"—A psychological condition as diagnosed by a physician or licensed psychologist caused by the acts or omissions—including the refusal of appropriate treatment—of the perpetrator which does one of the following:

(i) Renders the child chronically and severely anxious, agitated, depressed, socially withdrawn, psychotic or in reasonable fear that his life or safety is threatened.

(ii) Seriously interferes with the child's ability to accomplish age appropriate developmental and social tasks.

(5) "Serious physical injury"—Any injury caused by the acts or omissions of a perpetrator which does one of the following:

(i) Causes the child severe pain.

(ii) Significantly impairs the child's physical functioning, either temporarily or permanently.

(iii) Is accompanied by physical evidence of a continuous pattern of separate, unexplained injuries to the child.

(6)"Serious physical neglect"—A physical condition caused by the acts or omissions of a perpetrator which endangers the child's life or development or impairs his functioning and is the result of one of the following:

(i) Prolonged or repeated lack of supervision.

(ii) Failure to provide essentials of life, including adequate medical care.

Rhode Island

11-9-5. Cruelty to or neglect of child.

Every person having the custody or control of any child under the age of eighteen (18) years who shall abandon that child, or who shall treat such child with gross or habitual cruelty, or who shall wrongfully cause or permit that child to be an habitual sufferer for want of food, clothing, proper care, or oversight, or who shall use or permit the use of that child for any wanton, cruel, or improper purpose, or who shall compel, cause or permit that child to do any wanton or wrongful act, or who shall cause or permit that home of that child to be the resort of lewd, drunken, wanton, or dissolute persons, or who by reason of neglect, cruelty, drunkenness, or depravity, shall render the home of that child a place in which it is unfit for that child to live, or who shall neglect or refuse to pay the reasonable charges for the support of that child, whenever the child shall be placed by him or her in the custody of, or be assigned by any court to, any individual, association, or corporation, shall be guilty of a felony and shall for every such offense be imprisoned for not less than one year nor more than three (3) years, or be fined not exceeding one thousand dollars ($1000), or both, and such child may be proceeded against as a neglected child under the provisions of chapter 1 of title 14. In addition to any penalty provided herein, any person convicted or placed on probation for such offense may be required to receive psycho-sociological counseling in child growth, care and development as a part of that sentence or probation. For purposes of this section, providing a child treatment by spiritual means through prayer alone, in lieu of medical treatment, in accordance with a religious method of healing which has a reasonable, proven record of success, shall not be considered abusing or neglecting such child.

11-9-5.3. Child abuse

The following section shall be known and may be referred to as "Brenden's Law." Whenever a person having care of a child, as defined by § 40-11-2(2) whether assumed voluntarily or because of legal obligation, including any instance where a child has been placed by his or her parents, caretaker, or licensed or governmental child placement agency for treatment, knowingly or intentionally:

(1) Inflicts upon a child serious bodily injury shall be guilty of first degree child abuse.

(2) Inflicts upon a child any other serious physical injury shall be guilty of second degree child abuse.

For the purposes of this section, serious bodily injury shall mean physical injury that (1) creates a substantial risk of death or (2) causes protracted loss or impairment of the function of any bodily parts, member or organ, including any fractures of any bones, or (3) causes serious disfigurement. For the purposes of this section, serious physical injury shall be defined as any injury, other than serious bodily injury, which arises other than from the imposition of nonexcessive corporal punishment.

(a) Any person who commits first degree child abuse shall be imprisoned for not more than twenty (20) years, nor less than ten (10) years and fined not more that ten thousand dollars ($10,000). Any person who is convicted of second degree child abuse shall be imprisoned for not more that ten (10) years, nor less than five (5) years and fined not more than five thousand dollars ($5,000).

(b) Any person who commits first degree child abuse on a child age five (5) or under shall not on the first ten (10) years of his or her sentence be afforded the benefit of suspension or deferment of sentence nor of probation for penalties provided in this section; and provided further, that the court shall order the defendant to serve a minimum of eight and one-half (8 1/2) years or more of said sentence before he or she becomes eligible for parole.

(c) Any person who has been previously convicted of first or second degree child abuse under this section and thereafter commits first degree child abuse shall be imprisoned for not more than forty (40) years, nor less than twenty (20) years and fined not more than twenty thousand ($20,000) dollars and shall be subject to subsection (b) of this section if applicable. Any person who has been previously convicted of first or second degree child abuse under this section and thereafter commits second degree child abuse shall be imprisoned for not more than twenty (20) years, nor less than ten (10) years and fined not more than ten thousand ($10,000) dollars.

40-11-2. Definitions

When used in this chapter and unless the specific context indicates otherwise:

(1) "Abused and/or neglected child" means a child whose physical or mental health or welfare is harmed or threatened with harm when his or her parent or other person responsible for his or her welfare:

(i) Inflicts, or allows to be inflicted upon the child physical or mental injury, including excessive corporal punishment; or

(ii) Creates or allows to be created a substantial risk of physical or mental injury to the child, including excessive corporal punishment.

South Carolina

§ 20-7-50. Unlawful conduct towards child.

(A) It is unlawful for a person who has charge or custody of a child, who is the parent or guardian of a child, or who is responsible for the care and support of a child to:

(1) place the child at unreasonable risk of harm affecting the child's life, physical or mental health, or safety;

(2) do or cause to be done unlawfully or maliciously any bodily harm to the child so that the life or health of the child is endangered or likely to be endangered; or

(3) wilfully abandon the child.

(B) A person who violates subsection (A) is guilty of a felony and for each offense, upon conviction, must be fined in the discretion of the court or imprisonec' not more than ten years, or both.

§ 20-7-70. Cruelty to children.

Whoever cruelly ill-treats, deprives of necessary sustenance or shelter, or inflicts unnecessary pain or suffering upon a child or causes the same to be done, whether the person is the parent or guardian or has charge or custody of the child, for every offense, is guilty of a misdemeanor and, upon conviction, must be imprisoned not more than thirty days or fined not more than two hundred dollars, at the discretion of the magistrate.

§ 20-7-490. Definitions.

When used in this article and unless the specific context indicates otherwise:

(1) "Child" means a person under the age of eighteen.

(2) "Abused or neglected child" means a child whose death results from or whose physical or mental health or welfare is harmed or threatened with harm, as defined by items (3) and (4), by the acts or omissions of the child's parent, guardian, or other person responsible for his welfare.

(3) "Harm" to a child's health or welfare can occur when the parent, guardian, or other person responsible for the child's welfare:

(a) inflicts or allows to be inflicted upon the child physical or mental injury, including injuries sustained as a result of excessive corporal punishment, but excluding corporal punishment or physical discipline which:

(i) is administered by a parent or person in loco parentis;

(ii) is perpetrated for the sole purpose of restraining or correcting the child;

(iii) is reasonable in manner and moderate in degree;

(iv) has not brought about permanent or lasting damage to the child;

(v) is not reckless or grossly negligent behavior by the parents.

(4) "Threatened harm" means a substantial risk of harm, as defined by item (3).

(6) "Physical injury" means death or permanent or temporary disfigurement or impairment of any bodily organ or function.

(7) "Mental injury" means an injury to the intellectual or psychological capacity of a child as evidenced by a discernible and substantial impairment of the child's ability to function when the existence of that impairment is supported by the opinion of a mental health professional or medical professional.

(21) "Abandonment of a child" means a parent or guardian wilfully deserts a child or wilfully surrenders physical possession of a child without making adequate arrangements for the child's needs or the continuing care of the child.

South Dakota

26-8A-2. Abused or Neglected child defined. In this chapter and chapter 26-7A the term "abused or neglected child" means a child:

(1) Whose parent, guardian, or custodian has abandoned the child or has subjected the child to mistreatment or abuse;

(2) Who lacks proper parental care through the actions or omissions of the parent, guardian, or custodian;

(3) Whose environment is injurious to his welfare;

(4) Whose parent, guardian, or custodian fails or refuses to provide proper or necessary subsistence, supervision, education, medical care or any other care necessary for his health, guidance, or well-being; or

(5) Who is homeless, without proper care, or not domiciled with his parent, guardian, or custodian through no fault of his parent, guardian or custodian.

(6) Who is threatened with substantial harm.

(7) Who has sustained emotional harm or mental injury as indicated by an injury to his intellectual or psychological capacity evidenced by an observable and substantial impairment in his ability to function within his normal range of performance and behavior, with due regard to his culture.

(8) Who is subject to sexual abuse, sexual molestation or sexual exploitation by his parent, guardian, custodian or any other person responsible for his care.

26-10-1. Abuse of or cruelty to minor is felony. Any person who abuses, exposes, tortures, torments or cruelly punishes a minor in manner which does not constitute aggravated assault, is guilty of a Class 4 Felony.

22-6-1 Felony classes and penalties.

(6) Class 4 felony: ten years imprisonment in the state penitentiary. In addition, a fine of ten thousand dollars may be imposed;

The South Dakota Department of Social Services—Laws pertaining to child abuse and neglect.

Because of the variations among tribes it would be difficult to highlight tribal codes. It is important that staff who work in reservation areas become knowledgeable about the tribal code governing the respective reservations.

Tennessee

37-1-102(19). Severe Child Abuse.

"Severe child abuse" means:

(a) The knowing exposure of a child to or the knowing failure to protect a child from conditions of brutality, abuse or neglect that are likely to cause great bodily harm or death and the knowing use of force on a child that is likely to cause great bodily harm or death:

(b) Specific brutality, abuse, or neglect towards a child which in the opinion of qualified experts has caused or will reasonably be expected to produce severe psychosis, severe neurotic disorder, severe depression, severe developmental delay or retardation, or severe impairment of the child's ability to function adequately in his environment, and the knowing failure to protect a child from such conduct:

(c) The commission of any act towards the child prohibited by §§39-13-502, 39-13-503, 39-13-504, 39-13-510, 39-15-510, 39-15-302, 39-17-915 [repealed], and 39-17-916 [repealed], or the knowing failure to protect the child from the commission of any such act towards him.

37-1-401. Definitions

In this part, unless a different meaning is clearly intended:

(1) "Child" means a person who is under eighteen (18) years of age or who is reasonably presumed to be under eighteen (18) years of age;

39-4-401. Child Abuse and Neglect—Penalty—Procedure—Relation of Section to Other Law.

(a) Any person who maliciously, purposely, or knowingly, other than by accidental means, treats a child under eighteen (18) years of age in such a manner as to inflict injury or neglects such a child so as to adversely affect its health and welfare is guilty of a Class A misdemeanor.

(b)(1) Any juvenile court having reasonable cause to believe that a person is guilty of violating this section shall have the person brought before the court either by summons or warrant.

39-15-402. Aggravated Child Abuse.

(a) A person is guilty of the offense of aggravated child abuse who commits the offense of child abuse as defined in §39-15-402, and:

(1) The act of abuse results in the serious bodily injury of the child; or

(2) A deadly weapon is used to accomplish the act of abuse.

(b) A violation of this section is a Class B felony.

Texas

§ 261.001. Definitions

In this chapter:

(1) "Abuse" includes the following acts or omissions by a person:

(A) mental or emotional injury to a child that results in an observable and material impairment in the child's growth, development, or psychological functioning;

(B) causing or permitting the child to be in a situation in which the child sustains a mental or emotional injury that results in an observable and material impairment in the child's growth, development, or psychological functioning;

(C) physical injury that results in substantial harm to the child, or the genuine threat of substantial harm from physical injury to the child, including an injury that is at variance with the history or explanation given and excluding an accident or reasonable discipline by a parent, guardian, or managing or possessory conservator that does not expose the child to a substantial risk of harm;

(D) failure to make a reasonable effort to prevent an action by another person that results in physical injury that results in substantial harm to the child;

§ 262.008. Abandoned Children

(a) An authorized representative of the Department of Protective and Regulatory Services may assume the care, control, and custody of a child:

(1) who is abandoned without identification or a means for identifying the child; and

(2) whose identity cannot be ascertained by the exercise of reasonable diligence.

(b) The department shall immediately file a suit to terminate the parent-child relationship of a child under Subsection (a).

(c) A child for whom possession is assumed under this section need not be delivered to the court except on the order of the court.

§ 161.003. Involuntary Termination: Inability to Care for Child

(a) The court may order termination of the parent-child relationship in a suit filed by the Department of Protective and Regulatory Services if the court finds that:

(1) the parent has a mental or emotional illness or a mental deficiency that renders the parent unable to provide for the physical, emotional, and mental needs of the child;

(2) the illness or deficiency, in all reasonable probability, proved by clear and convincing evidence, will continue to render the parent unable to provide for the child's needs until the 18th birthday of the child;

(3) the department has been the temporary or sole managing conservator of the child of the parent for the six months preceding the filing of the petition;

(4) the department has made reasonable efforts to return the child to the parent; and

(5) the termination is in the best interest of the child.

Utah

76-5-109. Child abuse.

(1) As used in this section:

(b) "Child abuse" means any offense described in Subsection (2) or (3), or in Section 76-5-109.1.

(2) Any person who inflicts upon a child serious physical injury or, having a care or custody of such child, causes or permits another to inflict serious physical injury upon a child is guilty of an offense as follows:

(a) if done intentionally or knowingly, the offense is a felony of the second degree;

(b) if done recklessly, the offense is a felony of the third degree; or

(c) if done with criminal negligence, the offense is a class A misdemeanor.

(3) Any person who inflicts upon a child physical injury or, having the care or custody of such child, causes or permits another to inflict physical injury upon a child is guilty of an offense as follows:

(a) if done intentionally or knowingly, the offense is a class A misdemeanor;

(b) if done recklessly, the offense is a class B misdemeanor;

(c) if done with criminal negligence, the offense is a class C misdemeanor.

76-5-109.1 Definitions

(c) "Physical injury" means an injury to or condition of a child which impairs the physical condition of the child, including:

(i) a bruise or other contusion of the skin;

(ii) a minor laceration or abrasion;

(iii) failure to thrive or malnutrition; or

(iv) any other condition which imperils the child's health or welfare and which is not serious physical injury as defined in Subsection (1)(d).

(d) "Serious physical injury" means any physical injury or set of injuries which seriously impairs the child's health, or which involves physical torture or causes serious emotional harm to the child, or which involves a substantial risk of death to the child, including:

(i) fracture of any bone or bones;

(ii) intracranial bleeding, swelling or contusion of the brain, whether caused by blows, shaking, or causing the child's head to impact with an object or surface;

(iii) any burn, including burns inflicted by hot water, or those caused by placing a hot object upon the skin or body of the child;

(iv) any injury caused by use of a dangerous weapon as defined in Section 76-1-601;

(v) any combination of two or more physical injuries inflicted by the same person, either at the same time or on different occasions;

(vi) any damage to internal organs of the body;

(vii) any conduct toward a child which results in severe emotional harm, severe developmental delay or retardation, or severe impairment of the child's ability to function;

(viii) any injury which creates a permanent disfigurement or protracted loss or impairment of the function of a bodily member, limb, or organ;

(ix) any conduct which causes a child to cease breathing, even if resuscitation is successful following the conduct; or

(x) any conduct which results in starvation or failure to thrive or malnutrition that jeopardizes the child's life.

Vermont

§ 4912. Definitions.

As used in this subchapter:

(1) "Child" means any individual under the age of majority.

(2) An "abused or neglected child" means a child whose physical or mental health or welfare is harmed or threatened with harm by the acts or omissions of his parent or other person responsible for his welfare or a child who is sexually abused by any person

(3) "Harm" to a child's health or welfare can occur when the parent or other person responsible for his welfare:

(A) Inflicts, or allows to be inflicted, upon the child, physical or mental injury; or

(B) Commits, or allows to be committed, against the child, sexual abuse; or

(C) Fails to supply the child with adequate food, clothing, shelter or health care. For the purposes of this subchapter, "adequate health care" includes any medical or nonmedical remedial health care permitted or authorized under state law. Notwithstanding that a child might be found to be without proper parental care under chapter 55 of Title 33, a parent or other person responsible for a child's care legitimately

practicing his religious beliefs who thereby does not provide specified medical treatment for a child shall not be considered neglect for that reason alone; or

(D) Abandons the child.

(4) "Threatened harm" means a substantial risk of physical or mental injury to such child by other than accidental means which would likely to cause death or serious or protracted disfigurement, or protracted impairment of physical or mental health or protracted loss or impairment of the function of any bodily organ.

(6) "Physical injury" means death, or permanent or temporary disfigurement or impairment of any bodily organ or function by other than accidental means.

(7) "Mental injury" includes a state of substantially diminished psychological or intellectual functioning of a child as evidenced by an observable and substantial impairment; provided, however, that such impairment must be clearly attributable to the unwillingness or inability of the parent or guardian to exercise a minimum degree of care toward the child.

§ 1303. Abandonment or exposure of baby

A person who abandons or exposes a child under the age of two years, whereby the life or health of such child is endangered, shall be imprisoned not more than ten years or fined not more than $1000.00, or both.

§ 1304. Cruelty to children under ten by one over sixteen.

A person over the age of sixteen years, having the custody, charge or care of a child under ten years of age, who wilfully assault, ill treats, neglects or abandons or exposes such child, or causes or procures such child to be assaulted, ill-treated, neglected, abandoned or exposed, in a manner to cause such child unnecessary suffering, or to endanger his health, shall be imprisoned not more than two years or fined not more than $500.00, or both.

Virginia

§ 18.2-371.1 Abuse and neglect of children; penalty.

(A) Any parent, guardian, or other person responsible for the care of a child under the age of eighteen who by willful act or omission or refusal to provide any necessary care for the child's health causes or permits serious injury to the life or health of such child shall be guilty of a Class 4 felony. For the purposes of this subsection, "serious injury" shall include but not be limited to

(i) disfigurement,

(ii) a fracture,

(iii) a severe burn or laceration,

(iv) mutilation,

(v) maiming,

(vi) forced ingestion of dangerous substances, or

(vii) life-threatening internal injuries.

(B) Any parent, guardian, or other person responsible for the care of a child under the age of eighteen whose willful act or omission in the care of such child was so gross, wanton and culpable as to show a reckless disregard for human life shall be guilty of a Class 6 felony.

(C) Any parent, guardian or other person having care, custody or control of a minor child who in good faith is under treatment solely by spiritual means through prayer in accordance with the tenets and practices of a recognized church or religious denomination shall not, for that reason alone, be considered in violation of this section.

§ 18.2-10. Punishment for convictions of felony.

The authorized punishments for conviction of a felony are:

(d) For Class 4 felonies, a term of imprisonment of not less than two years nor more than ten years and, subject to subdivision (g), a fine of not more than $100.000.

(f) For Class 6 felonies, a term of imprisonment of not less than one year nor more than five years, or in the discretion of the jury or the court trying the case without a jury, confinement in jail for not more than twelve months and a fine of not more than $2,500, either or both.

§ 63.1-248.2. Definitions.

As used in this chapter unless the context requires a different meaning:

"Abused or neglected child" means any child less than eighteen years of age:

(1) Whose parents or other person responsible for his care creates or inflicts, threatens to create or inflict, or allows to be created or inflicted upon such child a physical or mental injury by other than accidental means, or creates a substantial risk of death, disfigurement, or impairment of bodily or mental functions;

(2) Whose parents or other person responsible for his care neglects or refuses to provide care necessary for his health. However, no child who in good faith is under treatment solely by spiritual means through prayer in accordance with the tenets and practices of a recognized church or religious denomination shall for that reason alone be considered to be an abused or neglected child;

(3) Whose parents or other person responsible for his care abandons such child;

(4) Whose parents or other person responsible for his care commits or allows to be committed any act of sexual exploitation or any sexual act upon any child in violation of the law; or

(5) Who is without parental care or guardianship caused by the unreasonable absence or the mental or physical incapacity of the child's parent, guardian, legal custodian or other person standing in loco parentis.

Washington

RCW 9A.42.010 Definitions. As used in this chapter:

(1) "Basic necessities of life" means food, water, shelter, clothing, and medically necessary health care, including but not limited to health-related treatment or activities, hygiene, oxygen, and medication.

(2)(a) "Bodily injury" means physical pain or injury, illness, or an impairment of physical condition;

(b) "Substantial bodily harm" means bodily injury which involves a temporary but substantial disfigurement, or which causes a temporary but substantial loss or impairment of the function of any bodily part or organ, or which causes a fracture of any bodily part;

(c) "Great bodily harm" means bodily injury which creates a high probability of death, or which causes serious permanent disfigurement, or which causes a permanent or protracted loss or impairment of the function of any bodily part or organ.

(3) "Child" means a person under eighteen years of age.

(6) "Parent" has its ordinary meaning and also includes a guardian and the authorized agent of a parent or guardian.

(7) "Abandons" means leaving a child or other dependent person without the means or ability to obtain one or more of the basic necessities of life.

RCW 9A.42.020 Criminal mistreatment in the first degree.

(1) A parent of a child, the person entrusted with the physical custody of a child or dependent person, or a person employed to provide to the child or dependent person the basic necessities of life is guilty of criminal mistreatment in the first degree if he or she recklessly, as defined in RCW 9A.08.010, causes great bodily harm to a child or dependent person by withholding any of the basic necessities of life.

(2) Criminal mistreatment in the first degree is a class B felony.

RCW 9A.42.030 Criminal mistreatment in the second degree.

(1) A parent of a child, the person entrusted with the physical custody of a child or dependent person, or a person employed to provide to the child or dependent person the basic necessities of life is guilty of criminal mistreatment in the second degree if he or she recklessly, as defined in RCW 9A.08.010, either

(a) creates an imminent and substantial risk of death or great bodily harm, or

(b) causes substantial bodily harm by withholding any of the basic necessities of life.

(2) Criminal mistreatment in the second degree is a class C felony.

West Virginia

§ 61-8B-1. Definition of terms.

In this article, unless a different meaning is plainly required:

(9) "Bodily injury" means substantial physical pain, illness or any impairment of physical condition.

(10) "Serious bodily injury" means bodily injury which creates a substantial risk of death, which causes serious or prolonged disfigurement, prolonged impairment of health or prolonged loss or impairment of the function of any bodily organ.

§ 61-8D-1. Definitions.

In this article, unless a different meaning plainly is required:

(1) "Abuse" means the infliction upon a minor of physical injury by other than accidental means.

(2) "Child" means any person under eighteen years of age not otherwise emancipated by law.

(6) "Neglect" means the unreasonable failure by a parent, guardian, or any person voluntarily accepting a supervisory role towards a minor child to exercise a minimum degree of care to assure said minor child's physical safety or health.

§ 61-8D-3. Child abuse resulting in injury; child abuse or neglect creating risk of injury; criminal penalties.

(a) If any parent, guardian or custodian shall abuse a child and by such abuse cause such child bodily injury as such term is defined in section one [§ 61-8B-1], article eight-b of this chapter, then such parent, guardian or custodian shall be guilty of a felony and, upon conviction thereof, shall be fined not less than one hundred nor more than one thousand dollars and committed to the custody of the division of corrections for not less than one nor more than five years, or in the discretion of the court, be confined in the county or regional jail for not more than one year.

(b) If any parent, guardian or custodian shall abuse a child and by such abuse cause said child serious bodily injury as such term is defined in section one, article eight-b of this chapter, then such parent, guardian or custodian shall be guilty of a felony and, upon conviction thereof, shall be fined not less than one thousand nor more than five thousand dollars and committed to the custody of the division of corrections for not less than two nor more than ten years.

(c) Any person who abuses a child and by the abuse creates a substantial risk of serious bodily injury or of death to the child is guilty of a felony and, upon conviction thereof, shall be fined not more than three thousand dollars and confined to the custody of the division of corrections for not less than one nor more than five years.

§ 61-8D-4. Child neglect resulting in injury; child neglect creating risk of injury; criminal penalties.

(a) If any parent, guardian or custodian shall neglect a child and by such neglect cause said child bodily injury, as such term is defined in section one [§ 61-8B-1], article eight-b of this chapter, then such parent, guardian or custodian shall be guilty of a felony and, upon conviction thereof, shall be fined not less than one hundred nor more than one thousand dollars or committed to the custody of the division of corrections for not less than one nor more than three years, or in the discretion of the court, be confined in the county jail for not more than one year, or both such fine and confinement or imprisonment.

(b) If any parent, guardian or custodian shall neglect a child and by such neglect cause said child serious bodily injury, as such term is defined in section one, article eight-b of this chapter, then such parent, guardian or custodian shall be guilty of a felony and, upon conviction thereof, shall be fined not less than three hundred nor more than three thousand dollars or committed to the custody of the division of corrections for not less than one nor more than ten years, or both such fine and imprisonment.

(c) The provisions of this section shall not apply if the neglect by the parent, guardian or custodian is due primarily to a lack of financial means on the part of such parent, guardian or custodian.

(d) The provisions of this section shall not apply to any parent, guardian or custodian who fails or refuses, or allows another person to fail or refuse, to supply a child under care, custody or control of such parent, guardian or custodian with necessary medical care, when such medical care conflicts with the tenets and practices of a recognized religious denomination or order of which such parent, guardian or custodian is an adherent or member.

(e) Any person who grossly neglects a child and by the gross neglect creates a substantial risk of serious bodily injury or of death to the child is guilty of a felony and, upon conviction thereof, shall be fined not more than three thousand dollars and confined to the custody of the division of corrections for not less than one nor more than five years.

§ 61-8D-7. Presentation of false information regarding child's injuries; penalty.

Any person who presents false information concerning acts or conduct which would constitute an offense under the provisions of this article to attending medical personnel shall be guilty of a misdemeanor, and, upon conviction thereof, shall be fined not less than one hundred dollars nor more than one thousand dollars, and shall be confined in the county jail not more than one year.

Wisconsin

948.03 Physical abuse of a child.

(1) Definitions. In this section, "recklessly" means conduct which creates a situation of unreasonable risk of harm to and demonstrates a conscious disregard for the safety of the child.

(2) Intentional causation of bodily harm.

(a) Whoever intentionally causes great bodily harm to a child is guilty of a Class C felony.

(b) Whoever intentionally causes bodily harm to a child is guilty of a Class D felony.

(c) Whoever intentionally causes bodily harm to a child by conduct which creates a high probability of great bodily harm is guilty of a Class C felony.

(3) Reckless causation of bodily harm.

(a) Whoever recklessly causes great bodily harm to a child is guilty of a Class D felony.

(b) Whoever recklessly causes bodily harm to a child is guilty of a Class E felony.

(c) Whoever recklessly causes bodily harm to a child by conduct which creates a high probability of great bodily harm is guilty of a Class D felony.

(4) Failing to act to prevent bodily harm.

(a) A person responsible for the child's welfare is guilty of a Class C felony if that person has knowledge that another person intends to cause, is causing or has intentionally or recklessly caused great bodily harm to the child and is physically and emotionally capable of taking action which will prevent the bodily harm from occurring or being repeated, fails to take that action and the failure to act exposes the child to an unreasonable risk of great bodily harm by the other person or facilitates the great bodily harm to the child that is caused by the other person.

(b) A person responsible for the child's welfare is guilty of a Class D felony if that person has knowledge that another person intends to cause, is causing or has intentionally or recklessly caused bodily harm to the child and is physically and emotionally capable of taking action which will prevent the bodily harm from occurring or being repeated, fails to take that action and the failure to act exposes the child to an unreasonable risk of bodily harm by the other person or facilitates the bodily harm to the child that is caused by the other person.

(5) Penalty enhancement; abuse by certain persons. If a person violates sub. (2) or (3) and person is responsible for the welfare of the child who is the victim of the violation, the maximum term of imprisonment may be increased by not more than 5 years.

(6) Treatment through prayer. A person is not guilty of an offense under this section solely because he or she provides a child with treatment by spiritual means through prayer alone for healing in accordance with the religious method of healing permitted under s. 48.981 (3) (c) 4. or 448.03 (6) in lieu of medical or surgical treatment.

948.21 Neglecting a child.

(1) Any person who is responsible for a child's welfare who, through his or her actions or failure to take action, intentionally contributes to the neglect of the child is guilty of a Class A misdemeanor or, if death is a consequence, a Class C felony.

(2) Under sub. (1), a person responsible for the child's welfare contributes to the neglect of the child although the child does not actually become neglected if the natural and probable consequences of the person's actions or failure to take action would be to cause the child to become neglected.

Wyoming

14-3-202. Definitions.

(a) As used in W.S. 14-3-201 through 14-3-215:

(ii) "Abuse" with respect to a child means inflicting or causing physical or mental injury, harm or imminent danger to the physical or mental health or welfare of a child other than by accidental means, including abandonment, excessive or unreasonable corporal punishment, malnutrition or substantial risk thereof by reason of intentional or unintentional neglect, and the commission or allowing the commission of a sexual offense against the child as defined by law:

(B) "Physical injury" means death or any harm to a child including but not limited to disfigurement, impairment of any bodily organ, skin bruising, bleeding, burns, fracture of any bone, subdural hematoma or substantial malnutrition;. . .

Endnotes

Introduction
1. Webster's *Thesaurus* (Landoll, Inc., 1992), 204.

Chapter 1
1. Michael Lemonick, "Spare the Rod? Maybe,"*Time* (August 25, 1997), 65.
2. Dr. James Dobson, *The Strong-Willed Child*, (Tyndale House Publishers, Inc., 1978). Used by permission; All rights reserved.
3. Ibid.

Chapter 2
1. From the seminar "How to Change Your Child's Behavior," Mr. Bob Reitman, March 7, 1997, used by permission.

Chapter 3
1. William Sears, M.D., and Martha Sears, R.N., *The Discipline Book*, (Little. Brown and Company, 1995).
2. http://www.religioustolerance.com.
3. RCox@cei.net.
4. Ibid.
5. Ibid.
6. Ibid.
7. Ibid.
8. Ibid.
9. Ibid.
10. Ibid.
11. Ibid.
12. Ibid.
13. Ibid.

Chapter 4
1. *Crime in the United States 1996*, Uniform Crime Reports, Federal Bureau of Investigation, iii.

2. *Crime in the United States 1996*, Uniform Crime Reports, Federal Bureau of Investigation, iv.

Chapter 5
1. 1989 House Bill 257, effective 08/03/89.
2. 1997 Senate Bill 60, effective 10/21/97.
3. 1998 House Bill 565, effective 03/30/99.
4. 1995 House Bill 4, effective 11/09/95.
5. 1996 House Bill 124, effective 09/30/97.
6. 1997 House Bill 238, effective 11/05/97.

Chapter 6
1. Cuyahoga County Department of Human Services, Child Abuse/ Neglect Report.
2. James F. Sweeney, "Welfare agency agrees to ask court before taking children," *The Cleveland Plain Dealer* (Saturday, May 30, 1998).
3. Ibid.
4. Ibid.
5. Ibid.
6. Ibid.

Chapter 7
1. Michael Lemonick, "Spare the Rod? Maybe,"*Time* (August 25, 1997), 65.
2. Ibid.
3. Ibid.
4. "Spanking by Parents and Subsequent Antisocial Behavior of Children," *Archives of Pediatrics and Adolescent Medicine* (August 1997).
5. Found in Julie V. Iovine, "Spanking gaining acceptance again," *The Cleveland Plain Dealer* (Saturday, November 11, 1996), 7-D.
6. Found in Julie V. Iovine, "Spanking gaining acceptance again," *The Cleveland Plain Dealer* (Saturday, November 11, 1996), 10-D.

7. Ibid.

8. Peter L. Benson, Ph.D., Judy Galbraith, M.A., and Pamela Espeland, *What Kids Need to Succeed*, (Reprinted by permission of Free Spirit Publishing, Minneapolis, Minn., 1998, 1-800-735-7323, www.freespirit.com).

9. Ibid.

10. Ibid.

11. Ibid.

12. Ibid.

13. Found in Joan Kirchner, "Pediatricians oppose spanking," *The Cleveland Plain Dealer* (Tuesday, April 7, 1998), 1-C.

Chapter 9

1. Michael K. McIntyre, "Opening Door to Woodshed," *The Cleveland Plain Dealer* (Saturday, November 28, 1996), 1-F.

2. http://www.stophitting.com.

3. Ibid.

4. Ibid.

5. Ibid.

6. Ibid.

7. Ibid.

8. nblock@infinet. com.

Chapter 10

1. William Sears, M.D., and Martha Sears, R.N., "You and your child," *Redbook*, (March 1995), 156–59.

2. http://www.positiveparenting.com/nospank.html.

3. Ibid.

4. http://www.cnet.unb.ca/orgs/prevention_cruelty/spank.htm.

5. http://www.cei.net/ ~rcox/embry.html.

6. http://www.naturalchild.com/jan_hunt/tenreasons.html.

7. http://www.ericps.urc.uiuc.edu.npin/respar/texts/fampeer/ discipli.html.

8. D. Fresee, W. Horn, and K. Bussman, *Violence Against Children* (Berlin and New York, 1996), 91–105.

9. http://www.religioustolerance.com.

Chapter 12

1. "Spanking by Parents and Subsequent Antisocial Behavior of Children,"*Archives of Pediatrics and Adolescents Medicine* (August 1997).

2. Michael Lemonick, "Spare the Rod? Maybe,"*Time* (August 25, 1997), 65.

3. Sylvia B. Rimm, "Spanking no solution to discipline problem," *The Cleveland Plain Dealer* (Saturday, January 24, 1998), 2-E.

4. Ibid.

5. Ibid.

6. William Sears, M.D., and Martha Sears, R.N., "You and your child," *Redbook*, (March 1995), 156–59.

8. Ibid.

9. Ibid.

10. Ibid.

11. Ibid.

12. Ibid.

13. William Sears, M.D., and Martha Sears, R.N., *The Discipline Book*, (Little, Brown and Company, 1995).

14. Ibid.

15. Ibid.

16. Ibid.

17. Ibid.

18. Ibid.

19. Ibid.

20. Ibid.

21. Ibid.

22. Ibid.

23. Marianne Neifert, M.D., "Beyond Time Out," *Parenting* (February 1998), 102–09.

24. Ibid.

25. Ibid.

26. Ibid.

27. Ibid.

28. Ibid.

29. Ibid.

30. Ibid.

Chapter 15

1. Julie Higgie, "Experts examine causes of school violence," *The Sun Herald* (Thursday, April 30, 1998), A-1.

Index

About the Author

Robert Surgenor was raised in a Christian home by a mother who taught his Sunday school class and a father who quit the steel mill when Robert was twelve to preach the gospel full time. He grew up in the Cleveland area and settled down with his own family in a Cleveland suburb.

Robert began his career in law enforcement in 1974 when he was hired as a theft investigator for a large retail organization in northern Ohio. In 1982, he was hired by a Cleveland area police department. Graduating from the Ohio State Highway Patrol Academy, he began his career as a police patrol officer.

Robert was one of the first police officers to install a video camera in his police cruiser, and in 1988, recorded the first high-speed stolen car chase ever video-taped in the world. His video footage has been aired numerous times on national television on programs such as Real TV, World's Scariest Police Chases, and World's Most Amazing Videos. Robert still utilizes videotape in his work with juvenile crime.

In 1995, Robert was assigned to the detective bureau and placed in charge of the juvenile crime unit. Amongst his responsibilities are the investigation of all juvenile offenses in his city and the filing of all criminal charges on offenders under eighteen years of age. He conducts interviews with the family and friends of all the juvenile offenders in his jurisdiction. He wrote the city's Daytime Curfew truancy ordinance making parents responsible for the actions of their children when they cut school. He was instrumental in the formation of the Youth Diversion Program, designed to offer juveniles who qualify an alternative to the juvenile justice system.

Robert has appeared on national television to debate members of the American Academy of Pediatrics and Dr. Murray Straus of the Family Research Laboratory on the subject of corporal punishment. Robert has also conducted seminars in cooperation with Robert Reitman on the subject of How To Change Your Child's Behavior, including the legal aspect of spanking and how parents can incorporate the assistance of the local police department in helping them to control their children.

Robert is married to his wife Nancy, and has five children. His oldest son, Rob, is twenty-six years old and is a deputy sheriff in the county in which he resides. His daughter Dawn is twenty-four and lives in Cleveland, Ohio. Bryan, twenty-one years old, lives in a Cleveland suburb and works for the security department of the Rock and Roll Hall of Fame in Cleveland. Michael is eighteen years old, and lives with his parents. He is currently attending college, majoring in criminal justice. The youngest son, Matt, is fifteen years old and attending high school. He also intends to enter law enforcement as a career.

238